W9-AEA-126

HARVARD STUDIES IN ROMANCE LANGUAGES

PUBLISHED UNDER THE DIRECTION OF THE
DEPARTMENT OF FRENCH AND OTHER
ROMANCE LANGUAGES AND LITERATURES

VOLUME XVIII

LONDON : HUMPHREY MILFORD
OXFORD UNIVERSITY PRESS

CRITICAL THEORY AND PRACTICE OF THE PLÉIADE

BY

ROBERT J. CLEMENTS
HARVARD UNIVERSITY

CAMBRIDGE
HARVARD UNIVERSITY PRESS
1942

PUBLISHED IN COÖPERATION WITH THE MODERN LANGUAGE ASSOCIATION OF AMERICA, WITH THE ASSISTANCE OF A GRANT AWARDED BY THE AMERICAN COUNCIL OF LEARNED SOCIETIES FROM A FUND PROVIDED BY THE CARNEGIE CORPORATION OF NEW YORK

PRINTED AT THE HARVARD UNIVERSITY PRESS
CAMBRIDGE, MASS., U.S.A.

To

GUERDON STEARNS HOLDEN

SCHOLAR AND FRIEND

CONTENTS

PLATES

FOREWORD

If one is willing to accept the Renaissance theory of "innutrition" as something more than an obsolete or merely academic issue, one becomes conscious that little he writes can be safely called his own creation. After subjecting the most inventive minds of sixteenth-century France to an intellectual perquisition only to find a great share of their ideas the integrated reiterations of yet earlier minds, one is obliged to conclude that it is indeed a wise scholar who knows his own brain child. If someone were to delve into the affinities or influences behind this present study, several debts would undoubtedly become apparent.

First among those to whom an obligation must be acknowledged is Professor William A. Nitze, who offered generous counsel during the composition of this work in its initial form. The communications and personal interest of Professor Paul Laumonier, whose courses on the Pléiade at the University of Bordeaux this writer was privileged to attend, have been a great satisfaction. Professors Robert Valentine Merrill and E. Preston Dargan of the University of Chicago and Samuel F. Will of the University of Illinois have made valuable suggestions during the course of this investigation. Professor Louis Cons of Harvard University has volunteered many critical ideas as we discussed problems raised in the following pages. Last, but by no means least, the author must express earnest thanks to Professor J. D. M. Ford, whose active interest has ensured the study's appearance in published form.

Each of these scholars has offered not only of his erudition but of his friendship.

> E quant' io l'abbia in grado, mentre io vivo
> Convien che nella mia lingua si scerna.

Beyond these individual acknowledgments, more impersonal but no less hearty thanks are due the Modern Language Association of America and the American Council of Learned Societies, who voted monies toward publication of this volume, and the Committee on Publication of the Department of Romance Languages of Harvard University, which granted a further subvention.

The editors of *Modern Philology* and the *PMLA Quarterly* of the Modern Language Association have consented that portions of this study already published in those journals be reproduced in the present volume.

R. J. C.

Cambridge, Massachusetts
January, 1942

INTRODUCTION

VARIOUS studies have been published on the linguistic and stylistic reforms of the Pléiade poets, the foremost literary "school" of Renaissance France. However, no single study devoted exclusively to a comprehensive view of their literary theory has yet been presented. Most of the discussions treating of this group (and the definitive history of the movement now being undertaken by Professor Henri Chamard is an example) have adopted the "historical method," and are consequently more concerned with the biographies, literary relationships, sources, and innovations of these poets than with their aesthetics. An occasional study on some individual member of the Pléiade has dealt with his literary ideas; but as yet none has been written giving undivided attention to the basic literary tenets shared by the entire group.

The Pléiade left no carefully articulated and formulated system of critical theory, of course, and the prefaces of Ronsard, Pontus de Tyard, Du Bellay, Peletier, and Sébilet afford only a fragmentary idea of their theory. Recent scholars, particularly those studying individual poets of the Pléiade, have attempted to codify certain critical notions of the group into a coherent body.[1] These scholars have coördinated the materials of the manifestoes mentioned above with observations of a critical nature found in the principal poems where the Pléiade wrote about the profession of letters. These are such familiar pieces as the "Ode à Michel de l'Hospital" of Ronsard, "Les

[1] *Cf.*, Paul Laumonier, *Ronsard, poète lyrique* (Paris: Hachette, 1909); H. Franchet, *Le poète et son œuvre d'après Ronsard* (Paris: Champion, 1922); H. Chamard, *La doctrine et l'œuvre poétique de la Pléiade* (Paris: Guillon, n. d.); Marcel Raymond, *Influence de Ronsard sur la poésie française* (Paris: Champion, 1927), 2 vols.; A. Rosenbauer, *Die Poetischen Theorien der Pleiade* (Leipzig: "Münchener Beiträge zur Romanischen und Englischen Philologie," 1895).

Muses" of Jean-Antoine de Baïf, and "A Bertran Bergier" of Du Bellay. These two separate materials the recent scholars have then woven into as whole a critical cloth as the meagre weft would allow. By such a synthesising process, they have acquainted us with certain general theories and reforms of the Pléiade.

Because of the scarcity of written aesthetic theory left by these poets, however, and since the position of the Pléiade in the history of criticism is a paramount one, it has seemed worth while to expand and fill in to a greater extent certain parts of this hypothetical or patchwork critical system, examining and revaluating their works more closely than had been done. Despite previous work on Pléiade literary theory, there remained one way by which this process of filling in a basic poetics might be successfully carried on. This was by an analysis of the judgments and opinions of the Pléiade on other writers. Such an analysis has been one of the principal purposes of this study.

The writings of the Pléiade are replete with references to other poets, orators, chroniclers, grammarians, and philosophers, ranging from the mythical Orpheus, whom Pontus de Tyard criticised for knowing only Greek,[2] down through their colleague Desportes, whose glory was to cast Ronsard into shadow during the reign of Henri III. The Laumonier-Lemerre edition of Ronsard [3] shows that the complete text, including all variants from 1550 to 1587, has better than a thousand references to other writers, many of these carrying judgments with them. These remarks about his confreres invade Ronsard's works of every genre, except, it must be granted, his orisons. Ronsard spares only his God from shop talk about literary acquaintances. The remainder of the Pléiade, although as individuals their production lacks this richness, show a propor-

[2] Pontus de Tyard, ed. by Ch. Marty-Laveaux (Paris: Lemerre, 1875), pp. 235–236.

[3] *Œuvres complètes de Pierre de Ronsard*, ed. by P. Laumonier (Paris: Lemerre, 1914–1919), 8 vols.

tionate interest in other writers. Unfortunately, their abundant remarks are not all of a competent critical nature. Some are commonplaces describing a friend as a favorite of the Nine Sisters or of Phoebus Apollo, some are personal remarks based on prejudice, while others are the insincere hyperbole necessitated by court life. Yet a great many remain which, once grouped and analysed, constitute a valuable complement to present-day knowledge of Pléiade aesthetics. Not only do these references and judgments help to clarify the sketchy ideas about nature against nurture, mimetic processes, poetic madness and divinity, and the like, which the prefaces and manifestoes presented, but they introduce new concepts and criteria entirely neglected in the manifestoes. These include such basic issues as truth and mendacity, sincerity and insincerity, clarity and obscurity, sweetness and utility, poetic glory and the revolt against glory. It is noteworthy that these became major criteria in practice, that is, in the criticisms and judgments which the Pléiade pronounced upon other writers, even though they remained minor in theory.

It is the aim of this volume to demonstrate, by inducing principles from specific judgments, that these issues must be included in any hypothetical system of criticism which might be set up for the Pléiade, to show how they were a part of the literary tradition which the Pléiade inherited, to indicate the extent to which they were used, and lastly, to quote from the specific judgments themselves. To summarise, then, this volume is to our knowledge the first attempt to create a latter-day poetics for the Pléiade movement, including, although not all, at least the most basic issues of their aesthetics.

A word must be said to establish which poets shall be examined under the title of "Pléiade." The Pléiade, as Laumonier has said, was composed of the inner circle of the Brigade,[4] and its constituency varied with the passing of the years, just as that of the Alexandrian group from which these poets took the

[4] Ronsard, Laumonier-Lemerre edition, VII, 301.

I. CONVENTIONAL POETIC THEORY FROM

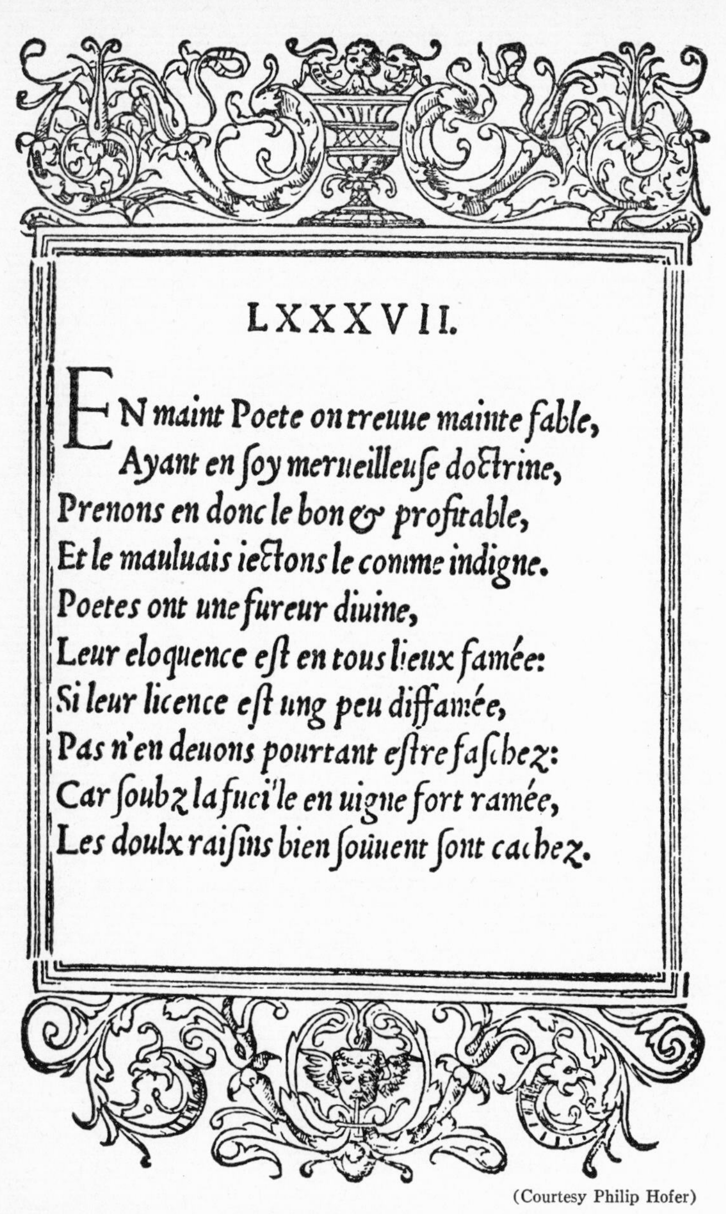

LXXXVII.

EN maint Poete on treuue mainte fable,
Ayant en ſoy merueilleuſe doctrine,
Prenons en donc le bon & profitable,
Et le mauluais iectons le comme indigne.
Poetes ont une fureur diuine,
Leur eloquence eſt en tous lieux famée:
Si leur licence eſt ung peu diffamée,
Pas n'en deuons pourtant eſtre faſchez:
Car ſoubz la fueille en uigne fort ramée,
Les doulx raiſins bien ſouuent ſont cachez.

(Courtesy Philip Hofer)

CONTEMPORARY EMBLEMATIC LITERATURE
(From the *Théâtre des bons engins*, 1539)

name of Pléiade had varied.[5] The attempt to restrict to the number of seven "les nouveaux Cignes, qui ores par la France vont chantant" [6] was a futile attempt to revive the Alexandrian nomenclature which their leaders at length abandoned. That it was soon recognised as such and discarded is evident from Ronsard's "Préface des nouvelles poésies," [7] where he recalls having once used the term Pléiade in the "Élégie à Christofle de Longueil." The popular retention of the word, both Laumonier and Chamard affirm, was due to the Huguenot poets, to whom it illustrated the vanity and pretentiousness of Ronsard.[8] Some personal observations about the meaning of the word "Pléiade" in the concluding chapter of this volume may serve to justify our acceptance of the term in its broadest sense.

In this volume, the Pléiade is considered as encompassing at least fifteen of the mid-century poets whose aims and educations coincided with those of Ronsard and Du Bellay. These will be selected from the register of names collected in the following works where the New Swans are mentioned: [9]

Ronsard:	Les isles fortunées (V, 157)
	Épître à Jean de la Péruse (V, 34)
	Élégie à Christofle de Longueil (V, 185)
	Hymne de Henry II (VII, 434)
	Binet's *Vie de Ronsard* (Laumonier edition, pp. 43–44)
	Dithyrambes à la pompe du bouc de Jodelle (VI, 186)
Baïf:	Les Muses (M.-L., II, 90)
Du Bellay:	Preface to the first edition of the *Olive*
	La Musagnœomachie (IV, 3)

[5] Henri Chamard, *La doctrine et l'œuvre poétique de la Pléiade* (Paris: Guillon, n. d.), p. 2.

[6] Du Bellay, *Œuvres poétiques françaises*, ed. by H. Chamard (Paris: "Société des textes français modernes," 1908–1919), IV, 51.

[7] Ronsard, Laumonier-Lemerre edition, VII, 38.

[8] Ronsard, Laumonier-Lemerre edition, VIII, 122; and Henri Chamard, *La doctrine et l'œuvre poétique*, pp. 2 ff.; also Chamard, *Histoire de la Pléiade* (Paris: Didier, 1939–), I, 2.

[9] For an explanation of the editions referred to in footnotes, see closing paragraph of this introduction.

Tyard:	Chant en faveur de quelques excellens poètes de ce temps (M.-L., p. 121)
	Épistre-préface aux *Erreurs amoureuses* (M.-L., p. 2)
Dorat:	Épithalame de Marie de Lorraine (M.-L., p. 22)

The poets to be studied, then, will include Ronsard, Du Bellay, Jean-Antoine de Baïf, Jodelle, Des Autels, La Péruse, Belleau, Dorat, Peletier, Pontus de Tyard, Héroët, Magny, Passerat, Tahureau, and Grévin. These are the most representative of a larger group which might include Paschal, Tagault, Gruget, Butet, Lancelot Carle, and several others.

It is the actual poems of these men which will serve as the prima materia of our investigation. However, their written theory is kept constantly under consideration, and this prose is correlated with their poetry when the occasion demands. This opposition of theory preached and theory applied is another primary objective of this study. To avoid viewing the Pléiade as an isolated and unrelated phenomenon, we parallel some of their ideas not only with the critics of classical antiquity, but with other French and even neo-Latin writers of their epoch.

The principal criteria or facets of their aesthetics which gradually emerge from the wealth of criticisms in the Pléiade poetry are the following:

Chapter I:	The Ethics of poetry (truth and sincerity)
Chapter II:	The Values of poetry (glory and the revolt against glory)
Chapter III:	The Communication of poetry (clarity and obscurity)
Chapter IV:	The Function of poetry (sweetness and utility)
Chapter V:	The Inspiration of poetry (art and nature)

Quotations from the poetry of Ronsard relate to the Laumonier edition published by Lemerre (1914–1919) unless otherwise indicated. References to Du Bellay's French verse apply to the Chamard edition; for Du Bellay's Latin poemata, to the Garnier edition. Passages from Baïf, Dorat, Tyard, Belleau, and Jodelle, unless otherwise indicated, are taken from the Marty-Laveaux series and designated by "M.-L." For the poetry of Magny, Héroët, Peletier, Des Autels, La Péruse, Grévin, Tahureau, and others, the footnote will indicate the standard edition used. Any reference to the "Société des textes français modernes" printing of Ronsard will be identified by "STFM." As this latter edition being prepared by Laumonier is not at this date sufficiently complete, we have consulted its valuable exegesis and quoted from its variants, but normally refer to the Laumonier-Lemerre edition. A description of these and other texts of the Pléiade poets may be found in the bibliography at the close of the volume. The footnote will record deviations from the practice outlined here, and references to the editions not published by Marty-Laveaux will be clearly indicated.

CRITICAL THEORY AND PRACTICE OF THE PLÉIADE

The Ethics of Poetry . . .

I

TRUTH AND SINCERITY

> This impression of reality is produced by truth only, and therefore the highest relation of an author to his subject is *sincerity*. The lowest limit, conversely, will be that in which the author's relation to his subject is not genuine but false. All works of art lie between these two limits.
>
> — LEO TOLSTOY, *On Art*

> Giacchè, o per sincerità s'intende il dovere morale di non ingannare il prossimo; e, in tal caso, è estranea all'artista. Il quale, infatti, non inganna nessuno, perchè dà forma a ciò ch'è già nel suo animo, e ingannerebbe solo se tradisse il suo dovere d'artista. . . . Se nel suo animo è l'inganno e la menzogna, la forma ch'egli dà a quei fatti . . . non può essere, essa, inganno o menzogna.
>
> — BENEDETTO CROCE, *Estetica*

ONE of the most common standards by which the Pléiade associates judged a writer was that of his truthfulness or sincerity. Although none could be more classically traditional or more psychologically obvious, the wide use of this criterion is surprising. For nowhere in the prose treatises of Du Bellay, Peletier, Sébilet, Ronsard, or the others, are mendacity and sincerity in literature discussed independently. Ronsard comments in brief fashion upon historical truth and verisimilitude in the "Abbrégé de l'art poétique" and in the 1587 preface to the *Franciade*,[1] but, as we shall explain below, it is truth as an ethical concept that is to be our concern here.

[1] Ronsard, VII, 52, 80.

It is within the poems themselves that one learns of the Pléiade's belief that deliberate falsehood and insincerity in literature are cardinal sins. One may feign — that is, conceal truth — but one may not lie. Feigning, as a matter of fact, was an important part of the primitive relationship existing between poetry and truth. The function of the poet was to interpret and embroider truth. In Pléiade theory, the process of feigning was entirely dissociated from the vice of lying. Poetry was at first an allegorical theology hiding verity behind style and ornament and had, according to Ronsard, the ultimate purpose of "admitting into the brains of primitive men by pleasant and colored fables secrets which they would not be able to understand if the truth were disclosed to them too openly."[2] Again, when Ronsard describes how he acquired the art of poetry, he relates that he learned from Dorat the science of properly disguising realities.[3] A further development of this conception of poetry as allegory or fabulation can be found in the fourth of the neo-Platonic *Dialogues philosophiques* by Louis Le Caron, in which feigning is the topic of an imaginary conversation among Ronsard, Jodelle, Claude Fauchet, and Pasquier:

> . . . Ainsi les poètes . . . pensant estre indignes de prostituer leurs sacrées inventions au profane vulgaire, les ont voulu couvrir de fables: afin qu'elles ne fussent entendues que des plus sages et doctes. Toutesfois si naïvement elles imitent et représentent la nature, qu'elles semblent estre tirées d'elle; les autres sont plus graves et éloignées de l'opinion commune, sous lesquelles aussi sont cachées les plus haultes et excellentes choses, mais si obscures, que l'ignorante multitude eût mal fait son profit, si autrement elles eussent été révélées. . . .[4]

The idea of a poet as a possessor of divine and arcane truths which he does his best to obscure or distort (*feindre*, *farder*,

[2] Ronsard, *Abbrégé de l'art poétique*, VII, 44–45.
[3] Ronsard, *Hymne de l'Automne*, IV, 313.
[4] Quoted in Marcel Raymond, *Influence de Ronsard sur la poésie française* (Paris: Champion, 1927), I, 315.

II. JEAN DORAT

Ainsi disoit la Nymphe, et de là je vins estre
Disciple de Dorat, qui longtemps fust mon maistre,
M'apprist la poésie, et me monstra comment
On doit feindre et cacher les fables proprement.
— RONSARD

(see page 4)

contrefaire) is an inevitable result of the Platonic or Pindaric view of the poet as an oracle or mouthpiece of the gods, which the Pléiade knew well. The idea had a Christian antecedence also, for Christ himself had elected to speak his truths in parables. At any rate, it was a widespread notion in the Middle Ages. Laumonier has shown it to result in part from mediaeval interpretations of pagan mythology, and finds a reference to feigning in Jean Lemaire.[5] D. L. Clark views feigning as a consequence of the allegorising of the Middle Ages which persisted far into the sixteenth century, citing the justification for allegory in Stephen Hawes's *Pastime of Pleasure*:

> To make of nought reason sentencious
> Clokynge a trouthe wyth colour tenebrous.
> For often under a fayre fayned fable
> A trouthe appereth gretely profitable.[6]

One might add that such a prescription exists in French as early as the *Archiloge Sophie* of Jacques Legrand.[7]

This conception of the creative writer's function is most common in the poetics of the middle and late sixteenth century. *Feindre* is the standard verb employed to describe the process. Among the Latin grammarians and rhetoricians, *fingere* had had the original meaning of creation or creative imitation, and as late as the *Genealogia Deorum*, XIV, one finds Boccaccio suggesting *fingo* as the equivalent of the Greek ποιέω. By the time of Vida [8] and the Pléiade, however, the verb *feindre* was only occasionally used in the original sense of imitation, and usually bore connotations of falsifying.[9] Thus, the evolution

[5] Paul Laumonier, *Ronsard, poète lyrique* (Paris, 1909 and 1933), pp. 300–301.

[6] D. L. Clark, *Rhetoric and Poetry in the Renaissance* (New York: Columbia University Press, 1922), p. 127.

[7] "Poétrie est science qui aprent à faindre et à fere ficcions, *etc.*," quoted in W. F. Patterson, *Three Centuries of French Poetic Theory* (Ann Arbor, 1935), I, 10.

[8] Vida, *De arte poetica*, II, 304–306, 315–319, 345.

[9] With meaning of "represent, imitate," see Du Bellay's *Deffence*, ed. by Chamard, p. 170. For representative uses with the meaning of "falsify," see:

from the idea of creative imitation to an idea of creative falsification admitted by both pagan and Christian theorists, is illustrated by the semasiological change of *fingere*.

There are several members of the Pléiade who mention this type of "cloaking." Ronsard has further references to it, as have Du Bellay, Belleau, Héroët, and Tahureau.[10] They all sanction the practice and, in fact, seem inclined toward Ronsard's view that "the poet who writes things as they are is not worth so much as the poet who feigns them." [11] Vauquelin de la Fresnaye echoes this at least three times.[12]

This distinction then must be clear at the outset. To ornament truth, to render its communication obscure with willful distortion, to reproduce its *Schein* rather than its *Sein*, as Hartmann would write, this is the traditional function of the poet. Insincerity, deliberate misrepresentation of facts or truths, on the other hand, involves ethics and is therefore a vice. In their criticisms of other writers, the Pléiade censured those who practised deliberate falsification and called them liars.

Another distinction must be made here. This chapter is concerned with the problem of mendacity rather than with the more complicated related problem of verisimilitude. It has no concern with "possible improbabilities" or "probable impossibilities." The difference will become apparent as the examples are set forth, but a few words may be ventured here. A poet may offend against conceivable truth (*νοητά*) in three ways. He may belie historical, logical, or poetic truth. There are two principal ways in which the poet most frequently belies truth. If the infraction is due to incompetent imitation itself, conscious or unconscious, the problem is one of logic and

---

Baïf, M.-L., I, 9, 348; V, 75, 214; Jodelle, M.-L., II, 13, 49, 149; Du Bellay, VI, 282, 331; Desportes (ed. by Michiels), pp. 64; *etc.*

[10] Ronsard, III, 343; Du Bellay, VI, 165; Belleau, M.-L., II, 157–158; Héroët, ed. by Gohin, p. 94; Tahureau, ed. by Blanchemain, I, 92.

[11] Ronsard, VII, 66–67.

[12] Vauquelin de la Fresnaye, *Art poétique* (Paris, 1885), pp. 53, 125, and 157–158.

of verisimilitude. If the infraction is due to insincere falsification of known truth, independent of media or imitation, the problem is one of mendacity and an ethical one.

Although some of the criticisms by the Pléiade involved verisimilitude, most of those bearing upon truth are concerned with the ethical practices and sincerity of the writer under discussion. The exact meaning of the word truth as it becomes a criterion in this chapter is rendered by the Greek grammarians' precise word *ἀλήθεια*. This term, as contrasted with other terms for truth, means truth based on good faith, evident truth the opposite of a lie. Hermogenes called *ἀλήθεια* one of the seven characteristics of good poetry.[13] Julian the Apostate speaks of poets and seers as *ἐνθουσιῶντες πρὸς τὴν ἀλήθειαν*,[14] and the century's leading grammarian, Julius-Caesar Scaliger, revived the term.[15]

The distinction, then, is entirely one of moral intention, involving "conscience." Our differentiation between these two categories of untruth is not unlike that which Montaigne makes in his essay "Des menteurs" between "to tell a lie" and "to lie":

> dire mensonge, c'est dire chose faulse, mais qu'on a prins pour vraye; et la définition du mot mentir en latin, d'où nostre françoys est party, porte autant comme aller contre sa conscience.

Having established these two basic distinctions anent feigning and verisimilitude, we may pass on to a discussion of the antecedence of the Pléiade's beliefs about poetry as untruth.

That poetry was wed to falsehood was an idea which had already made its way into France as a mediaeval Christian conviction before being reinforced by the translation of Plato's *Republic* in the Petit edition of Ficino in 1518. The suspicions of churchmen who refused to believe poetry a mere handmaid of theology were part of the heritage of the very Catholic

[13] Hermogenes, *Opera* (Leipzig: Bibliotheca Teubneriana, 1913), pp. 352–363.
[14] Julian the Apostate, *Orationes*, iv, 136.
[15] J.-C. Scaliger, *Poetices libri septem* (Heidelberg: Bibliopolio Commeliano, 1617), p. 403.

Pléiade. Such church fathers as Tertullian and Lactantius had held that poets falsify and distort basic truths of church teachings. That all these misgivings and objections reached the boiling point at the time of the Pléiade is evidenced by the foundation of the Congregation of the Index Expurgatorius in 1563. The church charged that the poets not only made free with poetic license, but that they had a deliberate intention to deceive as well. Both of these charges were included in the classical heritage represented by the *Republic* and the *Ion*, although Plato as a philosopher was more tolerant of poets than were some of the Christian philosophers.

An inquiry into the history of poetry as falsehood would encompass the entire problem of the moral justification of poetry, treated by Spingarn, Clark, and others.[16] This chapter will deal merely with those comments of the Pléiade treating of honesty and sincerity. Although honest or sincere intention would seem a basic issue in any discussion of the morality of poetry, we have not found a full discussion of its history up to the advent of the Renaissance. It is not our aim to trace such a history, but a summary of the attitudes of a few of the pagan and Christian apologists and grammarians who pronounced opinions upon the subject will help to clarify the tradition behind the remarks of the Pléiade to be recorded here. If treatises on verisimilitude are common, treatises on ἀλήθεια are rare.

⚜ ⚜ ⚜

The second, third, and last books of the *Republic* carry the implication that poets are liars, but the passage best suiting our purpose is the colloquy between Glaucon and Socrates in the second book. Glaucon asks wherein Hesiod and Homer

[16] J. E. Spingarn, *Literary Criticism in the Renaissance* (New York, 1908), and D. L. Clark, *Rhetoric and Poetry in the Renaissance* (New York: Columbia University Press, 1922).

are particularly reprehensible and is informed that there is one principal objection: . . . ἄλλως τε καὶ ἐάν τις μὴ καλῶς ψεύδηται. Socrates illustrates his charge by citing striking lies of these two early writers.

Others in the pagan tradition who agreed that poets were liars wrote in Latin. The young poet Gallus admitted that "saepe poetarum mendacia dulcia finxi."[17] Ovid speaks of the poet as one who takes full advantage of his license: "Exit in immensum foecunda licentia vatum."[17] In the first century of the Christian Era, Quintilian and Pliny concurred that poets shied away from truth,[18] the latter asking mischievously what poets have to do with truth ("tametsi quid poëtae cum fide?").

For their part, the church fathers were even more direct in their assertions that poets told falsehoods. The pope-apologist Eusebius writes simply that "licet poetis mentiri."[19] Saint Augustine warns that mimes, comedies, and poems may be "full of lies," and in his epistles holds that writers have no more license regarding truth than other men.[20] Two centuries later, another churchman, Isidore of Seville, discusses in his *Etymologiae* the untruths of poets, which are not "res factae sed tantum loquendo fictae."[21] Boccaccio, one of the greatest of the early humanists, will admit that poets lie,[22] but insists that this is the result of invention rather than deception. There are two types of liars, he contends, those who tell untruths intentionally and those telling them unintentionally. Only those of the first category are really liars, and, after all, philosophers are just as great prevaricators as poets. If Boccaccio's argument lacks logical sequence, it nevertheless shows how

[17] The references to Gallus and Ovid are from the *De Abusu Mendacii* of Gentili (see note 25).

[18] Quintilian, *Inst. Orat.* I, v, 12; Pliny, *Epist.* ix, 33.

[19] Eusebius, iv, 6.

[20] Augustinus, *Soliloquiorum Liber II*, cap. ix; in *Opera Omnia* (Basileae, MDLVI), I, 533.

[21] Isidore of Seville, *Etymologiae* i, 40.

[22] Boccaccio, *De Genealogia Deorum* xiv, 13.

important sincerity and intention had become as a means of judging the truthfulness of poets.

Neo-classic rhetoric declared that the purpose of the demonstrative faculty was the true; of the dialectic, the probable; of the rhetoric, the persuasive, and of the poetic, the false. Robortelli, commenting on the poetics of Aristotle, reintroduced these categorical purposes to the Renaissance.[23]

These representative examples must serve as a sketchy outline summary of the history of theories on poetic mendacity up to the Renaissance, upon which subject a volume might well be written.

At least two treatises known to France of the late sixteenth century attest the existence of a current "proverb" that poets are liars. The first, the *Politique Discourses upon Truth and Lying*, written in French by Martin Cognet and Englished by Sir Edward Holy in 1586, devotes a brief chapter to the proposition that "lying hath made poets and painters to be blamed."[24] Showing that Plato had condemned poetry, citing the banishment of Archilochus, Cognet concludes: "Hence grew the common proverb that all poets are Lyers." Another contemporary treatise on prevarication, the *De Abusu Mendacii* of Alberico Gentili, was of a more historical and less moral tone. Gentili also reveals the existence of a sixteenth-century dictum that poets were liars. The chapter devoted to poetry makes this charge in the initial sentence:

> Sed & poetae, qui item Logici sunt, multa soliti mentiri: ut vetus et proverbium est. Et nihil est magis ad manum, quam dicere, poetas esse mendaces. . . . Sic poetae non refugiunt a mendacio.[25]

Two other neo-Latin volumes, the *Poemata* of the Bordeaux humanist, George Buchanan, and the *Ata* of Julius-Caesar Scaliger, contain almost categorical pronouncements about the mendacity of poets:

[23] Toffanin, *Fine dell'umanesimo* (Torino, 1920), p. 96.

[24] Martin Cognet, *Politique Discourses upon Truth and Lying*, Eng. trans. (London, 1586), p. 159.

[25] Alberico Gentili, *Disputationes Duae* (Hanoviae, MDXCIX), p. 162.

Dixit; sed vates dicere falsa solent.[26]

(ast mentiuntur: ast hoc est
Peculiare ac proprium poetarum).[27]

With this dual heritage, pagan and Christian, coming down from the past, with the belief so common in the Renaissance as to become a familiar adage, one is surprised, as we have already observed, that there is no mention of poetic sincerity or mendacity as a basis of literary criticism in any of the Pléiade treatises.

However, these poets were concerned with the problem, "nihil magis ad manum," as Gentili put it. If there are no prefaces or entire poems devoted to mendacity, the subjoined collection of passages from their verse will attempt to show how mindful they were of the issue and how often it became the basis of their opinions on other writers. In the course of our collecting these opinions voiced by the Pléiade, it has become apparent that they hinged upon this one basis as frequently as on any single criterion of judgment.

It has already been stated that the problem of truth in this chapter is an ethical one, that verisimilitude is only contingent or secondary. Before passing to the individual judgments themselves, a few words must be said to amplify this. The Pléiade, as one will see, was most inconsistent about poetic truth or inventiveness. They confused poetic with other types of truth, and not all the reproaches of mendacity brought forward were relevant. Although they admit that poets may invent, and supposedly sanction the licenses of fiction, one will find them in the following pages criticising poets for indulging in what they claimed was *invraysemblance*. Sometimes they became as narrow in their conception of verisimilitude as was the seventeenth century, judging solely by standards of historical

[26] Buchanan, *Poemata quae extant*, editio postrema, Lugduni Batav. Ex officina Elzeviriana, 1628, p. 329.

[27] J.-C. Scaliger, *Ata*, in the *Poemata* (Heidelberg: "apud Petrum Santandreanum, MDXCI"), part II, p. 63. See also, Vulteius, *Hendecasyllaborum liber III* (Paris, 1538), p. 84, the piece entitled "Ad Villansium": "Quod non misceo fabulas libellis, *etc.*"

or scientific truth and censuring a poet for mere flights of imagination which should be his artistic birthright. The chief objection contained in such passages seems to be that the poet is dishonest, that he has a desire to deceive the reader. In view of this confusion of the Pléiade over the meaning and prerogatives of poetic truth, one must not be surprised when these writers censure the *merveilleux* of the old epics. The censure is really directed against the ethics of an author who would abuse the reader's credulity and good faith. All charges of mendacity, whether based on evidence or intention, will be listed together, for our arrangement of these passages is a purely chronological one, based on who told the lie rather than which type of lie it was. We have adopted the chronological arrangement in order that this chapter may be consistent with the following chapters.

The judgments of the Pléiade are not merely categorical statements that a given poet lied. Such may be the case, of course. But more frequently the remarks vary in tone from accusation to mild reproach. There are also a few instances where the ethical implications are so slight as to become negligible. In such cases the Pléiade will deny the truth of the writer's statement without charging him with an intent to deceive. In sum, certain of the observations will question only the truth of the poet's statement, certain others the sincerity of the poet himself, whereas the majority of them will question both. These many observations, approaching truth and sincerity from various sides, tend to show that remarks about the intellectual honesty of poets are not merely fortuitous or casual, that they derive from a definite principle.

The judgments or remarks will be considered in chronological order, from the ancient Greeks to the sixteenth-century French. At the close of the chapter a section will be devoted to studied lying and "silken words," as flattery was called.

⚜ ⚜ ⚜

The Pléiade poets as Hellenists were quite familiar with the Platonic suspicions concerning poetic mendacity: both Du Bellay and Jodelle mention them:

> Jadis le fameux inventeur
> De la doctrine Académique
> Chassoit le poète menteur
> Par les loix de sa république.[28]

> Celuy qui sa République
> Nous a laissée en portrait,
> Banissoit les faux Poëtes. . . .[29]

The lesson which the Pléiade learned from this was a simple one. If the ancients could not believe their own writers, then there was no logical reason why the sixteenth century should believe them. In the middle sixteenth century, then, the fact that a statement was uttered by a classic poet was not sufficient to stamp it as a truth. This we shall see proved many times. In this respect, the 1550's showed more *bon sens* than the early seventeenth century. A second reason made the Pléiade writer reticent about accepting unreservedly the authority of the past. Realising that he himself, as a practitioner, could fall into error, he became aware that even a Homer could nod, a bit of reasoning regarded as specious a few decades later. Literary, like ecclesiastical authoritarianism was suffering momentarily. Acceptance by formula, the *αὐτὸς ἔφη* of the Pythagoreans and the *ipse dixit* which had satisfied the Aristotelians, was now a thing of the past. Reason was replacing it. This at least was the contention of two of the group's spokesmen, Du Bellay and Tahureau:

> Mais si j'ay dict bien ou mal, je m'en rapporte à ceux qui sont plus amis de la vérité que de Platon ou Socrate, et ne sont imitateurs des Pythagoriques, qui pour toutes raisons n'alleguoint [*sic*] si non: Cetuy la l'a dit.[30]

[28] Du Bellay, IV, 138.

[29] Jodelle, M.-L., II, 332. See also, the *Uranie* of Du Bartas, vss. 97 ff.; and J.-C. Scaliger's "De poetis a Platone ejectis" in his *Apiculae* (*ed cit.*, I, 13).

[30] Du Bellay, *Deffence*, ed. by Chamard, p. 187.

> . . . ainsi que faisoient au temps passé les disciples de Pithagore, ne donnans autre raison de leurs opinions voire fussent elles les plus sottes & les plus lourdes du monde, fors qu'en disant αὐτὸς ἔφα, c'est à dire il l'a dit.[31]

It was then possible for them to weigh dispassionately the statements of the ancients as well as those of their contemporaries, despite their enthusiasm for classical literatures, and to accept or discard at will.

As an illustration of the incredulity of which this century was capable when the truth of the ancients was involved, we cite the following passage from the *Dialogues* of Tahureau. One of the collocutors, Le Democritic, cites the tale of Empedocles's freeing the Agrigentines from a windstorm by encircling the town with ramparts of asses' skins:

> LE COSMOPHILE: Ha ha ha! la grande folie que c'est d'avoir mis cette bourde là en escrit, comme une chose véritable.
>
> LE DEMOCRITIC: Comment, tu ne le croi donq' pas, & tant d'autheurs approuvés en ont fait mention!
>
> LE COSMOPHILE: Si nous voulions croire tout ce que nous voyons par escrit, enregistré comme histoires, il ne faudroit point aller chercher d'autres peaus pour destourner le vent que les nostres.[32]

The sincerity of the ancients is implicitly challenged as frequently as that of the moderns. Despite the Pléiade's Hellenism, they could not forget the notorious mendacity of Greek writers. Pontus de Tyard, in his *Erreurs amoureuses*, recalls the fabulous Helen of "la menteuse Grèce." [33] The same formula is found in the *Odes* of Jodelle, "la cauteleuse Grèce, la Grèce tousjours menteresse," [34] while Ronsard disowns the subject matter "des Grecs mensongers." [35] One may remember the reference to "cete Grèce menteresse" in the *Deffence*, which

[31] Tahureau, *Dialogues*, ed. by F. Conscience (Paris: Lemerre, 1870), p. 152.
[32] *Ibid.*, pp. 122–123.
[33] Pontus de Tyard, M.-L., p. 102.
[34] Jodelle, M.-L., II, 194.
[35] Ronsard, IV, 164.

Chamard traces to Juvenal's "Graecia mendax." [36] Of the literature of this lying nation Jodelle complains:

> Que diray je de mille songes,
> Mille fables, mille mensonges,
> Dont ils pensoyent orner leurs faits,
> Et leurs beaux escripts contrefaits? [37]

The very waters of Parnassus from which the ancients quaffed their inspiration were called "les flotz menteurs." [38]

In his exchange of sonnets with Jeanne d'Albret, Du Bellay seems to find that the artifice of the ancients diminishes the truth of their works.[39] To the lady's innuendo about his knowing how to "dextrement feindre," he replies that the ancients surpassed him at this. To sing her praises he will resort to neither artifice nor fables, as would a Homer, but will content himself with his natural expression, without trying to imitate the ancients: "Car si moins qu'eux j'estois ingénieux, plus véritable aussi qu'eux je serois." [40]

Ronsard could be most forthright. Hesiod becomes "le vieil Ascréan qui ment" when he writes that pity and justice have left the earth forever.[41] Ronsard accuses even his favorite Pindar with a blunt "tu mentois" in another poem published in 1555; it will be remembered that by 1555 his devotion to Pindar was on the wane.[42] Occasions like this one where the Pléiade openly calls a writer a liar are rare. More common is the politely reserved doubt, where the wording is subtle but the inference is plain.

It is while speaking of classic literature that Du Bellay introduces a phase of this problem of sincerity which we have not yet considered, but which regards the relationship between the

[36] *Deffence*, ed. by Chamard, p. 339.

[37] Jodelle, M.-L., II, 195.

[38] Ronsard, Laumonier-STFM edition, III, 104.

[39] Obviously, the pejorative meaning of artifice (falsehood) is intended here; for other meanings, see Chapter V.

[40] Du Bellay, II, 224.

[41] Ronsard, II, 441; also, VI, 340.

[42] *Ibid.*, II, 31.

author and the falsehoods in his work. It has been suggested by at least one modern literary critic that we cannot charge authors with deception if deceit is actually in their hearts or with lying if lies are in their hearts.[43] Thus a poet would be mendacious only if, he being guileless, his writings betrayed deceit, or he being guileful, his writings betrayed no deceit. This implication that the poem may be a lie while the poet remains ethically blameless is a bit of logic which Du Bellay foresaw and rejected instanter. To him the written word was an intimate expression not only of the artist's mind, but of his personality and ethos as well. If the forms of his expression are lies and deceit, then the poet himself is a liar and a deceiver; there is no way out through choplogic.

Quel esprit tant sourcilleux
Contemplant la *Thébaïde*
Ou le discours merveilleux
De l'immortelle *Énéide*
Se plaint que de ces autheurs
Les poèmes sont menteurs?
Ainsi l'Aveugle divin
Nous faict voir sous feint ouvrage
D'ung guerrier le fort courage
Et l'esprit d'ung homme fin.[44]

Verses not only represent what the poet is and what he thinks; they go further and reveal those innermost thoughts which he would not dare to speak. Both Du Bellay and Desportes admit this in almost identical wording. Du Bellay records that "verses sing for me what I dare not say," [45] and Desportes writes, "I write all night that which I dare not say." [46]

With the proposition established that as a man is, so will he reveal himself in his writings, let us proceed to further doubts of the Pléiade regarding the veracity of the ancient

[43] Benedetto Croce, *Estetica* (Bari, 1928), p. 62.
[44] Du Bellay, IV, 173–174.
[45] *Ibid.*, II, 63.
[46] Desportes, *Œuvres*, edition of Michiels (Paris, 1858), p. 116.

Greeks. Plato is arraigned several times. Ronsard says that the glory of Plato almost persuades him to believe the statement that the forms of all things exist in our souls, but that he still disbelieves it.[47] Jacques Grévin has his doubts about this very same affirmation of Plato, and he wonders "whether that could be true of which you dare assure us." [48] Ronsard accuses Plato of insincerity, not mendacity, in his "Hymne de l'or," observing that Plato was servile toward the Tyrant of Sicily, hoping to be financially rewarded.[49] He doubts Plato's cosmography,[50] and in another place objects to the subtle words of the great Plato who pretended that one could rule a city by paper and not by action.[51] Nor can this poet believe the philosopher's talk about the human mind's being an "influxion des cieux." [52] But the greatest accusation of intellectual dishonesty is found in the initial sonnet of the poem sequence to Hélène de Surgères:

> Lecteur, je ne veux estre escolier de Platon,
> Qui la vertu nous presche, et ne fait pas de mesme.[53]

By a coincidence which seems hardly accidental, Du Bellay, Jean-Antoine de Baïf, Ronsard, and Magny all question the position of Pythagoras on metempsychosis in similar fashion:

> Si lon doibt croire à Pythagore
> Qui les corps fait ranimer . . .[54]
>
> Si après que la mort nostre âge auroit finie,
> Comme dit Pythagore, il estoit vray . . .[55]
>
> Si ce qu'a dit Pythagore
> Pour vrai l'on veut estimer.[56]
>
> Si lon doit croire à Pythagore.[57]

[47] Ronsard, II, 269.
[48] Grévin, ed. by Pinvert, p. 293.
[49] Ronsard, IV, 339.
[50] *Ibid.*, I, 39.
[51] *Ibid.*, III, 279.
[52] *Ibid.*, I, 285.
[53] *Ibid.*, I, 295.
[54] Gohin edition of Héroët, p. 154.
[55] Baïf, M.-L., I, 185.
[56] Ronsard, VI, 119.
[57] Magny, edition of Courbet, I, 120.

Pontus de Tyard finds that mocking Aristophanes used deceit and falsehood in his *Clouds*.[58] Du Bellay grants that although Xenophon occasionally failed to tell the truth about Cyrus, his authority among the Greeks is still great.[59] Dorat, who seldom ventured a literary opinion in his pieces, holds that Homer "en plusieurs façons se souloit varier," and maintains that Proteus would never have let himself be caught napping, as Homer would have us believe.[60] Even the views of Epicurus on fortune are contradicted by this skeptical coterie.[61] By the way, the year 1566 marked the appearance of Henri Estienne's *Apologie pour Hérodote*, a work with the avowed purpose of proving the truthfulness of the Greek historian, the "father of history."

Ronsard accuses Homer of misguided reason when he recalls that Homer (the princeps read "Virgile" here) quite wrongfully called sleep the brother of death,[62] or when he described his favorite fountain as black in color,[63] but when Homer records that one of the horses of Achilles augured the death of his master, he becomes "le fantastique Homère." [64] And fantasy is conscious falsehood, as Ronsard shows elsewhere:

> Un discours fantastiq' ma raison ne contante:
> Je n'aime point le faux, j'aime la vérité.[65]

In the 1587 preface to the *Franciade*, however, he accuses Homer of outright falsifying. Showing how the epicist gave Greek names to the Phrygian soldiers of Troy, he concludes that the entire *Iliad* is an untruth: "ce n'est qu'une fiction de toute *l'Iliade*, et non vérité." [66]

The subject matter of epics in the Hellenic tradition often stirred up sharp, incredulous comment on the part of the Pléiade. Not only Homer, but the whole realm of pagan and pagan-Christian epic material from Homer to Ariosto, with

[58] Pontus de Tyard, M.-L., p. 134.
[59] Du Bellay, II, 215.
[60] Dorat, M.-L., p. 18.
[61] Ronsard, II, 10.
[62] *Ibid.*, II, 324.
[63] *Ibid.*, II, 428.
[64] *Ibid.*, V, 112.
[65] *Ibid.*, VI, 389.
[66] *Ibid.*, VII, 84.

all its magical trappings, is classed as untruth by Belleau. In his ode congratulating Nicolas Denisot for his *Cantiques du premier advènement de Jesus-Christ*, Belleau praises the Christian Muse and rejoices that, for a change, "Icy ne sont point chantez d'un son pippeur les mensonges, bois meuz, fleuves arrestez, ny d'un mont cornu les songes." [67] These *Cantiques* prompt Jodelle to echo this very thought. All of this, by the way, anticipates the future defenders of the *merveilleux chrétien*. Jodelle, too, congratulates Denisot on reviving the Christian Muse, asking,

Que nous sert plus de redire
Maint fatal enfantement,
Qu'en noz Menteurs on peut lire
Descrit fabuleusement?
Fuyons ces vois menteresses,
Que nous servent ces Déesses,
L'une sortant d'un cerveau:
L'autre de l'écume fille,
Qui aborde en sa coquille,
Virevoltante sus l'eau? [68]

The legend about Pallas Athene's birth was one of the commonplaces of pagan mythology which disturbed Du Bellay as well. Typically denying the epic writer the licenses of poetic imagination, Du Bellay in his *Regrets* classes all this narrative material as falsehood. "Paschal, I have no wish to assault Jupiter or break his skull, like Vulcan, to bring out a new Pallas."

D'un effroyable armet je ne la veulx armer,
Ny de ce que du nom d'une chèvre on appelle,
Et moins pour avoir veu sa Gorgonne cruelle,
Veulx-je en nouveaux cailloux les hommes transformer.
  Je ne veulx déguiser ma simple poésie
Sous le masque emprunté d'une fable moisie,
Ny souiller un beau nom de monstres tant hideux.[69]

[67] Belleau, M.-L., II, 454.
[68] Jodelle, M.-L., II, 331.
[69] Du Bellay, II, 201.

It was the *Iliad* and the *Odyssey*, of course, which were the sources of all this epic lying. J.-C. Scaliger himself held a brief for truth, taking the tragedians and epicists of antiquity to task: "Most men hate mendacity. That is why those battles at the walls of Thebes which last but two hours always displease me." [70] If others in the century were particularly harsh about Arthurian epic materials — Mellin calls the Perceforest "ces mensonges" and Marot refers to "Lancelot, le très plaisant menteur" — the Pléiade was no less severe regarding the classical epic.[71] In his "Discours de Jules César," Jodelle speaks of the *Iliad* as prevarications and impossibilities: Phoebus descending to preserve Hector, Minerva haranguing her father against Hector, and the rest. "To me this is nothing but empty and ponderous falsehood; I want to reprove the whole thing as a lie." [72] And Jacques Grévin begins his first book of amores, "I sing here no dusty victories the Greeks won on foreign strand, I describe here no dubious battles of banished Francion in some lying poem." [73] In branding as false the subject matter of the ancients, Jodelle includes the melic and tragic poets as well. This accusation occupies most of Branle II of his *Amours*. He complains that the ancients

> Des maux nous écrivent
> Qui onc à eux, ni aussi
> Onc à nul n'arrivent.[74]

The Sophists, too, came in for their share of reproof. Jean-Antoine de Baïf exclaims in his *Amours de Francine*:

> Sophistes, vous mentez, qui dites que l'amour
> Est une passion dedans une âme oisive:
> Sophistes, vous mentez. . . .[75]

[70] Scaliger, *Poetices libri septem* (edition of 1561), III, 97.
[71] Saint-Gelays, *Œuvres poétiques*, ed. by Blanchemain (Paris, 1873), II, 65; Marot, *Œuvres complètes* (Paris: Garnier, n. d.), I, 315.
[72] Jodelle, M.-L., II, 262.
[73] Grévin, edition of Pinvert, p. 243.
[74] Jodelle, M.-L., II, 55.
[75] Baïf, M.-L., I, 124.

Such are the passages treating of the mendacity of Hellenic writers. Of Hebrew literature nothing may be said in this section. As a group, the Pléiade did not read Hebrew, one of the "three languages" of the humanists. Héroët called it an excessively hated language.[76] The only Hebrew literature they knew was the Holy Writ. As both the Old and the New Testaments were inspired by the Christian God, it is not extraordinary that the Pléiade nowhere accuses their author of insincerity. Du Bartas, the Protestant, described the divine origin of the Old Testament, declaring it to have been openly drawn up by God, while Ronsard, writing on the tradition of the Roman Church, is witness to the divinity of the New Testament. Du Bartas recorded that God had "taken pains not only to give to the Jews exquisite nourishment, but also to give abundantly of his laws — Spirit to their spirit through the Spirit of his voice." [77] Ronsard stated that the Church "full of grace and the spirit of God, chose four witnesses, Saints John, Luke, Mark, Matthew, secretaries of Christ, and to make them believed by the baptised people approved their story." [78]

⚜ ⚜ ⚜

The Latins could be just as mendacious as the Greeks. Ronsard, reading a remark of Cicero's on infamy, cannot refrain from retorting, "Que tu es, Cicéron, un affetté menteur." [79] And Étienne Jodelle attacks the *De Bello Gallico* of Julius Caesar:

> Tu mens, Jules César, lache en son infortune
> Le François ne se montre. . . .[80]

[76] Héroët, *Œuvres*, ed. by F. Gohin (Paris: STFM, 1909), in dedication of the *Androgyne*, p. 81.

[77] Du Bartas, *Works*, ed. by U. T. Holmes, Jr. (Chapel Hill: University of North Carolina, 1935–40), II, 34.

[78] Ronsard, V, 409.

[79] *Ibid.*, VI, 229.

[80] Jodelle, M.-L., II, 105.

The question of credibility is applicable even to Vergil, although we have already found Vergil and Statius complimented upon writing as they really felt (*v. supra*, note 44). In at least two pieces Ronsard makes the reservation, "if one is to believe Vergil." [81] But once again the verb *mentir* is called into play when Ronsard reflects upon the Lesbian verses of Catullus. He quotes the Veronese poet on old age, but quickly adds, "Si Catulle a menti, ma faulte est à crédit." [82] Du Bellay also charged Catullus with either inaccuracy or insincerity, pointing out with curious logic that Catullus must have neither wished nor received so many kisses, since he was able to remember the exact count of them, according to his claims.[83]

Occasionally these humanists could sound like thin-lipped Councillors of Trent. When Du Bellay reflects upon the futility of passing one's time reading Petrarch, Vergil, Horace, Ovid, and the Greeks, as he does in the discourse to Macrin on virtue, he makes the observation that all the fine dreams of these people are lies.[84] *Songes* are no more than *mensonges*. What does one gain by reading them except to be caught up in the rapid sweep of the years? Here again the charge of mendacity is unspecified and arbitrary, illustrating the Pléiade's want of discrimination and analysis when treating of poetic license.

We have noted that the veracity of Statius is not questioned, oddly enough. Moreover, he is commended for having "suivi la vraysemblance." [85] As much cannot be said for Lucretius; because he described his frenzies which he thought to be true according to his sect "and since he did not build his work on verisimilitude and possibility, I deny him completely the name of poet, even though certain of his verses are divine." [86] This seems a strange contrariness on the part of Ronsard. Two tenets held in high esteem by the Pléiade, the sacred fury and sincerity of intention, seem to conflict with verisimilitude, and

[81] Ronsard, VI, 219; VII, 71.
[82] *Ibid.*, IV, 59.
[83] Du Bellay, V, 89.
[84] *Ibid.*, IV, 147.
[85] Ronsard, VII, 83.
[86] *Ibid.*, VII, 82.

Ronsard is unwilling to admit that the result is poetry. This is not consonant with his position elsewhere in his works — certainly a contradiction to Du Bellay — and results from the ill-defined distinction that Ronsard was wont to make between poetic and historical truth. Ronsard acknowledges in the "Ode à Michel de l'Hospital" that Orpheus, Amphion, and Arion were poets, without questioning their claim to the title on grounds of verisimilitude and plausibility. Verisimilitude should regard poetic, not historical, truth. Yet if Statius is commended for following verisimilitude or truth in the *Thebais* (Ronsard does not include the more imaginative *Silvae*, which he knew), it is certainly historical probability that Ronsard has in mind. And it is evidently not poetic truth he has in mind while criticising Lucretius. Thus, instead of agreeing, as he might have done at another time, that divinity and sincerity with poetic truth made Lucretius a great poet, he reasons that divinity and sincerity without historical truth deny him the title of poet.

An inconsistency anent truth is common to most of the members of the Pléiade. First they will accuse Plato of being an inveterate falsifier; in the next breath they will profess that the elegance of his style is nothing compared to the truth (*rayson*) of his doctrines.[87] But, inconsistent in this respect, they were thoroughly consistent about the immorality of insincerity, just as the earlier centuries had been. In a few cases, as with Lucretius, to be sincere is not enough to be commended; but to be insincere always brings a harsh judgment. Christian indignation at a lie was not dead yet.

⚜ ⚜ ⚜

Any discussion of sincerity and truth in the Pléiade must necessarily refer to Petrarchism. The definitive history of the Pléiade undertaken by Chamard reaffirms the Petrarchism of

[87] *Deffence*, ed. by Chamard, p. 142; for *rayson* as truth, see Du Bellay, III, 121.

the Pléiade, but concedes in passing that at least two of these poets reacted against Petrarch, adducing as evidence Du Bellay's poem, "A une Dame," later called "Contre les Pétrarquistes" and Ronsard's "Élégie à son livre."[88] Similar condemnations of Petrarchism by the French writers of the Middle Renaissance, however, could be multiplied severalfold.

In general, most literary historians have been content to accept the Pléiade poets as confirmed Petrarchists. Meozzo's recent study of European Petrarchism shares this view.[89] Arturo Graf, the first to record any reaction against Petrarchism, has shown how strong the reaction grew in Italy itself,[90] enabling Vianey to observe that anti-Petrarchism in France was a natural importation, like the rest of the ultramontane movements borrowed.[91] Neither Vianey nor Piéri, in his *Pétrarque et Ronsard*, attempts a survey of this reaction of the Pléiade. Vianey limits himself to the representative "A une Dame," while Piéri mentions only the admission of Jodelle, "How many times have my verses gilded those black locks worthy of a Medusa?" and Desportes's statement that love makes a man say "ce qui n'est point."[92]

These meagre samples of anti-Petrarchistic passages neither cover the ground nor lead to a full understanding of the ethical, almost moral, issue which underlay the Pléiade's objections. The reaction against Petrarchism which accompanied the reaction against Italianism was based on ethical grounds. Every reference of the Pléiade attacking Petrarch questions his sincerity, directly or indirectly. True, Petrarch had won their admiration for many reasons. Formally, they adopted the medium of the sonnet; linguistically, they admired his use of the vulgar tongue; artistically, they acknowledged Petrarch

[88] H. Chamard, *Histoire de la Pléiade* (Paris, 1939–), I, 274; II, 149.

[89] A. Meozzo, *Il Petrarchismo europeo* (Pisa, 1934), pp. 40–166.

[90] Arturo Graf, *Il Cinquecento* (Torino, 1888), pp. 3–86.

[91] J. Vianey, *Pétrarquisme en France au XVIe siècle* (Montpellier, 1909), p. 177.

[92] M. Piéri, *Pétrarque et Ronsard* (Marseille, 1896), p. 65.

as a model; [93] psychologically, they were awed before the glory which Petrarch had won for himself, his Laura, and his Tuscany, a glory which cast his predecessors so deeply into the shadow that Ronsard speaks of his appearance in the "night of Dante and Cavalcanti" [94] much as Rabelais speaks of the night of the Middle Ages. Du Bellay implies to the architect Pierre Lescot that the three greatest poets of the past were Homer, Vergil, and Petrarch.[95] But the renunciation of Petrarchism came fairly early in the Pléiade, even earlier than Du Bellay's "Contre les Pétrarquistes," written in 1553. Héroët, a Platonist who should certainly encourage any expression of idealistic love, is struck only by the insincerity of the plaints of Petrarch. Ideal, androgynous love has no place for plaints. These crocodile tears and sighs, this "cold contention," he writes in the *Parfaite Amie*, are intended for the consumption of servants. He condemns master and disciples alike:

> Tous les escripts et larmoyants autheurs,
> Tout le Pétrarque et ses imitateurs,
> Qui de souspirs et de froydes querelles
> Remplissent l'air en parlant aux estoilles.[96]

This is perhaps the first note of anti-Petrarchism in France, for it was published no later than 1542, before Petrarchism had become a stirring issue with the Pléiade.

The Pléiade could not believe in the purely chaste character of Petrarch's love. Agreeing with Du Bellay that a poem must honestly reflect the feelings of the author, they found it incredible that a man should spend thirty-one years sighing over a love purportedly on a *noli tangere* basis. (The same question did not arise regarding Dante or the troubadours, neither of whom the Pléiade knew well.) Ronsard was the

[93] Du Bellay, I, 8; Baïf, M.-L., I, 228; Pontus de Tyard, M.-L., p. 125; Du Bartas, *Works*, ed. by Holmes, II, 3.
[94] Ronsard, VI, 27.
[95] Du Bellay, II, 179.
[96] Héroët, *Parfaite Amye*, vss. 1511–14.

most vehement in his charges against the good faith of the Tuscan Apollo:

> Et que le bon Pétrarque un tel péché ne fist,
> Qui fut trente et un an [*sic*] amoureux de sa dame,
> Sans qu'un autre jamays luy peust eschauffer l'ame:
> Respons-luy je te pri', que Pétrarque sur moy
> N'avoit authorité de me donner sa loy . . .
> Luy mesme ne fut tel: car à voir son escrit
> Il estoit esveillé d'un trop gentil esprit
> Pour estre sot trente ans, abusant sa jeunesse
> Et sa Muse au giron d'une vieille maistresse:
> Ou bien il jouyssoit de sa Laurette, ou bien
> Il estoit un grand fat d'aimer sans avoir rien,
> Ce que je ne puis croire, aussi n'est-il croyable.[97]

This "elegy" beginning the second book of the *Amours* after 1560, appeared in 1556 at the close of the *Nouvelle continuation des Amours*. With Du Bellay's "A une Dame" appearing in 1553 and this poem in 1556, one realises how early the revolt took hold. There are other charges of insincerity in the first book of Ronsard's *Amours*. Witness Ronsard's admission that when he had been in the habit of reading the lamentable sonnets of the Florentine, he was incredulous and, in mocking him, could hardly keep from laughing.[98] In another piece, Ronsard writes to his lady that he is suffering too much to start lamenting and Petrarchising.[99] Later in his works he again employs the verb "Petrarchise" in this pejorative sense.[100]

In the afore-mentioned "A une Dame," Du Bellay considers Petrarchism studied hokum based upon falsification of one's emotions.

> J'ay oublié l'art de pétrarquizer.
> Je veulx d'amour franchement deviser
> Sans vous flater, et sans me déguiser.

[97] Ronsard, I, 126–127.
[98] *Ibid.*, I, 105.
[99] *Ibid.*, I, 60.
[100] *Ibid.*, VI, 227. A synonym for "pétrarquiser" was "castillaniser," used by Mellin, *ed. cit.*, I, 314.

Ceulx qui font tant de plaintes
N'ont pas le quart d'une vraye amytié,
Et n'ont pas tant de peine la moitié,
Comme leurs yeulx, pour vous faire pitié,
Getent de larmes feintes.[101]

Again in the same poem, Du Bellay regrets those good old days when Petrarch was unknown, and people talked to their lovers without the deceitful employment of falseness (*fard ou couverture*). This wish is reminiscent not only of Marot's "Amour du siècle antique," as Chamard points out, but also of Marot's "A une mal contente d'avoir esté sobrement louée." [102] It anticipates as well the complaint of Don Quixote (I, ix) where the knight regrets the passing of the golden age:

Entonces se decoraban los concetos amorosos del alma simple y sencillamente, del mesmo modo y manera que ella los concebía, sin buscar artificioso rodeo de palabras para encarecerlos. No había la fraude, el engaño ni la malicia mezcládose con la verdad y llaneza.

Similar complaints about the fraud and deceit of Petrarchistic verse are found in almost all of the Pléiade. In his *Amours diverses*, Baïf states that this is the reason why ladies no longer believe love sonnets: "they know our treachery, our fine reasonings, and our habit of deceiving." [103] Jodelle admits that he "hates the deceitful custom of crying of our lovers, who have only their tears as the subject of their verse." [104] And in another piece he writes that these sighs and tears are greater than the winds which Ulysses had enclosed on his ship, fine winds coming from their heads and not their hearts.[105] Tyard calls

[101] Du Bellay, IV, 205–206.

[102] J'en laisse faire à ces Italiens,
Ou Espagnols tumbés en vos liens,
Qui disent plus qu'oncques il ne penserent, . . .
Ne mon esprit est d'assez bonne marque
Pour suyvre ainsi leur Danthe ou leur Pétrarque.
Je diray bien, et ne mentiray point.

Regarding the author of this poem, see below, note 112.

[103] Baïf, M.-L., I, 348.

[104] Jodelle, M.-L., II, 19.

[105] *Ibid.*, II, 54.

this love verse "chants mensongers." [106] Again, Jodelle decries the fact that

> Tous les chants des amans sont
> Pleins d'un mal que point ils n'ont,
> Pleins de tourmens et de pleurs,
> De glaces et flames:
> Mais feintes sont leurs douleurs,
> Ainsi que leurs ames.[107]

Other indictments by Du Bellay are:

> Quant est de moy, je ne pris onq' plaisir
> A contre-faire un amoureux désir,
> Comme ceulx là qui ayment par la plume . . .
> Car je ne suis ny Tuscan, ny Lombard.[108]

> Et du Toscan le feu vingt ans durable
> Auprès du mien ne seroit que fumée.[109]

Jacques Tahureau is moved to hope that the variable style and "amours mensongers" of the foreign poets will not find their way into his poetry and falsify it.[110] So strong did the charge of insincerity and untruth in Petrarch therefore become that the Petrarchistic sonnet itself became suspect as a form of addressing one's love. It was certainly with the help of Petrarchism that love came to be known as "oracle de mensonge" by the mid-period of the Pléiade.[111] The sins of the followers perpetuated and even exceeded those of the master, as Ronsard observed to Del Bene.[112] Hence, as Petrarchism

[106] Pontus de Tyard, M.-L., p. 187.
[107] Jodelle, M.-L., II, 51.
[108] Du Bellay, V, 79.
[109] *Ibid.*, II, 236.
[110] Tahureau, *Poésies*, ed. by Blanchemain (Paris, 1870), I, 56.
[111] Desportes, *Œuvres* (Paris, 1858), p. 62.
[112] Ronsard, VI, 27. For similar examples of anti-Petrarchism outside the Pléiade, see "A une mal contente" of Saint-Gelays (Blanchemain edition, I, 196) also attributed to Marot (Garnier edition, I, 335), where Petrarch is mentioned by name; and the *Uranie* of Du Bartas (Holmes edition, Chapel Hill, 1935–40, II, 172), where the Muse Urania claims that French erotic poets have made bawds of her sisters.

became more questionable as a medium of expression, if a poet was to have a lady believe that his protestations were something more than mere flimflam, he had to take pains to assure her that he was not merely writing in the Petrarchistic vein. One finds all manner of these assurances in the Pléiade's amores. Belleau begins sonnets with, "Maistresse, croyez moy, je ne suis point menteur" and "Je n'en mentiray point, quand ce baiser je pris." [113] When Desportes sits down to compose his first book of amoristic poetry to Diane, he strikes an anti-Petrarchistic note in the very first sonnet: "I'll not aggrandise with rich fictions your beauties, your disdain, my faith and my passion; it will suffice that my pen adhere to the truth." [114] Baïf affixes this same type of disclaimer to his love sonnets to Francine no later than 1555: "As for me, there will be no lying in these songs; I'll describe our true friendship just as I feel the true stings of love." [115] (Nevertheless, Ronsard criticised Baïf for these very sonnets to Françoise de Gennes, judging them too Petrarchistic to sound genuine.) [116] Ronsard interpolates a similar disavowal which does not mince words, "Non, vous ne me pouvez reprocher que je sois un effronté menteur." [117] Olivier de Magny denies any note of falseness in his *Soupirs*; his love is too holy:

> Ce n'est pas moy qui sçait d'une voix feinte
> Ou d'un semblant traitrement déguisé,

[113] Belleau, M.-L., I, 146; II, 89.

[114] Desportes, ed. by Michiels, p. 13.

[115] Baïf, M.-L., I, 197.

[116] Ronsard, VI, 246.

[117] *Ibid.*, VI, 254. And yet Ronsard earned a reputation for insincere Petrarchising. Professor Robert V. Merrill kindly sends me the following evidence:

> Pétrarque loûra sa Laure,
> Et sa Cassandre Ronsard,
> Mais par feintise et par art
> Mes amours ie ne colore.
> Ie n'eus onc intention
> Que d'aimer d'affection.

From a *chanson* in *Les Œuvres de Claude de Pontoux, gentilhomme chalonnois, docteur en médecine* (Lyon, 1579).

Feindre mon cueur d'un amour embrasé
Pour à tous vents la flamme en estre esteinte.
Autre que moy d'une menteuse plainte
Aura l'honneur des dames abusé.[118]

Jacques Tahureau echoes this formula, "Ce n'est pas moy qui," adding the simple clause "qui veut, d'un feint ouvrage, par mille vers farder sa passion." [119] Desportes addresses his mistress in an elegy, "Mistress, writing thee, I have no wish to undertake to make my sorrows heard in a plaintive discourse. . . . The pain is not mortal that speaks and breathes; mine is an infinite pain which one could not describe." [120] Lastly, Baïf starts a quatrain of his *Devis amoureux*, "Mignonne, je jure ma foy, et ne t'en mentiray de rien." [121]

In many of these passages — and occasionally these disclaimers occupied entire stanzas [122] — it is no longer Petrarch himself, but rather the movement he initiated which incurs the suspicion of the Pléiade. If at times some of the quotations seem at several removes from Petrarch proper, do not mention Petrarch or Petrarchism by name, one must recall that artificiality of sentiment in one's sonnets was at length considered to be one and the same thing as Petrarchism by this sixteenth-century group. The reaction against this Italian movement was almost as vehement as the reaction against Italianism itself. To these poets Petrarchism came to imply two sorts of dishonesty. First, one exaggerated one's feelings for a lady, or, if no sentiment existed at all, one feigned some. Second, one stooped to inordinate flattery, a form of dishonesty to which a few pages will be devoted at the end of this chapter. Each of these, of course, was contrary to the poet's ethical duty to subscribe unerringly to truth. The reaction against Petrarchism, we have

[118] Magny, *Soupirs*, ed. by Courbet, p. 68.
[119] Tahureau, ed. by Blanchemain, II, 5.
[120] Desportes, *ed. cit.*, p. 269.
[121] Baïf, M.-L., IV, 381.
[122] Passerat, *Poésies françaises* (Paris, 1880), II, 13. *Cf.*, also, I, 55, where Passerat maintains the now familiar charge, "Trop peu sent de douleur qui sa douleur peut dire, *etc.*"

seen, became evident in 1542 with Héroët, but was not voiced by the leaders of the Pléiade until a decade later. Their greatest admiration for Petrarch may be said to have coincided with the *Blumzeit* of their Pindarism, occupying only the first half of the 1550's. Censure of Petrarch is noted as early and earlier than observations against Pindar. When, late in the following century, Boileau enunciates in his *Art poétique*:

> Je hais ces vains auteurs dont la muse forcée
> M'entretient de ses feux, toujours froide et glacée,
> Qui s'affligent par art, . . .[123]

he is merely echoing a prejudice which had become a commonplace with that generation of poets whom he valued so lightly.

⚜ ⚜ ⚜

After these outbursts against Petrarch and Petrarchism, the remarks of the Pléiade on Renaissance authors come as an anti-climax. Still following our chronological outline, we pass from the fourteenth century to the late fifteenth. Each of the following two writers was born, one in France and one in Italy, in the late Quattrocento and lived into the early sixteenth century. Each was a historian. Philippe de Commynes is praised as being more accurate and eloquent than Livy.[124] His honesty was so great, claims Ronsard, that he would describe only what he himself had seen; nor could any duke or king cause him to alter the true facts he had witnessed. Francesco Guicciardini is praised for the same reason: for refusing to alter truth, history he had witnessed, in order to flatter kings.[125] Both Commynes and Guicciardini conform to the offices of the historian as established in the preface to the *Franciade* (1587). The restrictions imposed on the chronicler's fictive talents are

[123] Boileau, *Art poétique*, II, 45–47.
[124] Ronsard, V, 290.
[125] *Ibid.*, VI, 422.

reminiscent of those to which the Pléiade often subjected the poet himself.

The most violent diatribe of any Pléiade member against a writer on grounds of dishonesty and insincerity is a poem of Ronsard published by his executors. Prefacing his invective with the statement that he dislikes Jews, he invokes the Emperor Vespasian's son Titus, asking why he did not do a thorough job of destroying the Jews:

> Jamais Léon Hébrieu des Juifs n'eust prins naissance,
> Léon Hébrieu, qui donne aux dames cognoissance
> D'un amour fabuleux, la mesme fiction:
> Faux, trompeur, mensonger, plein de fraude et d'astuce,
> Je croy qu'en luy coupant la peau de son prépuce,
> On luy coupa le cœur et toute affection.[126]

Even the accusations against the integrity of Calvin[127] and other *pseudoprophetae* whose religion he disliked[128] are milder than this excoriation of Leo the Jew.

The opening paragraphs of this chapter showed that in Renaissance opinion, the ability of the poet to cloak and disguise truth makes him a greater artist than one who writes simple unmitigated truths. But nothing in excess. Ronsard cannot swallow the extravagances of Ariosto in this regard. One must not "feindre une Poësie fantastique"[129] (we have already noted above that fantasy meant falsehood in the critical vocabulary of Ronsard) to the extent that Ariosto feigns in his counterfeit and monstrous epic, which seems more like the nightmare of a feverish invalid than the invention of a sane man. Jean de la Taille, by the way, classified the *Orlando Furioso* as a fabulous tale which was neither dictated by truth nor carried the safe-conduct of truth.[130]

Just as he had accused Plato of being inconsistent and in-

[126] *Ibid.*, VI, 60.
[127] *Ibid.*, V, 342.
[128] *Ibid.*, VI, 515.
[129] *Ibid.*, VII, 67.
[130] Jean de la Taille, *Art de la Tragédie* (Manchester, 1939), p. 31.

sincere, Ronsard assailed the honesty of the Platonists, those philosophers who reason eloquently about death, but once they grow old, begin to weep and wail to no purpose.[131]

The poets on the periphery of the Pléiade could call a spade a spade. Tahureau referred to Pierre Turel's volume on astrology as follies and calumnious lies.[132] Among the repercussions of the Sagon-Marot feud, Fontaine called La Huetterie a liar, and Saint-Gelays concurred.[133] Although minor stargazers might be subject to attack, it should be added that the celebrated Nostradamus was not discredited by the Pléiade. Ronsard even insisted that his prophecies were coming true. Only Scaliger remained to suggest that Nostradamus was a liar.[134]

The extreme discretion of the Pléiade in their relations with their contemporaries is attested by the fact that they do not censure poets by name for mendacity, or even for the lesser offense of insincerity. There is a slight implication of the latter in Ronsard's remark on the translations from Anacreon of Belleau: "Tu es un trop sec biberon pour un tourneur d'Anacréon." But this is too obviously a pleasantry to allow one to draw conclusions about the ethics of translation.[135]

Discreet toward their friends, the Pléiade did not temper their speech when disposing of their enemies. See, for example, the "ils ont menti . . . ils ont menti . . . ils ont menti" of Ronsard, reviling those who asserted that Du Bartas had done more in a *Semaine* than Ronsard had accomplished in a lifetime.[136] That category of nameless worthies to whom the Pléiade sent occasional mordant verses, "les mesdisants," received little shrift. Jean de la Péruse composes two poems

[131] Ronsard, IV, 369.

[132] Tahureau, *Dialogues*, *ed. cit.*, p. 129. Pierre Turel (or Turrel) of Autun was an author of almanacs. The book referred to was apparently his *Période*, which predicted by means of the planets the end of the world after some 270 years.

[133] Saint-Gelays, *Œuvres poétiques* (Paris, 1873), II, 42–43.

[134] J.-C. Scaliger, *Poemata* (Heidelberg: "Apud Petrum Santandreanum, MDXCI"), I, 447.

[135] Ronsard, II, 224.

[136] *Ibid.*, VI, 457.

"Contre un mesdisant," an anonymous critic, and is angered by "ton vers faussement léger" and "ta voix menteresse." [137] When the Pléiade found themselves attacked by some Malebouche, it was natural enough that they should defend themselves by branding the attack a falsehood.

These, then, are the judgments by which the Pléiade poets betray their interest in truth and sincerity as criteria of literary judgment. One special type of untruth or insincerity remains, however, and to it one must devote a few paragraphs. This type is flattery.

⚜ ⚜ ⚜

In principle, all of the Pléiade condemned flattery, or "words of silk," as Vauquelin defined it.[138] It is true that each of them practiced flattery in epithalamiums, odes, sonnets, and the like. Even those ivory tower dwellers on the perimeter of the Pléiade, Scève and Héroët, were offenders. Yet all of them recognised its traditional wickedness. Du Bellay, for example, swore that he made it a principle to be honest about poetry and wine.[139]

Pindar himself had warned against the blandishments of flatterers.[140] The *Ars poetica* of Horace had painted the flatterer in ridiculous colors.[141] Saint-Augustine had listed adulation in his *Liber Psalmorum* as one of the cardinal forms of lying.[142] Dante had cast flatterers into Hell. Vopiscus had set down flattery as the principal cause of the corruption of princes, an idea to which Commynes subscribed.[143] Martin Cognet, in his discourses on truth, likened sycophants to worms digging

[137] Jean de la Péruse, *Poésies* (Angoulême, 1866), pp. 163, 164.

[138] Vauquelin, *Art poétique*, ed. by Pellissier, p. 64.

[139] Du Bellay, I, 17.

[140] Pindar, *Pythian Odes*, i, 92.

[141] Horace, *Ars poetica*, vss. 419–437.

[142] Augustinus, *Liber Psalmorum*, "In Psalmum XLIX enarratio," (Basileae, MDLVI), VIII, 479.

[143] Both Vopiscus and Commynes are mentioned in Cognet, p. 170.

their way into fat living tissue.[144] In his *Emblemata* Alciatus writes that adulators are human chameleons and to be despised.[145] But the most famous deprecation of such hypocrites known to the sixteenth century was that Greek pun attributed to Antisthenes as well as Diogenes, which Erasmus reproduced in his *Apothegms*, and which Jacques Peletier translated (without the play on words) in the second book of his *Art poétique*:

Sache fere discrecion entre le vrai loueur et le flateur: se souvenant du mot d'Antistène, que les Corbeaus mangent les hommes mors; et les flateurs les mangent tous viz.[146]

The summa of the opinions of the Pléiade upon flatterers was the "Poète courtisan" of Du Bellay, where the poet-courtier is advised to seek the approval of those who find all works good.[147] These are the court heelers and, more particularly, the flatterers. There is a parallel development of this theme in the "Nouvelle manière de faire son profit des lettres" of the same author.[148] Both of these works date from 1559, according to the best evidence. But Du Bellay is interested in flattery at earlier periods, and in the *Regrets* is more than once ironic about liars at court.[149] Du Bellay had a more extensive opportunity than the others to study court flattery, having been present at both the French throne and the papal cathedra.

It was court life especially which incited flattery. Ronsard complained to Coligny that the crowd of writers and parasites at court were fair-weather friends and virtually wore their adulating countenances like masks.[150] Tahureau notes that those who refuse to flatter at court are considered presumptuous, indiscreet, and offensive.[151] And Jean de la Taille, whose

[144] *Politique Discourses*, *ed. cit.*, chapter on flattery, p. 169.

[145] *Emblemata Andreae Alciati* (*Frankfort-am-Mayn*, 1580), p. 206.

[146] Peletier, *Art poétique*, ed. by Boulanger, p. 219.

[147] Du Bellay, VI, 136–137.

[148] *Ibid.*, VI, 113. R. V. Merrill, "Lucian and Du Bellay's *Poète Courtisan*," *Modern Philology*, XXIX (1931), 11–20, shows that Du Bellay and Turnèbe derived these sentiments from Lucian's *Rhetoron Didaskalos*.

[149] Du Bellay, II, 168, 172.

[150] Ronsard, V, 180.

[151] Tahureau, *Dialogues*, *ed. cit.*, p. 69.

"Courtisan retiré" is a runner-up to Du Bellay's "Poète courtisan," amens ruefully, "A la cour le flateur on surnomme amiable." [152]

A justification of lying and flattering in good society as a solution to the conflict between the individual and the social *morale* is proposed by Baïf to Belot, voicing outright the thoughts which Philinthe was to express to Alceste in more covert terms:

> Laisse chez toy ta preudomie,
> Du vray la trop sévère amie;
> Si tu n'es flateur ou menteur,
> La vérité sçaches bien taire.
> Ne déplay ne pouvant complaire:
> Sois ou menteur ou lamenteur,
> La court requiert . . . que l'on mente.[153]

Here, in the plainest of language, Baïf presents the moral lesson of the *Misanthrope* several decades before the birth of Molière.

We cannot refrain from including here brief mention of a humorous quatrain by the Pléiade's contemporary, Julius-Caesar Scaliger. Entitled "In mutuos laudatores," it humorously compares poets who flatter each other to mules indulging in reciprocal scratching. We reproduce the Latin without further comment:

> Suos amicos quisque cum canit vates,
> Se mutuas captare sat docet laudes.
> Sic foeneratur ille nomen, et famam
> Verbum vetus fit: mutuum scabunt muli.[154]

Although they all recognised the truth it contained, none of the Pléiade was willing to repeat the moral tuition of Baïf quoted above. Instead, they decried flattery and its "sesquipedalian words" (Buchanan), each declaring it personally abhorrent and claiming that it was no indulgence of his. When

[152] Jean de la Taille, *Œuvres* (Paris, 1878–82), III, 35.
[153] Baïf, M.-L., II, 437.
[154] J.-C. Scaliger, *Poemata* (1591), I, 441.

Du Bellay pens laudatory verses in his series of sonnets to Diane de Poitiers, he makes the reassuring statement that "I am no inventor of frivolous fables, and do not embellish my verses with lying artifice. What I write to you is on everybody's lips."[155] Ronsard writes in "La salade" that people at court have to lie and flatter, but that he himself is too sickly, lazy, deaf, and fearful to be adept at this.[156] Magny says that he is too honest for his own good: "If I could flatter, play at court, and slander, be a good knave, invent quips, and be a complete hypocrite, I'd be well off; but because I am truthful and sincere, I have the ill will of everyone and they all speak ill of me."[157] Jodelle tells the monarch himself that he is unable to lie and flatter, but that no one will surpass his praises if the king deserves them.[158] Jacques Tahureau claims that court poetasters mask thousands upon thousands of falsehoods in their adulation, but that no one will ever find him disguising such lies.[159] Jean de la Taille's disavowal was no less forthright:

> Tu vois que je n'ensuy tant d'écrivains menteurs,
> Ains raptasseurs de vers, qui, serfs admirateurs,
> Idolatrent les grands par flatterie avare.
> Les Muses je ne veux faire ainsy valleter,
> Louer en mots tonnants ceux qu'on doit détester
> Et que princes on voit d'ignorance barbare.[160]

Establishing a principle of conduct by which the honest poet must abide, Tahureau avers in "De l'honneste liberté d'un poète":

> Au sucre d'une menterie
> Il n'allèche les grands seigneurs,
> Pipez souvent par les honneurs,
> Emmiellez de flatterie.[161]

155 Du Bellay, V, 388.
156 Ronsard, V, 78.
157 Magny, *Soupirs*, *ed. cit.*, p. 109.
158 Jodelle, M.-L., II, 130.
159 Tahureau, *ed. cit.*, I, 41.
160 Jean de la Taille, *Œuvres* (Paris, 1878–82), III, 86.
161 Tahureau, *ed. cit.*, I, 119.

Although no contemporaries are named as practitioners of this boot-licking, there are a few cases of poets or critics of antiquity judged by the standard of their critical honesty. These are praised for rising above flattery. First, there was Philoxenus, who asked the Tyrant Dionysius of Syracuse to put him in chains rather than have to listen to a certain poetaster and hear him praised.[162] One senses that Joachim had a certain admiration for Philoxenus. There was Aristarchus of Samothrace, a name used as a substantive meaning "honest critic."[163] There was Aristophanes of Byzantium, who had the frankness of a "sergent de bande."[164] Among those who were excessive, not in flattery but in censure, there were Bacchylides and Callimachus, mentioned by Ronsard, a pair who disapproved of their poetic rivals and particularly those who sought to "flatter the ears" of their monarchs.[165] Lastly, there was the frank Quintilius, first mentioned by Horace in the tract *Ad Pisones*. This proper name became a common noun with the meaning of severe critic. As such it is used in the *Deffence*, the *Quintil Horatian* of Barthélemy Aneau, the *Quintil Censeur* of Charles Fontaine, the *Art poétique* of Vauquelin,[166] and in the pseudonym, J. Quintil du Tronssay, under which Du Bellay published his "Poète courtisan."

⚜ ⚜ ⚜

A minimum recapitulation may be in order. The reaction against poetic mendacity and insincerity, like the reaction against the theme of glory, was part of the heritage left by

[162] Du Bellay, I, 17.

[163] Du Bellay, VI, 137; I, 17; *Deffence*, Chamard edition, p. 186. Du Bartas, however, employs it with a pejorative qualifier (Holmes edition, I, 220).

[164] *Deffence*, Chamard edition, p. 186.

[165] Ronsard, VII, 8.

[166] Vauquelin, *Art poétique*, *ed. cit.*, p. 177. For sincerity and flattery in literary criticism, see Horace, *Ad Pisones*, reference to Quintilius; Vida, *Ars poetica*, III, 462 ff.; Boileau, *Art poétique*, I, 186 ff.

the classic philosophers and the Christian apologists. Although the church recognised poetic license, it was suspicious of the libertarian possibilities of creative writing, and was quick to brand poets as liars. The age-old notion that poets were liars had become formulated into a popular byword by the time of the French Renaissance. Sixteenth-century treatises on mendacity state that nothing was more "ad manum" than this adage. One type of falsifying was approved, even preached, by members of the Pléiade. This was the process of feigning, which grew out of the Pindaric conception of the poet, as well as out of the mediaeval idea that pagan poets veiled Christian truth in their works. This widespread process of "cloaking," however, involved no ethical issue. As we have been concerned with the moral intention rather than the objective possibility and plausibility of the creative writer's work, we have perforce subordinated the problem of verisimilitude. One is not able to discard it completely, however, for the Pléiade poets confused poetic truth and poetic license with the ethics and the intentions of an author. Defined and limited in this way, the issue of truth and sincerity was not discussed in the manifestoes and prefaces of the time. It is rather from the judgments and criticisms in their poetry that one induces the Pléiade's ideas condemning mendacity and insincerity, their feelings regarding *Dichtung und Wahrheit*, and establishes their extremely traditionalist bias regarding truth.

The authority of the centuries did not spare the "unbroken packages" of antiquity, the classics, from a censure which varied from implied charges of insincerity to outright charges of lying. The Pléiade's confusion or inconsistency about poetic truth led them to make extravagant accusations; this was particularly evident in their criticisms of the epicists. Their chief difficulty resulted from their inability to keep poetic truth away from the narrow precincts of historical truth, and their failure to recognise completely the fictive privileges of the creative artist. Petrarchism was universally acknowledged as the archetype of literary untruth and dishonesty within the century. Petrarch's statements were questioned more frequently than those of any other author, including Homer and Plato. The many criticisms on Petrarch or on Petrarchism have an ethical basis and show that Petrarchism became synonymous with insincerity, with *mellitae mendacia linguae*. The reaction against Petrarch started as early as 1542 with Héroët, but the Pléiade's leaders did not participate in it until the early 1550's; as a matter of fact, these poets continued to practice Petrarchism long after they had begun their revolt against it. The Pléiade passed through a Petrarchistic as well as a Pindaric period during the first years of this decade, both a part of their youthful enthusiasms and hopes. With the passing of this early poetic self-consciousness, a reaction against Petrarch germinated within the Pléiade concurrent with the reaction against Pindar. The revival of Anacreon by Belleau in 1556 may likely have been instrumental in the Greek lyrist's supplanting Petrarch for a short time as the model love poet.

Incidentally, before dismissing the subject of the Pléiade's anti-Petrarchism, it might be appropriate to recall to the reader another parallel literary revolt. The middle sixteenth century was a period productive of a wealth of anterotic verse. The *contr' amour* was one of the most widespread poetic themes. There quite possibly remains a correlation to be established between the anteroticism of the period and the contemporary anti-Petrarchism.

It must be granted that, whereas any number of authors are blamed for deviating from truth, seldom is a writer praised for his veracity. Exceptions are Commynes and Guicciardini.

Few charges of insincerity and dishonesty were directed at their contemporaries by name, for the Pléiade members became discreet if not insincere themselves. Similarly, they practised and condemned flattery in the same breath. Economic necessity and ambition incited them to flatter not only the nobles, but also those writers who were favorites at court.

Conscious of a strong tendency toward insincerity in themselves, they were quick to detect such a penchant in others. Just as their own indulgence in Petrarchism made them sensitive to its insincerity, so did their practice of flattery make them discountenance flattery of all sorts in others. Their objections to flattery, like their objections to insincerity of all types, had a moral as well as an ethical basis. That is, not only did they find it personally distasteful, but they recognised as well all of its inherent vice for which the church had condemned it. These objections impelled the Pléiade to react unconsciously, to accept and apply a conservative canon of criticism which they never formulated, but which an inspection of their verse shows to be an integral part of their literary theory.

II

POETIC GLORY AND THE REVOLT AGAINST GLORY

As to his glory, let time be challenged to declare whether the fame of any other institutor of human life be comparable to that of a poet. That he is the wisest, the happiest, and the best, inasmuch as he is a poet, is equally incontrovertible.

— PERCY BYSSHE SHELLEY, *A Defence of Poetry*

Poor starv'ling Bard, how small thy Gains!
How unproportioned to thy Pains!

— JONATHAN SWIFT, *On Poetry: A Rapsody*

THAT the poet is an individual apart from and above his fellows is no Romanticist discovery. The poet's traditional monopoly of glory arises in the Platonic or Orphic idea that poets and rhapsodists are touched with divinity, theoleptic, even if that divinity is a sort of madness. As a recorded idea it antedates Plato. Pindar had already noted that the Muses awarded glory to mortals, thanks to their being the daughters of Zeus; he had presented the postulate of double poetic immortality, the notion that both the poet and the individual he celebrates win eternal fame.[1] When, in the *Ion*, the rhapsodist tells Socrates that poets are interpreters of the gods, and when Diotima in the *Symposium* shows how lovers and poets desire immortality, the two bases of this classical tradition of glory are established. It reappeared in every age. Cicero composed two treatises entitled *De Gloria* which have remained lost since

[1] Pindar, *Pythian Odes* i, 111–112; *Isthmian Odes* i, 45–47; vii, 23–26.

the fourteenth century; they very possibly centered about the proposition of Cicero's *De Officiis* that glory was worth striving for, that one could attain glory in certain specified ways, including eloquence.[2] Horace kept the tradition alive by the familiar observations that his work was a monument more lasting than bronze and that the Muses grant heaven to mortals.[3] The *Somnium Scipionis* (xxiii-xxiv) of Cicero recorded by Macrobius,[4] the opening verses of the *Erec and Enid* of Chrétien de Troyes,[5] the conversation between Dante and Ser Brunetto in the *Inferno*, the *Trionfo della fama* and the *De Gloria* of Petrarch, and the fourteenth chapter of the *Genealogia Deorum Gentilium* [6] are the most conspicuous examples in an evolution which we cannot fully trace here. In the early sixteenth century, Lemaire's *Épître de l'amant verd* showed how the Horatian *exegi monumentum* was still remembered:

> Et lui fut fait ce monument, et tumbe
> Dessus lequel pluye et rousée tombe
> Si auray je (par faveur supernelle)
> Louange et bruyt en mémoire éternelle.[7]

Among the earliest of the neo-classical doctrines to burst through the broken floodgates of scholasticism, this became such a common notion that the poets found themselves at a loss to find original ways of expressing it, once Ronsard had presented it in its essential Horatian form:

> Plus dur que fer, j'ay fini cest ouvrage,
> Que l'an dispos à démener les pas,

[2] Cicero, *De Officiis* (London: Heinemann, 1928), pp. 199 ff.
[3] Horace, *Odes* iii, 30 and iv, 8.
[4] Cicero, *De Re Publica* vi (London: Heinemann, 1928), p. 279.
[5] *Erec et Enide*, ed. by Foerster (Halle, 1890), vss. 23–26:

> Des or comencerai l'estoire
> Qui toz jorz mes iert an memoire
> Tant con durra crestientez
> De ce s'est Crestiens vantez.

[6] Chapter XIV: "It is perfectly obvious that the songs of the poets, like the names of the composers, are almost immortal."
[7] Lemaire, "Épître de l'amant verd," I, vss. 245–248.

Que l'eau rongearde, ou des frères la rage
Qui rompent tout, ne ru'ront point à bas.

Le mesme jour que le dernier trespas
M'assoupira d'un somme dur, à l'heure
Sous le tombeau tout Ronsard n'ira pas,
Restant de luy la part qui est meilleure.[8]

The facets of this immortalising were as many and varied as they had been in classical literature. One immortalised oneself, one's works, one's friends, one's mistress, one's monarch, one's province, one's river. As a scholar one could immortalise one's language. As a bard one could pay homage to virtue and to gods Christian or pagan. One's glory would set one apart as a social individualist having no commerce with the inglorious, whether they were courtiers or commoners.

The Pléiade accepted the doctrine of glory so dutifully that it almost lost its meaning through constant use and abuse. The treatises of Peletier, Du Bellay, Ronsard, and others took it for granted. It became a repetitious, sometimes pointless, theme of their poetry. The Pléiade referred so often to the glory of writers ancient and modern that we cannot undertake in this chapter to set down a register of these authors smiled upon by fame or fortune. In becoming a poetic theme, the doctrine of glory encouraged the pernicious use of flattery and insincerity which weakened the Pléiade's verse. It swelled the already inflated egotism of the competent and the incompetent among them.

Nevertheless, the Pléiade alternately espoused and renounced this cult of glory. The present chapter will study in turn their acceptance of and revolt against this doctrine. It will be shown later that the disbelief was no less extensive and hearty than the belief itself.

For the members of the Pléiade, poetic glory rested upon three indisputable conditions, to which we shall give their brief classical etiquettes and describe as follows:

[8] Ronsard, II, 462.

I. The *exegi monumentum* condition: The poet and his works may achieve lasting fame or immortality; they may confer immortality upon the poet's friends.

II. The *doctus poeta* condition: The poet is born with an infinite wisdom which study may temper but not increase.

III. The *odi profanum* condition: The poet is a social individualist living in an ivory tower and apart from the indiscriminate masses of the town or the court.

We have shown immediately above how the conviction of the *exegi monumentum*, a standard part of the baggage of classical poetics, was accepted and reproduced by the sixteenth century. There were so many repetitions of this credo that we cannot attempt to present any sort of anthology of them here. One encounters them at every turn among the pieces of Ronsard:

Le marbre, ou l'airain vêtu
D'un labeur vif par l'enclume
N'animent pas la vertu
Comme je fai par ma plume.[9]

Aussi le Roy, quelque chose qu'il face,
Meurt sans honneur, s'il n'achete pas la grace
Par maints presens d'un Poëte sçavant
Qui du tombeau le déterre vivant,
Et fait tousjours d'une plume animée
Voler par tout sa vive renommée.[10]

Faisant un vers plus durable
Qu'un colosse elabouré,
Ou la tumbe memorable
Dont Mausole est honoré.[11]

Mais en mille papiers ton renom se lira,
Et ne pourra la mort dedans la fange noire
De Styx, faire enfondrer ta vivante memoire,
Tant un chacun de toy ourdira de beaux vers.[12]

[9] Ronsard, STFM, I, 92 and 87.
[10] Ronsard, V, 37.
[11] *Ibid.*, VI, 122.
[12] *Ibid.*, IV, 230, var.

Within the greater Brigade group there were so many paraphrases of the Horatian tenet that one is confronted with an *embarras du choix* in selecting typical extracts. Preachments about the gloriosity of the writer are found in the ode, "De l'immortalité des Poètes," at the close of the *Vers lyriques*, composed when Du Bellay was twenty-seven and, as Chamard observes, already claiming immortality. It might be said parenthetically that this frequent use of the capital initial letter of the word "Poète" in the French Renaissance is not without significance to a study of poetic glory. To note how standardised the conception of poetic works as imperishable monuments became, compare the following lines from Du Bellay's lyrics with Ronsard's stanza just quoted:

Ton œuvre sera plus durable
Qu'un Théatre ou un Colisée,
Ou qu'un Mauséole admirable,
Dont l'étophe si fort prisée
Par le tens a été brisée,
Ou que tout autre œuvre excellant
De la main de l'ouvrier volant.[13]

Other versions of this theme are the paraphrase of Ovid by Antoine de Harsy,

Dieu est en nous, et par luy poussés sommes,
Nostre œuvre point ne procède des hommes;
Ce que contient cette machine basse
Périra tout, nos vers demeureront:
Bref, toute chose par le temps se fracasse,
Mais nos écrits à jamais floriront.[14]

and the following rhetorical question by Mellin de Saint-Gelays,

Estimes-tu que César ou Camille
Doivent le cours de leur claire memoire
Au marbre, au fer, au ciseau, ou enclume?
Toute statue, ou médaille est fragile

[13] Du Bellay, III, 41.
[14] Mellin de Saint-Gelays, ed. by Blanchemain, I, 140.

> Au fil des ans; mais la durable gloire
> Vient de main docte, et bien disante plume.[15]

Later in the century, when the sacred fury had abated somewhat, D'Aubigné looked back upon the mid-century period and confessed his excesses: "At that time I adored naught but the vain image of renown, renown anxiously awaited."[16]

As for the *doctus poeta* theme — once again, the verses illustrating this conviction are far too numerous for us to endeavor to catalogue them here — it should be remembered that the entire campaign of reform which the Pléiade attempted was directed against ignorance and apathy. "Ce fut une belle guerre que l'on entreprit lors contre l'ignorance," Pasquier recalled in his *Recherches*.[17] The war against the monster Ignorance undertaken by the Pléiade was commemorated, of course, in the *Musagnœomachie* of Du Bellay. Like Siegfrieds destroying dragons, each poet took pride in his rôle of killing "le vilain monstre Ignorance, qui souloit toute la France dessous son ventre couver."[18]

These theorists, who accepted the "recte sapere" of Horace as meaning knowledge, "le sçavoir," could imagine no greater tribute to pay a friend than to address him as "the learned." Such compliments crop out too frequently and indiscriminately in their verse. Learning to them meant book learning, with stress placed on the humanities, languages of the past and present, ancient literatures, music, and the fine arts. It will be noted that the ideal of erudition no longer set a premium upon ecclesiastical knowledge. Writing on this shifting emphasis from an ideal of theological wisdom to that of humanistic learning, Professor Louis Cons observes, "Si nous passons à l'activité intellectuelle nous voyons que la notion de *Savant* substitutée à celle de *Clerc* est un des exemples les plus nets de la tendance

[15] *Ibid.*, II, 300–301.
[16] D'Aubigné, *Tragiques*, préface: "L'autheur à son livre."
[17] Pasquier, *Recherches*, VII, vi.
[18] Ronsard, II, 99.

sécularisatrice de la Renaissance."[19] The Pléiade felt a genuine enthusiasm for the Renaissance Mind, a mind versed in many arts and sciences. They admired Nicolas Denisot for knowing other arts than literature, and especially painting. However, the Pléiade did not praise the universal minds of those, like Sébilet, who combined the arts and law, or those, like Rabelais, who combined the arts and medicine, for they were disposed to share the Renaissance suspicions of lawyers and medicos. Although there was no Da Vinci among them, the Pléiade could boast of one Renaissance Mind, one member competent in several arts and sciences. This was Pontus de Tyard.

"La science fait tout," wrote Ronsard as a typical representative of the New Learning which characterised the advent of humanism and the Renaissance itself. The only difficulty was that this knowledge or *doctrine* was very sparingly parceled among mankind. The Pléiade knew that they themselves possessed it, but beyond themselves there were only, to quote Stendhal, "the happy few."

When one considers with what alacrity these poets accepted the Horatian precept of "odi profanum vulgus et arceo," how completely they ignored the public and felt their own works to be caviar to the general, one perceives that this was one of the fundamental weaknesses of the Pléiade. To accomplish their reforms, to combat ignorance, to establish a great literature in the vernacular by putting that literature into everyone's hands, as had been done in Italy, this should have been a frankly avowed program of theirs. If the leaders of the Pléiade really believed that the purpose of poetry was to "esmouvoir les passions et affections de l'âme"[20] and to "faire indigner, apayser, éjouyr, douloir, aymer, haïr, admirer, bref, tenir la bride des affections" (*Deffence*, II, xi), they must have realised that these are not the aims of class or closet literature, but rather of great universal literature. Not only did the Pléiade

[19] Cons, *Anthologie littéraire de la Renaissance française* (New York, 1931), p. xxvi.

[20] Ronsard, VII, 90.

choose to ignore the mass of the populace, but felt themselves obliged as well to heap abuse on that populace in the classical tradition. Du Bellay could be as haughty as any: "Rien ne me plaist, fors ce qui peut déplaire au jugement du rude populaire."[21] Or again, he advises the poet to flee "that ignorant public, public inimical to all rare and ancient learning."[22]

The ideal of sublimity or altitude of style which had caused the classical critics to legislate that literature should eschew mean subjects and humble people may have been an indirect factor in shaping the Pléiade's conviction that poetry should not be written for the masses. As one later critic was to put it, "L'écrivain qui pense beaucoup ne sera jamais l'écrivain de la multitude. Elle ne saurait monter jusqu'à lui; et il ne peut descendre jusqu'à elle qu'en se rabaissant."[23] This disdain of the common taste was to remain one of the most inherent characteristics of French literature for two hundred years. In the following century it was to lure French letters into the artificiality of preciosity, to the persuasion of Somaize that a thought understood by the masses was of no value whatsoever.

Tolstoy maintained that the class-consciousness of art was coming into being at the time of the French Renaissance, and that the exclusive art of the upper classes broke away from universal art at this moment. It is no doubt true that a sort of scorn for the masses grew out of art's new aim to cultivate the wealthy and the influential, as well as from a miscarried acceptance of sublimity. Yet this was to some extent a doctrinary hate as well as an actual one. Laumonier claims that Pindar first initiated Ronsard to the cult of the intellectual aristocracy.[24] Horace was no less instrumental, and after Horace there was Petrarch reviling "la turba al vil guadagno intesa." At any rate, one could make a lengthy compendium, once again, of the pejorative epithets by which the Pléiade designated the

[21] Du Bellay, III, 52; also *Deffence* (*ed. cit.*), pp. 316–317.
[22] *Deffence*, ed. by Chamard, p. 316.
[23] L'abbé Trublet, *Essais*, I, 1.
[24] Laumonier, *Ronsard, poète lyrique*, p. 334.

public. Ronsard spoke of it as "ce monstre têtu," and De la Porte, in his preface to the dialogues of Tahureau, employs this identical phrase.[25] Tahureau himself paraphrases this with "grand' beste de plusieurs testes," referring later to "ce sot et inconstant vulgaire" and "beste populaire." [26] Jacques Grévin vituperates "ce sot populaire," and Sébilet the "tourbe ignare." [27] The invective was almost as common outside the ranks of the Pléiade, for there was Mellin de Saint-Gelays scorning the "ignorante et sotte multitude" [28] and Scève echoing with "sot peuple." [29] But there is scant need for us to multiply these instances; the reader has only to open the works of any member of the Pléiade and he will find many more.

It must be granted that if scorn of the multitude was first taught these writers by their study of older literatures, their immediate situation encouraged their wholehearted acceptance of it. Most of them, members of the petty nobility, proud of the particules in their names, found it easy to indulge in this aristocratic prejudice. Not without a modicum of race prejudice [30] and religious intolerance,[31] they could logically be class conscious as well. The ivory tower attitude was a natural result of this class consciousness. So great an individualist was one of them, Tyard, that he adopted as his personal mottoes, inscribed in his philosophical discourses, "Nec turbae nec in turbam" and "Solitudo mihi provincia est."

As we shall be obliged to repeat more than once, the *profanum* signified for these poets not only the unschooled masses, the great unwashed, but the privileged classes and the courtiers

[25] Ronsard, I, 131.

[26] Tahureau, *Dialogues* (Paris, 1870), pp. v and 5; pp. 63 and 180.

[27] Grévin, edition of Pinvert, p. 290; Sébilet, *Art poétique*, Bk. I, ii.

[28] Mellin de Saint-Gelays, *Œuvres poétiques* (Paris, 1873), II, 203.

[29] Maurice Scève, *Délie*, ed. by Parturier, p. 281.

[30] As examples of the anti-Semitism of these poets, see Ronsard's excoriation of Leo the Jew in the preceding chapter; Marot speaks of the Jews as the Crows who killed the Pelican (Garnier edition, I, 353); Jean de la Taille's *Negromant* as an example of the crafty Semites (II, cxlix).

[31] See the Pléiade's attacks upon the *pseudoprophetae* of Geneva.

who failed to understand the abilities and licenses of the Poet and who shared in the widespread lack of critical taste characteristic of the century. Among the privileged classes incapable of appreciating genuine poetry were those court versifiers whom Ronsard dismissed with the epithet, "soldars de l'Ignorance," or whom he called "vermin" and "croaking frogs" when in a less indulgent mood.[32]

That this professional haughtiness was recognised as a weakness before the century was over is evident from the *Recherches* of Étienne Pasquier. Mild but just in his remarks, he found that one of the essential characteristics of the members of this school had been that they made a profession of contenting rather their own minds than the opinion of the common people, and Pasquier deemed this a fault.[33]

This chapter is not concerned exclusively with the conventional theme of glory. The pro-glory convictions of this school are too familiar to students of the Renaissance to merit further amplification here. Almost every critic who has written on the mid-century poetic theory has noted this banal motif. Particularly competent is the third chapter of Henri Franchet's study of the literary doctrine of Ronsard. What such literary histories of our time, as well as the manifestoes of the sixteenth century, fail to record is the great reaction against the ideal of glory, a reaction which existed throughout the entire critical evolution of the Pléiade, and in which all of this group participated.

⚜ ⚜ ⚜

Like Glory, the anti-Glory became a poetic theme. The idea that poets are as inglorious as other mortals, that they are favored by neither the gods nor by friends, that both they and

[32] Ronsard, II, 143; VII, 7; STFM, VIII, 351.
[33] Pasquier, *Recherches*, VII, vii.

their works perish, no matter what their excellence, that they are after all merely tradesmen, was not new at the time of the Renaissance.

Pindar had given sad testimony to the fact that poets had become mere hirelings, lending their tongues for silver.[34] In his *Ad Pisones,* Horace grants that we all must die, even the poet.[35] Cicero, in the *Somnium Scipionis,* notes pessimistically that "fame among men can hardly endure for the small part of a single year." [36] Seneca preached that the end of all good acts is merely death.[37] And if Ovid says in his *Amores* that his verses have given his lady glory, he nevertheless feels that verses may do more harm than good: "An prosint, dubium, nocuerunt carmina semper. . . ." [38] The Senecan tradition was kept alive in the time of the Pléiade by Montaigne, who comments favorably on Seneca's belief that any virtuous work is its own reward,[39] and finds reputation and glory "the most useless, futile, and false currency that we have in our employ." [40] Glory was also suspect to two neo-Latin humanists known to the Pléiade. George Buchanan decried "fleeting fame, lying glory, which soon dies away as the south wind," and Scaliger assented: "Mundi gloria fumus et absque igne favilla." [41]

The notion that an author could gain immortality through his works had been denied by Christians and pagans alike. It was consonant with neither the preachments of Christ on humility nor with the *memento mori* which the Pléiade had heard from their schoolmasters during their clerical education. Not only were they conscious of the Biblical reminder that all things

[34] Pindar, *Pythian Odes* xi, 41–44.
[35] Horace, *Ad Pisones*, vs. 63.
[36] Cicero, *De Re Publica* (London: Heinemann, 1928), p. 279.
[37] Seneca, *Epist.* lxxi, 15.
[38] Ovid, *Amores* iii, 12, 13.
[39] *Essais*, Bk. II, chap. xvi.
[40] *Ibid*., Bk. I, chap. xxxviii.
[41] Buchanan, *Poemata quae extant* (Lugduni, 1628), p. 340; J.-C. Scaliger, *ed. cit*., II, 316.

have their term, but they translated this grim reminder into such works as the "Discours de la vanité" of Belleau and the "Epitaphe de Jan Martin" of Ronsard.[42] And it was Ronsard who recalled Solomon's omniscient pity for those who "wished to train their minds by study to ascend to a heaven they could never reach." [43]

The revolt against the idea of glory, moreover, was not merely a reaction against the belief in poetic immortality and divinity. It went even so far as to question whether writing was a worth-while profession to follow. It questioned the doctrine that poets are born, not made, which Peletier had first championed. It challenged the view that the song of the Swan was any more appreciated than the caw of the Crow. It had many facets, this reaction, and their diversity becomes apparent when one studies the poets' remarks and opinions on other writers. Just as the ideal of glory became a basis of their criticism (*e.g.*, Homer enjoyed perennial glory; *ergo*, Homer was a great author), so did its counterpart, the theme of anti-glory (*e.g.*, the court lets Du Bellay die in poverty; *ergo*, Du Bellay is a great poet). Their disenchantment over poetry colors their judgments in many ways.

As has been stated, the whole matter of the revolt against glory will be examined on the basis of remarks found throughout the *canzoniere* of the Pléiade, for no literary pamphleteer or prefacist of the 1550's would have openly voiced sustained objections to the value of poetry. To the conservative Pléiade, the literary arbiters and cognoscenti of the time, such a policy would have been radical and even anti-social. But occasional mentions of these objections found their way into verse. These apparently harmless *obiter dicta* accumulate and assume considerable proportions. From them one learns of the powerful undercurrent which passed unnoticed in the great abundance of prose literary theory of sixteenth-century France.

[42] Belleau, M.-L., II, 271, and Ronsard, VI, 201.
[43] Ronsard, IV, 93.

The revolt against the theme of glory involved the following major objections, made manifest in the comments of the Pléiade on other writers:

I. Poetry gives the maker no divinity or immortality, as the experience of the past shows.

II. Lack of discrimination robs the poet of glory even during his lifetime. Society cannot distinguish good poets from bad, as the experiences of present-day poets show.

III. Poetry is a trade and, as such, profitless and foolish.

⚜ ⚜ ⚜

As might be expected, the remarks of the Pléiade on the futility of poetry start with the earliest Greeks. What is less to be anticipated is the charge that Orpheus, the first bard and greatest prototype of the lyric art, should have abandoned poetry:

> Orphé que t'a servi ta mère Calliope,
> D'avoir trainé d'une rempante trope
> Les forests après toy? avoir parmi les bois
> De-sauvagé les fères sous ta vois? . . .
> Rien: car vous estes mort.[44]

The piece asks the same question of Linus, Pindar, and Homer. Elsewhere Ronsard asks again what Homer cares whether his name flourishes or not, while he lies "down there" without a whole head or limb.[45] Nor did it help Homer to have written such a great quantity of verse; verses will not save him from enduring the heavy weight of the tomb.[46]

In the *Dialogues* of Tahureau (1565), the cynical dialectician Democritic echoes apropos of Demosthenes the very question of Ronsard:

> Cuidés-vous que la louange que l'on donne à Demosthène ou à Cicéron leur chatouille bien maintenant les oreilles aus lieus où ils sont allés?

[44] *Ibid.*, V, 274; also V, 317.
[45] *Ibid.*, VI, 308.
[46] *Ibid.*, II, 438.

. . . Je ne veux pas dire qu'il faille délaisser pour cela d'estre affecté à la vertu, de profiter au public, de composer livres, et faire quelques autres choses dignes de mémoire, mais je veus bien maintenir qu'une heure de louange que lon reçoit durant la vie fait plus de bien à la personne que cent mille ans après la mort.[47]

As Byron phrased it (after Martial), "Post-obits rarely reach a poet." Such reflections make Ronsard gloomy concerning his own fate:

> Je pose le cas que mes vers
> De mon labeur en contr'eschange,
> Dix ou vingt ans par l'univers
> M'apportent un peu de louange.
>   Que faut-il pour le consumer,
> Et pour mon livre oster de terre,
> Qu'un feu qui le vienne allumer,
> Ou qu'un esclandre de la guerre? [48]

As a matter of fact, he writes to Catherine de Médicis, it was only through the humanistic patronage of the Medici family that Homer, Plato, and Socrates were saved from an eternal death, so precariously does Fortune deal with the greatest of poets.[49]

Homer never possessed a farthing and had to beg from door to door.[50] Ruminating upon the lot of Homer, Ronsard becomes convinced that the solution is to expect nothing of the future, or even of the present. Poetry is a form of virtue,[51] and as Claudian wrote, "virtus pretium sibi," virtue is its own reward. Better this small consolation than wait for an eternity of dust and emptiness:

> Chacun de son labeur doit en ce Monde attendre
> L'usufruit seulement, que présent il doit prendre,
> Sans se paistre d'attente et d'une éternité
> Qui n'est rien que fumée et pure vanité.[52]

[47] Tahureau, *Dialogues*, *ed. cit.*, p. 172.
[48] Ronsard, II, 438.
[49] *Ibid.*, III, 296. A similar tribute to the Medici as the restorers of classical culture is found in the poetics of Vida, Bk. I, vss. 192 ff.
[50] Ronsard, V, 175.
[51] *Ibid.*, III, 339.
[52] *Ibid.*, VI, 24.

If Homer were to see his valiant Aeacides today, he would no longer know him as his own son, any more than Vergil would recognise his Phrygian Aeneas: "Ainsi le froid giron de la tombe assoupist tous les sens de nature, qui sont deus à la terre et à la pourriture." [53]

As one gathers from these selections, it was Ronsard especially who brooded over death and its conquest of poetry, or of Time over Fame, as Petrarch had termed it. One finds this preoccupation in passages which do not deal with particular writers, such as the epitaph to his uncle Jehan de Ronsard. Here he asks what it avails to lucubrate, to burn the midnight oil in pursuit of Apollo and the Muses, when neither Apollo nor his poor feeble troupe are strong enough to preserve us from death.[54] And most somber is his elegy to Desportes:

> Nous devons à la Mort et nous et nos ouvrages,
> Nous mourons les premiers, le long reply des âges
> En roulant engloutist nos œuvres à la fin:
> Ainsi le veut Nature et le puissant Destin.[55]

In an elegy on death, the same poet recalls that for all the fine talk about poets being the interpreters of the gods, "death soils her hands in the blood of holy poets as she soils them in the blood of the meanest men." [56]

The eternal struggle for fame is in itself a martyrdom which the poet undergoes. Homer, Anacreon, Pindar, Hesiod, Bion sought fame, but none of them cares now what good or bad is spoken of him. Nor will he himself, adds Ronsard, hear anything under the earth, as he curiously explains, after a century or two.[57] There is an interesting sidelight to be noted here. In 1555, in the ode to Jacques de Rubampré quoted above, Ronsard gives his works ten or twenty years of posthumous fame, and just one year later he is willing to extend this period to a century or two. Is this then the limit of time which he

[53] *Idem.*
[54] *Ibid.*, VI, 215.
[55] *Ibid.*, VI, 23.
[56] *Ibid.*, V, 274.
[57] *Ibid.*, II, 303.

really predicted for his works, despite "Ode XIX" and despite his formal assertions elsewhere that his works would outlast bronze? One is reminded of Mark Twain's remark on literary immortality, "By forever I mean thirty years."

Poetry is not saved from the ravages of time by its being a form of virtue, as we have seen above. But Ronsard — and it is generally Ronsard who uses Greek authors to illustrate this aspect of the futility of creative writing — will go further than that. He will accuse virtue itself of being deceitful, of making men spend their lives vainly in the pursuits of philosophy and poetry, sealing their eyes with cunning. And virtue makes men oppose nature, a deceit which Ronsard condemns with a Romanticist conviction. Even the ancients succumbed to this lure:

> La Nature y repugne, et vous monstre combien
> Vertu pipe vos cœurs sous ombre d'un faux bien:
> Celuy qui suit Nature est sage, et ne se laisse
> Séduire des appas de telle enchanteresse.
> Qu'acquist jadis Socrate, Aristote, et Platon,
> Pythagore, Thales, Theophraste, et Criton
> Pour aimer la Vertu, fors une renommée
> Qui sera par les ans, comme ils sont, consommée?
> Dequoy sert le renom au mort qui ne sent rien? [58]

And again he refers to Plato, writing to Jean Martin; Plato, who felt the inexorable law of Pluto, for all his exploring the skies and prying into the secrets of Nature.[59]

In a piece bemoaning the decease of his friend Ronsard, Jean Passerat echoes this very thought about Plato: "Que me servira Platon pour n'aller point chez Pluton, veu qu'il y suivit Socrate?" [60]

The biographies of these ancients illustrate another truth to Jean-Antoine de Baïf. Although it was generally the misfortunes of themselves and their contemporaries which brought home to the Pléiade the sad truth that good poets do not

[58] *Ibid.*, III, 339.
[59] *Ibid.*, VI, 202.
[60] Passerat, *Poésies françaises* (Paris, 1880), I, 140.

achieve fame during their own lifetimes, Baïf finds the truth revealed by the lives of the Greeks and Romans as well:

> Mais d'où vient cela, je te prie,
> Peletier, que durant sa vie
> Le Poète mieux accomply
> Ne se veoit jamais anobly,
> Et bien peu souvent se voit lire
> Quelque beau vers qu'il puisse écrire:
> Et que toujours on prise mieux
> Que les plus jeunes les plus vieux? . . .
> Son aage se moquoit d'Homere;
> On lisoit Enne le vieil père,
> Que Rome avoit Maron vivant.
> Jamays comme l'âge suyvant,
> On n'a vu que le présent âge
> Donnast l'honneur et l'avantage
> A qui le meritant vivoit
> Aussi grand que le mort l'avoit.[61]

The following section of this chapter, devoted to the general proposition that poets cannot win true fame within their lifetimes, documents Baïf's charge with sixteenth-century illustrations.

Continuing in this same vein, Jean Passerat repeats the harsh truth that the great ancients got anything but glory for their pains, showing how Orpheus, Homer, Euripides, Archilochus, Lycophron, Aeschylus, Alcman, Sappho, among the Greeks, and Lucretius, Ovid, Plautus, and Lucan were mortally dealt with by fortune.[62] Among the ancients there were those whose works survived them and whose glory died nevertheless. Then there were also those who strove for glory, but whose works were destroyed by the will of God. Among the latter were Simonides, Alcman, Bacchylides, Alcaeus, and Stesichorus, all of whom wrote beautiful verses grave and sweet which could be read by schoolboys even today. But their glory is lost forever. "God does not will it, who covers under the earth so

[61] Baïf, M.-L., IV, 408–409.
[62] Passerat, *ed. cit.*, I, 90–91.

many lost books, shipwrecks of war, so much laborious art." [63]

The Latin writers have fared just as poorly in the matter of glory. Olivier de Magny regrets that all those who would like to revive the masterpieces of classic literature or sing ancient verses are received with cold disdain. These Romans have no more glory:

> Plus ne sont leuz d'un Ovide les vers,
> Plus ne sont veuz en pris par l'univers
> Catulle, Galle, et Properce, et Tibulle,
> Plus on n'entend les chansons de Marulle,
> Tous sont esteintz et le monde aujourd'huy
> D'eux et de moy ne reçoit qu'un ennuy.[64]

Ronsard uses this very fact as an argument against the neo-Latin writers. So completely lost is the glory of such ancients as Statius and Seneca that they are seldom heard of any more.

> Comment veux-tu qu'on te lise, Latineur, quand à peine lit-on Stace, Lucain, Seneque, Silius, et Claudian, qui ne servent que d'ombre muette en une estude, ausquels on ne parle jamais que deux ou troys foys en la vie, encore qu'ils fussent grands maistres en leur langue maternelle? [65]

Most of the Pléiade were just as certain as Ronsard that the writings of the neo-Latins could never last. But Ronsard, taking a long, historical perspective, fears that French verse will be forgotten just as completely as Latin works, even as completely as the works of the Medes and the Greeks. For nothing of human creation has ever resisted death.[66]

Du Bellay, in his "Discours à Macrin sur la Vertu," likewise carries this *cui bono* doctrine into Roman literature. Poetry as an interest as well as a pursuit is condemned. What has he gained except old age by embracing Ovid, Petrarch, Vergil, Horace, and the rest? [67] Du Bellay was one of the frankest of the Pléiade group, the closest to Montaigne's conception

[63] Ronsard, V, 187.
[64] Magny, *Odes*, *ed. cit.*, I, 66.
[65] Ronsard, VII, 97.
[66] *Ibid.*, VI, 309.
[67] Du Bellay, IV, 147.

of the "honnête homme." His candor and humility were honest, not a pose, or at least became so with time. A drafter of the principles of the Pléiade, he was sometimes the readiest to reject in later years what he had formulated. Although he taught the doctrine of the *altiloque*, or sublimity of tone, he himself avoided it whenever possible soon after 1550. Although he preached the doctrine of immortality through verse, he came to feel that this, too, was all pure vanity. In his *Regrets*, he removes himself from those who subscribe to the *exegi monumentum* of Horace:

> Aussi n'ay-je entrepris d'imiter en ce livre
> Ceulx qui par leurs escriptz se vantent de revivre
> Et se tirer tous vifz dehors des monumens.[68]

If Du Bellay accepts the theory of Horace about keeping one's works until the ninth year before publishing them, he is nevertheless opposed to those who guard their works religiously, like sacred relics, to be printed posthumously, "sçachant bien que tout ainsy que les mors ne mordent point, aussi ne sentent-ilz les morsures." [69] Just as one cannot partake of glory after death, one cannot partake of censure.

Whatever their opinion of Julius-Caesar Scaliger's other ideas, the Pléiade must have applauded his comparison of thirst for eternal fame with a quick-spreading poison.[70] Scaliger himself expressed some doubt in his piece "In barbariem huius saeculi" that the ancient poets were held in honor, but adds that whether or not they were, those of today are definitely unhonored.[71] Which leads us conveniently to our next consideration.

⚜ ⚜ ⚜

From the remarks of the Pléiade upon writers of classical antiquity one learns that hope for honor long after death is

[68] *Ibid.*, II, 55.
[69] *Ibid.*, I, 14.
[70] J.-C. Scaliger, *Poemata* (Heidelberg, 1591), Bk. I, 10.
[71] *Ibid.*, Bk. I, 211.

well-nigh an impossibility. Death destroys any hope of poetic immortality, and if Fame triumphs for a while over Death, Time, as their master Petrarch had taught them, triumphs over Fame. This lesson of Petrarch so impressed Du Bellay, by the way, that he used it as a theme of his "A Salmon Macrin, sur la mort de sa Gelonis." [72] From the Pléiade's observations on their contemporaries, on the other hand, one gathers that honor during his lifetime was an impossibility for the poet of the middle sixteenth century. One reason was the lack of discrimination or taste, an idea developed below. Just as serious as the inability of society to distinguish between good and bad poets was its inability to appreciate poets as a class or singly. So the poet must in turn despise and remain aloof from his century. The ivory tower has existed in every century since Orpheus and Amphion, for every century is parsimonious in honoring its poets and prompt to forget those whom it has deigned momentarily to honor.

> Combien avons nous veu d'hommes vertueux survivre à leur propre reputation, qui ont veu et souffert esteindre en leur présence l'honneur et la gloire très justement acquise en leur jeunes ans?

queries Montaigne in the *Essays*.[73]

That the Pléiade poets considered themselves anti-social individualists is common knowledge, but it is interesting to note their admission that any glory they might win depended upon their contemporaries. We have already suggested that the *profanum* meant for them not only the uneducated populace, but the insincere and incompetent upper classes as well. As a matter of fact, the Pléiade deplored the wretched judgment of court society even more than that of the humbler classes. In Ronsard's "A un sien ami, fasché de suivre la Court," he likens courtly favor to the shifting tide of the sea.[74] This simile pleases Ronsard and he uses it elsewhere.

[72] Du Bellay, IV, 29.
[73] Montaigne, *Essays*, Bk. II, chap. xvi.
[74] Ronsard, VI, 153.

Many are the indictments of the Pléiade against the society of their day. Long before Ronsard complained of a "France ingrate," [75] Marot had deplored "l'ingrate France, ingratissime à son poète." [76] Belleau, writing on the researches of Pasquier, pens a representative complaint:

> Celuy qui docte se propose
> Bastir aujourd'huy quelque chose,
> Est né sous un ciel malheureux:
> Car toute œuvre laborieuse,
> Qui part de main industrieuse,
> Demande un siècle plus heureux.[77]

A century, Belleau explains, which will esteem the poet without defrauding him of his honor and letting his works dissolve into dust. Belleau finds that mediocrity prevails even upon the stage, and in a sonnet to Garnier he bemoans a situation where a divine mind like Garnier's, fertile and learned, gets nowhere whereas charlatans succeed.[78] Jean de la Péruse composes a "Sonnet perdu à la rafle" to Baïf,

> Ha! mon Baïf, les Poètes n'ont plus d'heur,
> Les vers n'ont plus faveur que bien petite,
> Ce siècle d'or n'a esgard au mérite
> Des bons espris, le seul or a faveur.
> Cessera donq' nostre noble entreprise?
> Si nous n'avons qui nos vers favorise,
> Cessera donq' le doux de nostre voix? [79]

Jacques Tahureau claims that the only way for the poet of today to receive the laurel is to give it to himself:

> Mais où est maintenant le Poète,
> Où est, je vous pry, l'écrivain,
> Tant ayt-il la plume parfaite,
> Qui n'aille travaillant en vain?

[75] *Ibid.*, III, 424.
[76] Marot (Paris, Garnier, n. d.), I, 205.
[77] Belleau, M.-L., I, 117.
[78] *Ibid.*, II, 462.
[79] Jean de la Péruse, *Poésies* (Angoulême, 1866), II, 205.

Il ne peut pas d'une couronne
Se voyr guerdonné seulement,
Si luy-mesme ne se la donne,
Servant encor d'esbattement.[80]

In his elegy to Desportes, Ronsard declares that he would rather have thirty years of fame during his lifetime than a thousand years of fame during his afterlife, while he is changing, in true Pythagorean fashion, into another form.[81]

Jean Passerat wrote two pieces assailing the treatment of the writer in his day.[82] The more forthright and brutal of the pair is entitled "Contre Phébus et les Muses." With sixteenth-century candor he explains to what uses the printed page of poetry is put. It is used by the greengrocer to wrap vegetables, by the husbandman to deliver butter, and has even more ignoble uses than these. In the second work, a *plainte*, the poet declares that he has served the public for forty years, teaching virtue and knowledge, without being rewarded; he regrets the passing of the great Francis I, who gave writers benefices, estates, and offices, of his own volition.

Beyond this opinion of the Pléiade that as a class they are victims of a want of sympathy or understanding on the part of their contemporaries, there is a group of judgments which center about a more specific complaint. The glory of the good poet is imperilled by the inability of his contemporaries to recognise his superiority over the bad poets. Poetasters are praised and true poets ignored. We learn from the "Poète courtisan" how many of the courtiers made it a practice to deem the works of the swans and the crows equally good. Even worse than these hypocrites were those courtiers who awarded praise to the crows and none to the swans, that ilk decried in Ronsard's "Élégie en forme d'invective."[83] It nettled the

[80] Tahureau, *Poésies* (Paris, 1870), I, 114–115.
[81] Ronsard, VI, 25.
[82] Jean Passerat, *Poésies françaises* (Paris, 1880), I, 86; II, 62–63.
[83] Ronsard, IV, 146.

Pléiade to see inferior poets, or poets they considered inferior to themselves, win greater glory and honoraria. That these "poetasters, poetito's, parcel-poets, poet-apes, and philo-poets," to quote Jonathan Swift, should win greater rewards elicited the complaints recorded in the following paragraphs.

Chamard has established that the later years of Du Bellay were neither very happy nor illustrious ones. This inglorious end of one of the two leading poets of the century shocked and impressed his fellow writers deeply as an example of the unfairness and lack of taste of the age. Ronsard, addressing Cardinal Charles of Lorraine, is most indignant. His own Du Bellay, who had scaled Parnassus with him,

> Ne fut, siècle de fer! d'un seul bien avancé.
> O cruauté du ciel, o maligne contrée,
> Où jamais la vertu qu'en fard ne s'est monstrée!
> Puis que les fols, les sots, les jeunes courtisans
> Sont poussez en crédit devant les mieux disans! [84]

This same idea is forcefully presented by Rémy Belleau, in his "Complainte d'une nymphe sur la mort de Joachim du Bellay." He compares Du Bellay to a peasant who has sown industriously, and after waiting for a rich harvest, has to content himself with the barest of gleanings. "Ainsi nous a deceus l'attente tromperesse que nous avions de luy pour sa docte jeunesse." [85]

Indeed, this death of Du Bellay and the ignominy of the fate of Jodelle, described by Pierre de l'Estoile,[86] illustrated the truth of the despairing remarks of Baïf that "good poets are scorned. Since people have changed about and hate praiseworthy acts, praise has no more value." [87] And well might Magny sigh over this situation in his *Soupirs*:

> Les sçavans aujourd'huy sont tous mis à mespris,
> Et les grands au sçavoir ne daignent plus attendre,

[84] *Ibid.*, III, 274.
[85] Belleau, M.-L., II, 134.
[86] *Cf.*, H. Chamard, *Histoire de la Pléiade* (Paris: Didier, 1939–), I, 29.
[87] Baïf, M.-L., V, 221.

> Les bouffons seulement ils se plaisent d'entendre,
> Et ceux qui font service au mestier de Cypris.[88]

And why should Baïf, Magny, or any Pléiade poet resent so deeply the fact that great writers are no longer prized? Because each of them accepted this as a personal tragedy. "I, who by no means hide my works, don't win sufficient recognition," admits Baïf.[89] The fault, he adds, lies with the indiscriminate minds which unthinkingly award wealth to poets whose greatest abilities are mercenary rather than literary. Elsewhere, Baïf phrases all these sentiments most succinctly,

> Poésie est donc terrassée!
> Coyonerie est avancée.[90]

Oddly enough, one of the poets whom the Pléiade inwardly considered favored by the lack of literary taste at court is cited as one slighted by the ignorant throng. This is Saint-Gelays. If a well-known jealous rivalry caused the Pléiade to dislike Mellin for a time, we should like to venture another reason why the Pléiade held him in low esteem, a reason which has occurred to us in the course of this investigation. This is the fact that nowhere in all his verse did Mellin entertain or expound a single critical or aesthetic idea of any consequence. He steadfastly refused to talk shop, so to speak, and the Pléiade could not forgive him this. At any rate, Ronsard penned in 1565, long after Mellin had died and there would be no further occasion for flattery, "Saint-Gelays was the ornament of our age. He saw (o miserable profession!) an infinite throng of poltroons advanced, and little did it profit him that his lute was the most skilled of all." [91] The manner by which these poltroons got ahead at court is described by Magny in the *Odes*. They would march about holding a Vergil, Ovid, Horace, or some other Latin volume in their hand for the world to see. They would occasionally read or recite a bit of

[88] Magny, *Soupirs*, *ed. cit.*, p. 84.
[89] Baïf, M.-L., II, 433.
[90] *Ibid.*, V, 211.
[91] Ronsard, III, 274.

Petrarch. And posing as great literators, they would pass judgments on their contemporaries.[92]

All the poets grumbled over the superabundance of poetasters in France, and some of the better poets, echoing a favorite complaint of the contemporary clergy, despaired that the art of printing was now so widespread that any fool could break into print.[93] If one were to believe the Pléiade, Renaissance France resembled nothing so much as present-day Japan, where everyone from prince to pauper spends his leisure time scribbling tanka and hokku.

Du Bellay advises his friend Ronsard not to be dismayed at the large number of inferior poets arising in France;[94] these rhymers are not guided by the Demon of poetry, and so will have no safe-conduct to glory.[95] This was wishful thinking designed to comfort his friend, however, rather than a conviction. One suspects that his remarks to Magny reveal more genuine feelings:

> Un tas de sots imitateurs
> Enflans leurs vaines poésies
> De monstrueuses fantasies,
> Ont tout gasté: et ceulx qui ont
> Le mieulx escrit, pour ce qu'ilz sont
> Pressez de la tourbe ignorante,
> Leur gloire n'est point apparente.[96]

The inability of society to distinguish between the swans and the crows was perhaps as instrumental as their Horatian temperament in making ivory tower dwellers of the Pléiade poets. The number of those whom they would acknowledge as pos-

[92] Magny, *Odes*, *ed. cit.*, I, 48.

[93] Jean de la Taille, *Art de la Tragédie* (Manchester, 1939), p. 29.

[94] These second-rate poets are also mentioned in the "Ode à Christofle de Longueil" of Ronsard (V, 184); in Du Bellay's *Regrets* (II, 101); in Du Bellay's "Épître à Madame Marguerite" (III, 57); see Marot's condemnation of them in "Fripelipes, Valet de Marot, à Sagon"; also Antoine de Harsy's reference to them in 1574 in Saint-Gelays, *Œuvres*, dedicatory epistle (Paris, 1873), I, 143.

[95] Du Bellay, II, 170.

[96] *Ibid.*, V, 66.

sessing any literary discrimination was extremely limited. In his first preface to the *Olive*, Du Bellay would reduce this number further than any of his colleagues. "I'm not seeking popular plaudits. It is enough for me to have as readers a Saint-Gelays, an Héroët, a Ronsard, a Carle, a Scève, a Bouju, a Salel, a Martin, and possibly a few others might be placed in this group." (We suggest that the reader confront this passage with one from the *Giudicio* of Bartolommeo Cavalcanti, written in July, 1543, "Vi dico che è meglio a meritar loda appresso dieci, o quindici giuditiosi huomini, che guadagnare il favore di tutto il vulgo, *etc.*")[97] A book might then mean to the Pléiade approximately what it meant to R. L. Stevenson, "in an intimate sense, a circular letter to the friends of him who writes it."

Thus, ill treatment by contemporary society caused the Pléiade to withdraw within itself, to cry with Jean-Antoine de Baïf, "Le peuple ny les rois contenter ne me chaut."[98] Ronsard's discourse to Louis des Masures contains this disclaimer. "By neither edict nor public decree do I constrain anyone to read my poetry; let him read it or buy it who will."[99] Du Bellay, too, is disillusioned,

> Voyant en ce siècle où nous sommes
> Sans faveur les plus doctes hommes,
> Les arts d'Apollon en mespris,
> Les Muses servir de risée,
> Et la gloire aussi peu prisée
> Que les vertus en peu de pris.[100]

This reaction against their contemporaries encouraged them to accept only one another as literary arbiters, to look askance at honors which they themselves did not receive, to deprecate those who did receive them, and to assure themselves that another age might recognise them,

[97] Bartolommeo Cavalcanti, *Giudicio sopra la tragedia di Canace* (Venice, 1566), the concluding speech of the *Giudicio*.

[98] Baïf, M.-L., I, 102.

[99] Ronsard, V, 363.

[100] Du Bellay, V, 348–349; *cf.*, Belleau, I, 118.

Et ne faut point que lon escrive,
En espoir qu'au monde lon vive,
Sinon par la postérité . . .[101]

all with the mental reservation, as one has noted from their remarks on the classic writers, that another age might not.[102]

⚜ ⚜ ⚜

The inability of poetry to give them a profitable living was the third cause of the Pléiade's revolt against the will-o'-the-wisp of glory. They believed poets consorts of Poverty. When, occasionally, some court poet capitalised on his ability to rhyme, this isolated instance did not renew their faith in Gloria, but only made them more resentful. The Pléiade did not know the statement of a later critic about Desportes: "Plus on cherche dans sa vie, plus on y trouve des abbayes," [103] but by the facts behind it they were impressed indeed. After all, there is a certain type of glory which one may receive for his efforts which all the ivory tower convictions of the Pléiade fought against. This was material remuneration: abbeys, sinecures, hard cash. Ambition and acquisitiveness were failings which these poets possessed so keenly that they felt it necessary to disown them. They had read in their favorite, Horace, that the ideal life of the poet is a sheltered, country existence, free from ambition and care. Vida, whose opinions they valued so highly, also emphasised that the ideal poet must be apathetic about money: "Hic laeti haud magnis opibus, non divite cultu vitam agitant vates, *etc.*," and suggested again for him a retired, unambitious, bucolic life.[104]

[101] Jodelle, M.-L., II, 209.

[102] One way of course for the poet to lose that glory which the years might bestow is to be superseded by another, as Commynes surpassed Livy (Ronsard, V, 290), or Castiglione surpassed Homer, Pindar, Vergil, and Horace (La Boétie, edition of Bonnefon, sonnet xii).

[103] On the financial rewards of Desportes, as contrasted with his fellow poets, see Jacques Lavaud, *Un poète de cour, Philippe Desportes* (Paris: Droz, 1936), pp. 315 ff.

[104] Vida, *De arte poetica*, I, 492–493.

Like good disciples, the Pléiade poets spread the doctrine of their masters. One of the first was Peletier, "Know then, whoever would profess the religion of the Muses, that their holy grottoes are inaccessible to him who will be avaricious of anything other than honor." [105] The idea is found in Jean-Antoine de Baïf as often as in any other. A piece entitled "Du Contentement" is devoted to the proposition that great poets are apathetic about wealth.[106] In a poem to the king which stresses both the notion of apathy and that of isolation, Baïf describes the disdain for riches of his father, Lazare de Baïf, "Good Lazarus, untouched by avarice and even less by ambition, follows his Muse in Anjou . . . not far from the Loir." [107] In other places the idea is presented more objectively, as a formal principle:

> La tromperesse Ambition
> Un vray Poète n'enveloppe, . . .
> Ny aux richesses il ne bâille.[108]

Again, Baïf presents this disdain as a phase of the ivory tower maxim:

> Toujours franc depuis j'ay vescu
> De l'ambition populaire,
> Et dans moy s'est tapy vaincu
> Tout ce que domte le vulgaire.[109]

It found its way into the *Art poétique* of Vauquelin: "The poet is in no way avaricious: he loves his labours, his only purpose and joy," [110] as well as into the *Art Poétique* of Boileau a century later.[111] Even Desportes, whose ambitions were satisfied more liberally than those of his fellow poets, echoes this same refrain, deprecating those who, thirsty for honors and riches, press about the king.[112]

[105] Peletier, *Art poétique*, ed. by Boulanger, p. 218.
[106] Baïf, M.-L., IV, 359.
[107] *Ibid.*, I, iv.
[108] *Ibid.*, II, 392.
[109] *Ibid.*, II, 161.
[110] Vauquelin, *ed. cit.*, p. 96.
[111] Boileau, *Art poétique*, IV, 174–176.
[112] Desportes, *ed. cit.*, p. 29.

These sentiments, coined in such an *altiloque* manner, expressed wishful thinking rather than honest opinion. An author may be divine, he may be a learned individualist, but he has to eat and live. Even Pindar had written, "Every man strives to defend his belly from bitter hunger." Most of the members of the Pléiade, as has been noted earlier, were members of the petty aristocracy, and none experienced the days of hunger of a Dante. But because they had aristocratic origins, they shared none of Boccaccio's love for Lady Poverty.[113] They wanted an affluent living and were quite chagrined when literature failed to give it to them. They contradicted all of the old talk about the poet being an oracle or minister and poetry a divine, occult frenzy. Versifying became a *métier*,[114] just like law, medicine, soldiery, or as La Bruyère was to claim a century later, like clockmaking. With one difference, however: poetry failed to provide a satisfactory living. In his hymn on gold, Ronsard denies that even the greatest of writers can create their masterworks unless materially provided for.[115] Moreover, he shows how shabbily Fortune has dealt with many a fine writer. Small wonder that the Pléiade felt theirs to be the most inglorious of all professions.[116]

This is precisely the burden of the verses of Du Bellay to Baïf, advising him to leave poetry for law or some more worthwhile profession:

[113] Boccaccio, *De Genealogia Deorum* xiv.

[114] The Pléiade poets were not reticent about using the word "métier" for poetry. *Cf.*, Baïf, M.-L., II, 296, 436; Jodelle, II, 118; Du Bellay, II, 175; Ronsard, VII, 29; Ronsard, STFM, X, 213, *etc.*

[115] Ronsard, IV, 336; for same advice, *cf.*, Ronsard, V, 175. Peletier's *Art poétique* recalls wistfully that the Emperor had given Vergil so much money that Vergil had made the Emperor and Maecenas his heirs (*Art poétique*, ed. by Boulanger, p. 69). A similar reminiscence occurs in Ronsard (VI, 293).

[116] Outside the Pléiade, Julius-Caesar Scaliger acknowledged this miserable treatment of poets in his "De poetis":

> Si haec est conditio miserae Solimane Poesis,
> Post neglecta suos ut iaceat cineres:
> Ah ego vos mutas optem siluisse, Camoenae: *etc.*

Poemata (1591), I, 184.

Si tu m'en crois (Baïf) tu changeras Parnasse
Au Palais de Paris, Helicon au parquet,
Ton laurier en un sac, et ta lyre au caquet
De ceulx qui, pour serrer, la main n'ont jamais lasse.
C'est à ce mestier là que les biens on amasse,
Non à celuy des vers, ou moins y a d'acquêt
Qu'au mestier d'un boufon ou celuy d'un naquet.[117]

Du Bellay, it might be added, complained more of his poverty than any other of the Pléiade.[118] Ronsard, who called Lady Poverty "the most filthy harpy in this world," [119] gives Rubampré much the same counsel that his friend had given Baïf,

Non — non, il vaut mieux, Rubampré,
Son âge en trafiques despendre,
Ou devant un Sénat pourpré
Pour de l'argent sa langue vendre,
Que de suivre l'ocieux train
De ceste pauvre Calliope
Qui tousjours fait mourir de faim
Les meilleurs chantres de sa trope.[120]

This same disillusioned advice Du Bellay gives to Jodelle in another piece of the *Regrets*, pointing out that all professions have their rewards except tragic poetry, which does not bring even the reward of a laurel:

Pourquoy donc fais-tu tant lamenter Calliope
Du peu de bien qu'on fait à sa gentille trope?
Il fault (Jodelle) il fault aultre labeur choisir
Que celuy de la Muse, à qui veut qu'on l'avance.[121]

Twice in his works Baïf relates how the lean slattern Poverty was scolding him. "Smash thy flutes, break thy pipes, cease this wretched commerce with the Muses. Poor fellow, give thyself rather to some craft where thou may'st earn." [122] Another time "pale poverty takes him by the ear." She urges him

[117] Du Bellay, II, 175.
[118] *Ibid.*, II, 63, 70, 74, 85, 95, *etc.*
[119] Ronsard, IV, 351.
[120] *Ibid.*, II, 438.
[121] Du Bellay, II, 175.
[122] Baïf, M.-L., III, 7.

again to renounce the Muses, for winter is coming and he will have to eat.[123]

The lengthiest sustained objection to poetry as a profession which we have discovered in the Pléiade's *canzoniere* is the work of Jean Passerat mentioned earlier and entitled "Contre Phébus et les Muses." Passerat takes leave of Apollo and then of the Muses. He has been the slave of Apollo and of poverty too long:

> Les Muses ay suivy et leur mestier appry,
> Mestier sans nul profit, trompeur des bons esprits.[124]

He then cites the now familiar story of the great writers of antiquity who were not spared from misfortunes, even though they were thorough masters of their craft. Poetry is a *métier* and a poor one.

If the Pléiade writers were somewhat bitter about the affluent living of the politicians and lawyers, the favor which the architects enjoyed piqued them as well. Reflecting upon those splendid new châteaux which were being constructed in sixteenth-century France, Ronsard noted with regret that an architect or a mason enjoyed a better living than a poet.[125] And what future did Ronsard predict for these Renaissance châteaux which are even today one of the glories of France? He objected that they would endure less than a hundred years, that the contemporary poets' creations would outlast them by far.[126]

When the Pléiade reflected upon the poverty which Du Bellay described succinctly as the heritage of the Muses,[127] they sometimes became vehement in their denunciations of poetry. After all, the disciplines of the art were tremendous. They robbed one of his forces, made him catarrhal, sickly, weak, solitary, irascible, taciturn, and dreamy.[128] Furthermore, they made him pale, puffy, grey-haired, gouty, congested even

[123] *Ibid.*, IV, 323.
[124] Jean Passerat, *Poésies françaises* (Paris, 1880), I, 87.
[125] Ronsard, VI, 309.
[126] *Ibid.*, IV, 185.
[127] Du Bellay, VI, 137.
[128] *Ibid.*, VI, 131.

in his youth.[129] Or if not grey-haired, then bald.[130] As if this were not enough, they made him thin, sallow, worn, wrinkled, rheumatic, discourteous, sullen, distracted, and rude.[131] Letters become not only a profitless profession, but a foolish and stupid one, as both Baïf and Ronsard testify. "En cette sote fantaisie, le métier de la Poésie, j'ay mené bien près de vingt ans: j'esperoy quelque récompense, quand ne faisoy que perdre tems." [132] And to M. de Villeroy Baïf admits that when he thinks about the time he has spent in rhyming, he has to laugh at his long folly.[133] Ronsard's prose carries the same theme as his poetry. Of verse he writes, "S'il faut dire vray, un folastre mestier duquel on ne peut retirer beaucoup d'avancement, ny de profit." [134]

In many cases the fault is with the monarchs, who are unappreciative of the services which the poets render them and their countries. This fact Ronsard openly tells Troussily, of the King's Council, and Catherine de Médicis herself.

> Je pleurois du Bellay qui estoit de mon âge,
> De mon art, de mes mœurs, et de mon parentage,
> Lequel après avoir d'une si docte vois
> Tant de fois rechanté les Princes et les Rois,
> Est mort pauvre chétif, sans nulle récompense,
> Sinon du fameux bruit que luy garde la France.[135]
>
> J'ay remply de leurs noms les terres et les cieux:
> Et si de mes labeurs qui honorent la France
> Je ne remporte rien qu'un rien pour recompense.[136]

And in his caustic "Responce à quelque Ministre," Ronsard insists that he has lived as a true, disinterested poet; that royal favor has never been liberal toward him.[137]

Two pieces of this period mention the court's ill treatment

[129] Ronsard, VI, 294.
[130] *Ibid.*, VI, 307.
[131] *Ibid.*, V, 174.
[132] Baïf, M.-L., II, 437.
[133] *Ibid.*, V, 41.
[134] Ronsard, VII, 29.
[135] *Ibid.*, III, 289.
[136] *Ibid.*, III, 315.
[137] *Ibid.*, V, 424.

of authors with bitter irony. There is the backhanded slap in the poemata of George Buchanan, the Bordeaux correspondent of the Pléiade, which begins, "Vulgus me vocat et putat poetam; aula non putat et vocat poetam." [138] Then, there is the written request of Jean Passerat that Henri III make him the successor to the recently deceased court jester. Poets and fools are of a kindred nature. At least, if he were the king's jester, his financial circumstances would be improved. He compares writers and clowns to the disadvantage of the former:

> Le plus grand différent qui se trouve entre nous,
> C'est qu'on dict que tousjours fortune aime les fouls
> Et qu'elle est peu souvent favorable aus poètes.[139]

Ronsard himself expressed a wish that he might have been born a humpback or a hairy savage instead of a poet, in order to win the monarch's favor.[140]

As long as there will be royal courts, there will probably be sarcasm of this sort. Years later, Jonathan Swift wrote in his "rapsody" on poetry, "The vilest verse thrives best at court." When one reads all the trite verse written to and apparently welcomed by the courtiers of the French Renaissance, one must grant that the court by and large did have poor taste. The Pléiade wrote more competently to the good writers and scholars than they wrote to kings and nobles. Thus, when Ronsard pens a poem to Salel, his style is superior to that he employs in verses to Charles IX. This is one further reason why the celebrated ode to the chancellor Michel de l'Hospital is an exceptional work.

Poets must have material rewards, there is no doubt about it. In his hymn on gold to Dorat, Ronsard insisted on this, as well as in his ode to King Charles IX:

[138] Buchanan, *Poemata* (Lugduni, 1628), p. 356. This friend of the Pléiade also composed a diatribe against ignorant materialistic prelates who have no use for poets:

> Carmina portanti, Praesul, janua tua clausa est, *etc.*

Ibid., pp. 352–353.

[139] Passerat, *Poésies françaises* (Paris, 1880), II, 14–15.

[140] Ronsard, VI, 341.

Car sans honneur la Muse consommée
De long travail s'alambique en fumée,
Et l'escrivain qui n'a le plus souvent
Qu'une promesse aussi froide que vent,
Devient poussif et rétif à l'ouvrage.[141]

If one does not receive these honors, the only alternative is to ask for them. If intangible honors and kudos are such that they flee those who seek them too ardently, as Peletier claimed,[142] material honors are not so elusive, and one should demand to receive. After all, even the dignified neo-Latins made such demands.[143] As if in direct response to Ronsard's complaint that "je ne remporte rien qu'un rien" came Baïf's,

Frape, demande à toutes portes:
Autrement tu n'emportes rien.[144]

What a complete contrast this is to Carducci's proud claim that poets are not beggars, in his famous "Congedo": "Il poeta, o vulgo sciocco, un pitocco non è già."

It is too bad that one must be so outspoken. But if those in power are Philistines and Boeotians, there is no other course. Unfortunately, the courtiers of the Valois régime did not possess the gentlemanly discrimination and judgment which Castiglione's popular manual said they should. Ronsard was not afraid to state in forthright language what poor judgment was to be found at court. At a court so blind that it would have failed to recognise the merits of Vergil himself, what has he, Ronsard, gained in his campaign against ignorance? "What has it availed me to toil so hard overcoming Ignorance, if she is admittedly growing all the stronger, if those in power pay her court, impassioned by a deceitful language that the Nine Sisters would never recognise as their own? . . . Even if

[141] *Ibid.*, III, 237.
[142] Peletier, *Art poëtique*, ed. by Boulanger, p. 218.
[143] Take for example Buchanan's distich:

Das inopi dives, sed qualia reddere possit
Munera. Nonne hoc est dicere? Redde mihi.

Buchanan, *Poemata quae extant* (Lugduni, 1628), p. 338.
[144] Baïf, M.-L., II, 437.

Vergil himself showed up in their sight, I'm sure that they would find him a bore." [145] And when these courtiers chanced to encounter one of their finest contemporary poets on the street, they didn't know him from some African or Asiatic.[146] At the conclusion of the "Ode à Troussily" in the *Bocage*, Ronsard set down several bitter lines on courtiers which appeared in the edition of 1560, but which were removed from the 1567 printing. In these lines the real meaning of the epithet *corbeau* is specified. These poetasters and courtiers were birds of prey (*cf.*, the *corbeaux* of Henri Becque) who usurped the rights and riches which were the due of the Pléiade. They were the hangers-on, the perennial satellites.[147] They were the intruders, the falsifiers, the crows poaching on the wealth and glory of the swans. It nettled Ronsard to watch these ravagers pose as Ciceros at court, reaping rich rewards:

> Qui comme potirons, à la court sont venuz,
> Vieux Corbeaux affamez qui faucement heritent
> Des biens et des honneurs que les autres meritent.[148]

If they acknowledged, then, that good poets ought openly to ask for money to protect their interests from such interlopers, did the Pléiade carry this solution into actual practice? To be sure they did. Not always were they so cordially blunt in their demands as Marot had been in such pieces as his "Au roy, pour estre remis en son estat." As one of many examples of the mid-century poet asking for direct financial aid, we refer the reader to Jean Passerat's plea "Au thresorier de l'espargne":

> Mes vers, Monsieur, c'est peu de chose:
> Et Dieu mercy, je le sçay bien:
> Mais vous ferés beaucoup de rien
> Si les changés à vostre prose.[149]

[145] Ronsard, VI, 63.
[146] *Ibid.*, II, 305.
[147] *Ibid.*, V, 180.
[148] *Ibid.*, VII, 382; also IV, 352.
[149] Passerat, *ed. cit.*, II, 132.

Many pieces of the Pléiade reminded the rulers that poets had to market their verses, like other merchants. Ronsard suggested to Henri II that the two of them barter (*troque pour troque*) what each had to offer.[150] The same writer attempts to explain to Coligny how poets have to keep requesting favors as a fly keeps returning to milk or honey even though threatened with annihilation. He claims that poets receive so few favors that they are obliged to become veritable bloodsuckers.[151]

⚜ ⚜ ⚜

Granting, then, all the injustices perpetrated upon the poets, why did the Pléiade coterie cherish their profession so much? If the path up Parnassus is "harsh, steep, rough, and thorny," as Baïf said,[152] if poets are "advanced only in poverty," as Ronsard complained,[153] and if they reap no harvest of glory, why do they continue to write?

Both Du Bellay and his dear friend Olivier de Magny undertake to explain this paradox, in similar terms. Poetry, despite all these shortcomings, has therapeutic spiritual qualities which soothe and charm its practitioners. Here they are speaking not only for their own group, but for all writers:

> Bien qu'un art sans profit ne plaise au courtisan,
> Bien qu'on ne paye en vers l'œuvre d'un artisan,
> Bien que la Muse soit de pauvreté suivie,
> Si ne veulx-je pourtant délaisser de chanter,

[150] Ronsard, II, 90. Other typical requests for money are found in Passerat's "Au Roy, pour estre payé de quinze mois de sa pension"; Ronsard's ode "Au Roy" (II, 236) and his "Suite de l'hymne de Charles Cardinal de Lorraine," where he revives the legend of Simonides's disdain for praises and preference for hard cash (STFM, IX, 152). Ronsard suppressed these outspoken verses in 1578.

[151] Ronsard, V, 156.

[152] Baïf, M.-L., II, 392.

[153] Ronsard, III, 292. These objections were summarised later in Vauquelin de la Fresnaye's description of poetry as "cet art, où souvent les sçavants indiscrets n'emportent que du vent."

Puis que le seul chant peult mes ennuys enchanter,
Et qu'aux Muses je doy bien six ans de ma vie.[154]

Les seuls vers de la Muse allègent mes ennuys
Et seuls me font passer et les jours et les nuicts.[155]

This reminiscence of Cicero is repeated in the *Deffence*.[156] Looking into the correspondence of Du Bellay with his uncle, one finds still another version of this reasoning. When his uncle chided him for the type of versifying in which he had indulged while sojourning at Rome, Joachim explains that he had spent time rhyming in French and Latin "non tant pour plaisir que je y prisse que pour ung relaschement de mon esperit occupé aux affaires." [157]

Baïf and Ronsard interpret the paradox in like wise,

C'est seulement pour tromper les ennuis
De la fortune où trop pauvre je suis.[158]

La seule lyre douce
L'ennuy des cœurs repousse.[159]

Thus, this therapeutic function is represented by four verbs, but always the same substantive:

enchanter les ennuis
alléger les ennuis
tromper les ennuis
repousser les ennuis

The finest justification of the impoverished Muse arises in the distinction which the Pléiade was capable of making between spiritual wealth and material wealth. There is, as Baïf reminds us in the *Passetemps*, more than one kind of poverty. Many a man who might be envied by the poets in their mo-

[154] Du Bellay, II, 61.
[155] Magny, *Soupirs*, ed. by Courbet, p. 38.
[156] *Deffence*, *ed. cit.*, p. 197.
[157] Du Bellay, *Lettres*, ed. by Nolhac (Paris, 1883), p. 43.
[158] Baïf, M.-L., II, 91.
[159] Ronsard, II, 318; Ronsard adds "charmer nos ennuis" to this list (VI, 84).

III. JEAN-ANTOINE DE BAÏF

Quant est de moy, ô misérable Muse,
Si quelque fois à tes dons ie m'amuse
C'est seulement pour tromper les ennuis
De la fortune où trop pauvre je suis.

(see page 78)

ments of dissatisfaction, that is, a man rich in gold and offices, could justly be considered "pauvre, non de l'avoir, mais dedans son âme."[160] Ronsard makes this distinction twice. At one time he concedes that although the wealth he has received from the Muse is negligible, it is still greater by his own standards than the most precious treasures of the Orient.[161] Again, he cries indignantly, "Non, la Richesse, non, ne se mesure pas aux escus amassez l'un sur l'autre à grand tas, mais au contentement: celuy qui se contente vit très-riche, et n'eust-il qu'une moyenne rente."[162] Du Bellay perceives that poetry must have had this therapeutic value for the ancients as well, despite everything:

> Je ne veux plus de ces poètes vieux
> Plaindre le sort et la fortune amère:
> Je ne veux plus pauvre appeller Homère.[163]

Is it not quite possible, then, that Du Bellay, Ronsard, Baïf, and their fellow poets, consorts of Dame Poverty though they may have been, remained withal the richest mortals of Renaissance France?

⚜ ⚜ ⚜

The Pléiade's formal adherence to the cult of glory was one which the treatises on Renaissance criticism seldom fail to mention. In addition to reproducing some of the passages for which this belief was responsible, we have tried to show that three definite classical traditions lay behind it. These traditions may be summarily given their Latin etiquettes of the *exegi monumentum*, the *doctus poeta*, and the *odi profanum*. The three may be recalled briefly in that order: Through his works the poet builds a glorious monument to himself, his friends, or his patrons. The creative writer is the wisest and

[160] Baïf, M.-L., IV, 426.
[161] Ronsard, II, 230.
[162] *Ibid.*, IV, 353.
[163] Du Bellay, II, 229.

most gifted member of his society, not only in the field of literature, but in all branches of the humanities. The poet or artist is a social individualist, living apart from the throng in spirit if not in body; the vulgar throng, by the way, includes courtiers and commoners alike, and even those versifiers who would pose as rivals of the Poets, a word to be written with a capital initial letter.

Like the theme of poetic glory itself, the reaction against glory was part of the ideological heritage of the Pléiade from the classic poets and from the Christian philosophers. Not mentioned in formal treatises by the Pléiade, quite unlike its counterpart, the Gloria theme, this reaction has passed unnoticed by literary historians of that time as well as those of the present day. Its importance as a literary idea with the Pléiade becomes apparent only from an examination of the remarks and judgments of this group on other writers.

The experience of the ancients, both Greek and Roman, demonstrates that literature gives the maker no immortality, no real fame after his death. Furthermore, if any of them are occasionally read by some humanist of the present, what difference could this make to them, dust in their tombs? The experience of all ages, and particularly of sixteenth-century France, shows that poets as a class are not appreciated by society. The Pléiade's works show a revolt against social prestige, against the lack of sympathy and understanding of society — almost a *Weltschmerz*. Society and especially those in power cannot distinguish genuine poetry from doggerel, *rythmasseries*. The vulgar throng, as we have observed, included not only the "monstre têtu" or Caliban, but the wealthy classes as well. The Pléiade's grievances against the nobles and the privileged were, as a matter of fact, greater than those against the less educated classes. Not only their society, but their century, was resented by them. It was, as their contemporary Julius-Caesar Scaliger described it, a "seculum gustu insipido marcidum, inertique palato."[164] It was also a century

[164] J.-C. Scaliger, *Poemata*, *ed. cit.*, II, 137.

which favored men of action, courtiers, and those whose political utility was unquestioned. If poetry's utilitarian value was a mooted question in the literary debates of the time, others than the literati set little or no premium on verse. And even one of the literati, Malherbe, was to hold that a good poet was of no more use to the state than a good ten-pin player.

Just as readily as a Tolstoy or a Balzac, the Pléiade viewed literature as a profession, a trade, and one which afforded fewer rewards than other trades. Despite their disclaimers that the true poet does not possess ambition or avarice, the inability of letters to win them either kudos or economic gain led them to brand poetry foolish, stupid, and wasteful. Having just mentioned Scaliger, we submit that even this serious scholar of the art of writing admitted in his poem "Quare versus faciat" that to compose verses, one's mind must be bereft of reason.[165]

Such in brief was the Pléiade's stand on the glory and the futility of literature. We do not propose that the revolt against poetic glory was stronger or even more sincere than their belief in Gloria itself. As students of the classics they were quite willing to put faith in Pindar's preachments about the illustrious poet. But in their own lives, in the lives of their confreres, and in those of earlier authors, they saw real dissatisfactions and disillusions. Ill health, financial distress, court favoritism and intrigue all contributed to discredit the Pindaric and Horatian ideal. We have studied the chronology of the passages quoted in this chapter, hoping to establish a correlation between these moments of disenchantment and the personal events in the poets' lives. Had this been possible, one might interpret many of these passages as expressions of momentary dissatisfaction and vexation rather than a consistent philosophical conviction. Such a correlation was scarcely possible. The remarks are distributed throughout the entire productive period of the Pléiade, being somewhat more common after 1555 than before. They apparently cannot be traced to particular dis-

[165] *Ibid.*, I, 2.

appointments immediately discernible in the biographies of the poets. There are a few exceptions. During the years that Du Bellay played a sycophant's rôle in Italy, there was a pronounced reaction against verse and poetic penury in his works. Magny's unhappy stay in Italy also made him react visibly against the profession. Ronsard's deafness, ill health, and retirement from court accentuated the note of apathy about glory in his writings. Jodelle and Jean de la Taille had undergone days of privation, and even Ronsard was given by Dorat the epitaph, "Hei, vereor ne uno sit Maecenate carendum." The inglorious death of Du Bellay (1560) also impressed upon the Pléiade the futility of a poetic career; for this reason several of the eulogies commemorating that death echo the familiar *vanitas vanitatum*, applying it specifically to the fate of the poet.

Generally, however, this was a sustained revolt based on deep inrooted convictions, with objections to the poetic career likely to emerge at any moment. The examples of classic writers without honor which they have recalled here they knew from their student days and had before them all their lives; there was no reason why these should be evoked as object lessons at any given time. The only chronological consistency about these objections is in the fact of their rarity during the earliest 1550's. Similarly, it was during the first few years following the publication of the *Deffence* that the most extravagant and intransigent pretensions to glory were penned. But by 1555 one finds Ronsard predicting for his works the fame of a mere twenty years. After this time there was an evenly distributed outcropping of anti-Gloria passages, betraying neither a progression toward glory nor away from it. But the other values of poetry were now so seriously compromised that the therapeutic values were called upon to reinforce them. Certainly, the events of their lives contributed indirectly toward this reaction against the Pindaric ideal, but save for the exceptions conceded just above, no immediate correlation may be made between their *curricula vitae* and the three facets of their revolt, nor can a mass progression toward pessimism be established. For this reason, one must recognise the anti-Gloria as no less important than the Gloria as a sustained philosophical conviction and poetic motif in Pléiade theory.

III

CLARITY AND OBSCURITY

Car nous voulons la Nuance encor,
Pas la couleur, rien que la nuance!
Oh! la nuance seule fiance
Le rêve au rêve et la flûte au cor!
— PAUL VERLAINE, *Art poëtique*

It has finally come to this: that not only are haziness, mysteriousness, obscurity, and exclusiveness elevated to the rank of a merit and a condition of poetic art, but even inaccuracy, indefiniteness, and lack of eloquence, are held in esteem. — LEO TOLSTOY, *What is Art?*

THE third criterion of judgment which becomes apparent from the poetry of the Pléiade concerns clarity and obscurity. Unlike those of truth and glory, this issue is touched upon in two critical works of the Pléiade, the *Solitaire premier, ou Discours des Muses* (1552) of Pontus de Tyard and the *Art poétique* of Peletier.

The matter of literary obscurity was a delicate one in the 1550's, for the poet was caught in the path of two opposing currents. One literary tradition, the Hellenic or Orphic, held that the poet must be obscure. This was endorsed by more recent justifications of obscurantism, such as the "trobar clus" of the Provençals and the "difficulté à vaincre" of the mediaeval poets and the pre-Renaissance *rhétoriqueurs*. Moreover, there was before them the example of Biblical allegory, with the conscious obscurity of the *Canticum Canticorum* and the

Apocalypsis. The contrary tradition which insisted on clarity existed not only as a heritage from the classical grammarians, but as a universal doctrine of good sense.

As an oracle, a *μουσοπάταγος*, to use a word which caught the fancy of Du Bellay,[1] the poet has an obligation to disguise. He must cloak truth which he, as an interpreter of divine and arcanal wisdom, imparts to human minds.[2] This, we have seen, is a natural consequence of the Pindaric conception of the bard. Perhaps another contributory factor encouraging obscurity in ancient aesthetics was the belief that only the difficult was beautiful. This crystallised into the Hellenic proverb, *τὰ χαλεπὰ καλά.*

Nevertheless, attacks on obscurity were launched throughout antiquity by the rhetoricians, beginning with Aristotle himself. A considerable section of his *Poetics* is devoted to instruction on the art of being clear but not commonplace.[3] These attacks were seldom formal or complete. They generally disregarded the intention of the author. They were often concerned exclusively with problems of grammatical logic such as word order, brevity, prolixity, orthology, and asyndeta, discussing each as a detached phenomenon rather than part of the greater problem of obscurity. That we may gain an idea of the objections to incomprehensibility which the rhetoricians and logicians had recorded and which were to be revaluated by the Pléiade, they will be reviewed briefly.

Almost all the classical rhetoricians warned against lack of moderation in regard to brevity and prolixity (*αὔξησις* or *amplificatio*). Excess in either direction would lead to obscuration. Aristotle in his *Rhetoric* shows that asyndeta are a form of brevity which results in ambiguity and obscurity.[4] In another place, Aristotle mentions obscurity of style through thought order and word order, and finds that abstrusity results

[1] Du Bellay, *Deffence*, ed. by Chamard, II, xi.
[2] *Vide supra*, Chap. I.
[3] Aristotle, *Poetics* xxii, 1.
[4] Aristotle, *Rhetoric* iii, 12, 4.

when explanatory material that belongs to the beginning is inserted later in the narration.[5]

Other Greek references to obscurity are encountered in the works of Demetrius, Hermogenes of Tarsus, and the ideas of Theophrastus reproduced in Demetrius, Dionysius of Halicarnassus, and Ammonius Hermeiou. Hermogenes placed clarity (σαφήνεια) as the first of the seven basic ideas of diction.[6] According to Dionysius, clarity was one of the great virtues of style, and he regretted that Thucydides and Demosthenes were so obscure as to demand commentaries; [7] elsewhere he noted that Theophrastus praised clarity and saw obscurity resulting from use of foreign, archaic, equivocal words and homonyms. Theophrastus grants that brevity may lead to unintelligibility, but adds that some points must always be left to the ingenuity of the reader.[8] This same brevity against which Theophrastus cautions is praised by Dionysius of Halicarnassus, representing a stoic love of simplicity.[9]

One of the very few Hellenic writers to evaluate the psychological rather than purely syntactical or logical aspects of obscurity was Demetrius: "And strangely enough, obscurity (ἀσάφεια) may well make a deep impression, for what is distinctly hinted at is more impressive, while that which is clearly stated is looked down upon." [10]

Among the Latins, σαφήνεια and ἀσάφεια were treated as *perspicuitas* and *obscuritas*.[11] The most complete analysis of the subject was made by Quintilian, but Cicero was concerned with it in at least two passages of his *De Oratore*. Crassus, in the third book, speaks of the merits of "plane dicendi," and

[5] *Ibid.*, iii, 5, 7.

[6] Hermogenes, *Peri Ideon* (Lipsiae: Teubner, 1913), p. 226. Quoted by Scaliger, *Poetices libri* (Heidelberg, 1617), p. 403.

[7] Dionysius of Halicarnassus, *On Lysias* iv.

[8] In Demetrius, *On Style* (London: Heinemann, 1932), p. 439.

[9] For a competent condensed discussion of obscurity among Greek writers and theorists, see W. R. Roberts, *Dionysius of Halicarnassus, on Literary Composition* (London, 1910), pp. 335–341.

[10] Demetrius, *On Style* v, 254.

[11] Or *explanatio*, by Cornificius, *Rhetorica* iv, 17.

in the second book the writer distinguishes between obscurity in various parts of the composition, the consequences being graver in some parts than in others: "et maiore etiam periculo haec pars (*i.e.*, narratio) orationis obscura est quam caeterae." Three ways to avoid obscurity are suggested. "Erit autem perspicua narratio, si verbis usitatis, si ordine temporum conservato, si non interrupte narrabitur." [12]

Quintilian devotes an entire section of his manual on oratory to clarity and obscurity.[13] Clarity centers principally about *proprietas*, or that precision of wording which makes the thought comprehensible. Unintelligibility results from archaic, technical, dialectal words, as Cicero and others had established. A greater occasion for obscurity is found in the ambiguous or poorly ordered combination of words. The type of abstrusity which was most criticised by the Pléiade in their remarks on Scève and Pontus de Tyard is mentioned in Quintilian. This is the type resulting from the writer's attempt to avoid the commonplace, a tendency which Ronsard recognised in himself. It is the incomprehensibility which Rabelais is satirising when he makes his scholar recall that "l'origine primève de mes aves et ataves fut indigène des régions Lémoviques," instead of stating merely, as one would have said or written at that time, "je suis Limosin." Quintilian censures this consciously involved style which some misguided writers try to acquire. Indeed, he recalls Livy's telling of a pedagogue who urged his pupils to make all that they said obscure.[14] Other forms of obscuration are excessive brevity, misuse of figures, and *adianoeta*, or figures having both an overt and covert meaning. Quintilian then concludes that perspicuity is to him the primary virtue and suggests that the orator be ever ready for the suggestion: "Quae causa utique nostra culpa dicta obscurius est: ad planiora et communia magis verba descendimus." [15]

In the *Ars poetica*, Horace touches upon obscurity in at

[12] *De Oratore* iii, 50, 52; ii, 329.
[13] *Inst. Orat.* viii, 2.
[14] *Ibid.*, viii, 2, 18.
[15] *Ibid.*, viii, 2, 24.

least three passages. His "scribendi recte sapere," which Ronsard used as the motto for his *Abbrégé*, is a monition on clear thinking and clear writing. His admission that in trying to be brief he becomes obscure seems to imply that brevity alone is no safeguard against obscurity.[16] And his honest critic Quintilius makes it a point to insist that ornament be cleared and light shed upon the vague and the ambiguous.[17]

These quotations must serve as the brief of a chapter on the history of poetic obscurity in Hellenic and Roman treatises that may some day be written. A synthesis of this representative classical heritage reveals that obscurity may result from the following diverse causes: abstruse thinking, orthological difficulties, illogical development, phraseological ambiguity, prolixity, excessive brevity, mixed imagery, and conscious obscuration. Seven of these causes deal with unconscious obscuration, a fault which the poet or orator avoids whenever he is able. Only the last cause is the product of intention on his part. If obscurantism, or willful obscuration, had been a literary phenomenon almost nonexistent in the literature of the ancients, excepting, let us say, Lycophron, Heraclitus, and Persius, it was a very live issue in the period of the Pléiade, just as it was to be later when it reëmerged with Mallarmé and the Decadents. This does not mean that the first seven types will not receive a considerable share of attention in the French Renaissance. But one general point of variance may be kept in mind while the remarks of the Pléiade are being read. The ancients fought unintentional obscuration, hardly having the occasion to caution against any other kind; the Pléiade campaigned most of all against intentional obscurity, for they had to deal, as we shall observe, with several types of deliberately abstruse verse: neo-Pindarism, erudition and pedantry, symbolism in the manner of Scève, and even vestiges of *rhétoriqueur* complication.

Between classical antiquity and the Renaissance, three pe-

[16] Horace, *Ad Pisones* vs. 25.

[17] *Ibid.*, vss. 445–450.

riods, the mediaeval-allegorical, the Provençal, and the *rhétoriqueur*, all witnessed a reflorescence of conscious obscuration. There was nothing so dear to the hearts of the mediaeval poets as the unintelligible matter of allegory, numerology, gematria, dreams, visions, and symbolism. An example of this mediaeval tendency is the *Vita Nuova* of Dante, filled with dreams and symbols — or the *Commedia*, with its "Pape Satan aleppe" of Plutus and the "Rafel mai amech zabi almi" of the titan Nimrod, just as baffling as any sonnet about vowels of modern times. Not everyone in the Middle Ages espoused obscurantism, of course. The mediaeval *artes dictandi* often emphasised that clarity was an essential of good style, and the dictamina were generally models of perspicuity. Yet clarity was certainly not the mot d'ordre of the period.

Obscurantism was a mooted question in the Old French period. Professor Nitze has shown that it was opposed by several of the principal authors of romances.[18] In his discussion of *sens* and *matière* in early France, he quotes several passages proving that their desire for glory led them to eschew unintelligibility, esteeming the ancients who were clear more highly than those who demanded exegesis:

Qui sages est nel deit celer,
Ainz por ço doit son sens monstrer.
Que, quant serra del siècle alez,
En seit pues toz jorz remembrez.
Se danz Homers et danz Platon
Et Vergiles et Ciceron
Lor sapience celissant
Ja ne fust d'eus parlé avant.[19]

Costume fu as anciens,
Ceo testimoine Preciens,
Es livres que jadis faiseient
Assez oscurement diseient,

[18] Wm. A. Nitze, *Romania*, XLIV (1915–17), 14–36.
[19] *Thèbes*, vss. 7–16.

Pur cels ki a venir esteient
E ki aprendre les deveient,
Qui peussent gloser la letre
E de lur sen le surplus metre.[20]

The "trobar clus" of the troubadours was based on the postulate that poetic truths exist in nature to be found by the *trouvère* or finder, and that, on the other hand, hermetic ideas are to be enclosed in the verse to be discovered by the reader, a notable example of art imitating the processes of nature. While their love of kudos decided the Old French romance writers against obscurantism, it was this same gloriosity which made the Provençals renounce clarity. This view is presented by Raimbaut d'Orange in his partimen with Giraut de Borneil on the intelligibility of poetry:

Giraut, sol que'l melhs aparelh
E di' ades e trai'enan.
Me no chal si tan no s'espan
  C' anc grans viltatz
  No fo denhtatz;
Per so prez'om mais aur que sal
E de chan es tot atretal.[21]

It is true, of course, that the Pléiade knew little or nothing of the "trobar clus" school, as they were not familiar with Provençal literature, but the idea was not lost to the Renaissance, being actively resurrected in the sonnets of Michelangelo. One phase of the "trobar clus" is found in a sonnet of Desportes copied from Michelangelo.[22]

The mediaeval authors' convention of the "difficulté vaincue," with their passion for acrostics, equivocation, anagrams, complex verse forms, leonine rimes, *rime enchaynée*, *rime batelée*,

[20] Marie de France, *Lais*, proemium, vss. 9–17.

[21] *Nouvelle Anthologie des troubadours*, ed. by J. Audiau and R. Lavaud (Paris: Delagrave, 1928), p. 191.

[22] *Lettere di Michelangelo Buonarroti*, ed. by Papini (Lanciano, 1913), letter lxv, and Desportes, *Poésies*, ed. by Michiels (Paris: Delahays, 1858), p. 186. For further discussion of this matter, see the paragraphs treating of sensory inspiration in Chapter V.

all such devices were cordially adopted by the *rhétoriqueurs*, whose art Henry Guy has called a "très patiente chinoiserie." A list of these cunning forms is presented by Pasquier in his *Recherches* (VII, 13–15). That this byplay which made poetry more a pastime than an art was not only tolerated by the critics of the time, but even standardised and recommended, is gathered from an inspection of the manuals of second rhetoric of the fifteenth and early sixteenth centuries, following the precepts of Molinet. Of the seven vices of poetry mentioned in the *Instructif de la seconde rhétorique*, none is obscurity. We are a long way from Quintilian.

J. C. Lyons has recalled that the most important of the French poets immediately preceding the Pléiade, LeMaire des Belges, expressed the opinion that the poet should be a "man of mystery." [23] Thus, much of the Pléiade's critical heritage recommended obscuration. As no generation can completely discard the customs of its fathers, the Pléiade composed "temples," practiced anagrams, aenigmata, acrostics, wrote in leonine rime. As will be seen presently, they indulged in conscious obscuration of a type which they themselves identified as "Pindaric," and in another type (*viz.*, Scève) which we may classify as symbolistic. As J.-C. Scaliger allowed, the laborious Muses in their idle moments may devise puzzlers (*struere insidias*) and exchange brain-teasers.[24]

Beyond and above these several traditions, and dating from long before the classic grammarians, was the commonsensical conviction that communicability must be the first criterion of value of any art or literature, whether its purpose is the "useful" or the "sweet." An idea existed in the Renaissance that poets should be clear and philosophers obscure. This was expressed in the *Apology for Poetrie* of Philip Sydney: "I say the Philosopher teacheth, but he teacheth obscurely . . . but the Poet is foode for the tenderest stomacks." The poet is the

[23] *Vide infra*, note 102.
[24] J.-C. Scaliger, *ed. cit.*, I, 546.

monarch of all philosophers and artists, for he "beginneth not with obscure definitions which must blur the margent with interpretations and load the memory with doubtfulness." [25]

We have observed the Pléiade poet caught between two opposing families of tradition. The contemporary treatises on second rhetoric which he read during his youth showed an indulgent sympathy for mediaeval obscurantism and complexity. The classic treatises with which his humanistic education acquainted him taught the opposite lesson. If we weigh his love of Greece against his disdain for "notz majeurs," it will not be difficult for us at this point to predict which school of thought was eventually to win out.

⚜ ⚜ ⚜

Unlike the contemporary poetic manuals in Italy,[26] the *Deffence* of Du Bellay has no mention of obscurity other than a veiled reference to Scève in the register of living French writers.[27] There is in addition, it is true, a passing reflection that posterity will probably give "foy auz choses douteuses, lumière aux obscures"; that for this reason the poet should write as he sees fit, disdaining the judgment or incomprehension of his own generation.

It was neither Du Bellay nor Ronsard who led the fight against obscurity in the early 1550's. No one man could claim this distinction, least of all Ronsard. It is well known how the learned abstrusity of the first book of his *Amours* caused such unfavorable comment among his readers that Muret decided to append a commentary to the edition of 1553. It also

[25] Sir Philip Sydney, *Apology for Poetrie*, in "Elizabethan Essays," ed. by Gregory Smith (1904), pp. 167, 172.

[26] Vida, *De arte poetica*, iii, 15 ff.: "Verborum in primis tenebras fuge nubilaque atra, *etc.*," and Scaliger, *Poetices libri*, IV, 1, contain a brief history of clarity and obscurity, with examples. J. C. Lyons has noted that Speroni, Bembo, Equicola, Castiglione, and others admitted the justifiability of unintelligible poetry (*vide infra*, note 102).

[27] Du Bellay, *Deffence*, ed. by Chamard, pp. 182–183.

won him the Greek motto of σοφὰ ἀλλ' ἀσαφῆ from the humanist Dorat. And Pierre de Nolhac has shown that the heavily learned impedimenta of the *Odes* exceeds even that of the *Amours*.[28] No, it was certainly not Ronsard who led the campaign. Probably the most articulate was Peletier, and alongside him should be placed Mellin, who, according to Laumonier,[29] led the reaction against obscurity at court; Barthélemy Aneau, who felt that poems should be as clear as paintings, and illustrated this theory with a book; [30] and Jacques Tahureau du Mans. The only apologist for the opposite side seems to be Tyard, and we shall consider his reckoning first.

The defense of Tyard comes relatively early, being contained in the *Solitaire premier, ou Discours des Muses et de la fureur poétique* (1552). In the dialogue between Pasithée and the poet, the *doctus poeta* is defended against his carping critics by recourse to the early Pléiade device of identifying unintelligibility with erudition.

> Mais (repliqua-elle) que respondrez vous à ce qu'ils dient, que si par estranges façons de parler vous taschez d'obscurcir et ensevelir dans voz vers voz conceptions tellement, que les simples et les vulgaires, qui sont (iurent-ils) hommes de ce monde comme vous, n'y peuvent recognoistre leur langue, pource qu'elle est masquée et desguisée de certains accoustremens estrangers, vous eussiez encor mieux fait, pour atteindre à ce but de non estre entendus, de rien n'escrire du tout? [31]

This last sentence recalls the wording of the objection to obscurity that Peletier had voiced in his "A un poète escrivant obscurement" of 1547, five years earlier than the *Solitaire*. That Pontus had this poem of Peletier's in mind is quite possible, since it had been rather favorably received. The Solitaire now replies:

[28] Pierre de Nolhac, *Ronsard et l'humanisme* (Paris: Champion, 1921), pp. 92–99.

[29] P. Laumonier, *Revue de la Renaissance*, I (1901), 256.

[30] Barthélemy Aneau, *Picta poesis* (Lugduni: Pesnot, 1564).

[31] Pontus de Tyard, *Discours philosophiques* (Paris: L'Angelier, 1587), fol. 32r.

Je leur respondray (dy-je) que l'intention du bon Poète n'est de non estre entendu, ny aussi de se baisser et accommoder à la vilté du vulgaire (duquel ils sont le chef) pour n'attendre autre jugement de ses œuvres que celuy qui naistroit d'une tant lourde cognoissance. Aussi n'est-ce en si sterile terroir qu'il désire semer la semence qui luy rapporte louange. Bien desireroit-il que ces chassieux (mais aveugles) eussent la veue bonne, et peussent cognoistre que ce qu'ilz cerchent sous nom de facilité n'est rien moins que facilité: mais doit avoir nom d'ignorance painte aux rudes linéamens de leurs grossières inventions.

In addition to this vigorous counter-attack, there are those lines in which he defends the poet Scève in particular, to be quoted in our discussion of Scève.

Jacques Peletier devotes several paragraphs of his *Art poétique* (1555) to the problem of clarity, this being the greatest amount of space that any associate of the Pléiade reserved for the issue. In the ninth chapter of his first book, he embarks on the question, but immediately defers it to his following chapter, "Des vices de Poësie." His remarks reveal that he knew the passages of Quintilian discussed above. Recalling Quintilian's "nobis prima sit virtus perspicuitas," he begins his chapter IX:

La première et plus dine vertu du Poème est la Clarté: einsi même que le parler commun nous témoigne, quand on dit par singularité de louange, cete chose ou celle là avoit été éclercie et ilustrée par un tel ou un tel. Au contrère, par manière d'accusation et désestime, avoir été obscurcie et avilie. Et cete ci est la beauté universele, laquele doit aparoir par tout le cors du Poème.[32]

Logically enough, if clarity is the first virtue of poetry, obscurity will be the primary vice of poetry. Remembering the epigrammatic *pointe* to his "A un poëte escrivant obscurement,"[33] Peletier echoes this *pointe*. Moreover, he now adds a new thought concerning the poet's obligation to the reader.

[32] Peletier, *Art Poétique*, ed. by J. Boulanger (Paris: "Les Belles Lettres," 1930), p. 126.

[33] *Vide infra*, note 71.

This latter thought refutes the objection of the Solitaire to Peletier's *pointe* of 1547:

Car il n'i a point de diférance entre ne parler point, et n'être point entendu; Ancor penseroe-je etre plus mal fait de parler obscurement, que de ne parler point du tout: Car on tient le tans d'un homme qui s'amuseroet alheurs.

He thereupon proceeds to enumerate the various types of obscuration of which a poet may be guilty: an affected or incorrect vocabulary (*mots espaves*, as Rabelais called them); excessive brevity; illogical order of ideas. This is a simplification of the statement of Quintilian, with one variation. Where Quintilian had cautioned against prolixity, Peletier sees the danger in excessive brevity. Peletier next outlines those instances where the fault may be the reader's rather than the poet's. The reader may not understand the reference to some fable; he might fail to follow some philosophical problem (*neu*) brought up; he might be ignorant of some historical allusion. Let him blame himself alone. (Du Bellay had recourse to this reasoning in the first preface to the *Olive*, discounting "those who would not wish to accept this kind of writing because it exceeds their understanding.") Peletier then cites the case of Saint Jerome, who found Persius so obscure that he threw his writings into the fire, an illustration Peletier may have borrowed from the *Réplique aux furieuses defenses de Louis Meigret*, written by Des Autels four years before. The final method of deciding what is vicious poetic obscurity is noteworthy. (Peletier's reformed spelling was itself a striving for clarity.)

Quand, pour exemple, an Latin vous voyez quelque Poète obscur an un Suget qui de soe est bien tretable: et qu'on peut facilement juger que si un Virgile l'ut u an mein, il ne l'ut pas einsi randu dificile: eins l'ut orné, eclerci e ambeli: Lors on se peut assurer que c'est Vice.[34]

The fortunate poet never chooses an obscure argument, as

[34] Peletier, *Art poétique*, *ed. cit.*, p. 140.

Peletier has already noted in his first translation of Horace's *Poetics*. However, Lucretius was one poet who did not follow this rule. He was a great poet (quite the contrary to Ronsard's opinion, which denied Lucretius the very name of poet) [35] even though he had chosen subject matter in itself obscure and "maltretable." [36] But Lucretius was an exception, and the poet of today must not emulate him. Let the poet have as his first care the clarity of his work. Let him realise that the time is past for those who delight in abstruse things, only to take pride in understanding them.

After this lengthy, although hardly comprehensive treatment of obscurity by Peletier, the remarks by other contemporary theorists seem meagre indeed. There was nevertheless a continuity to these arguments throughout the last half of the sixteenth century. More of these remarks will be mentioned before passing to the actual judgments upon individual writers made by the Pléiade.

In 1554, a year before the treatise of Peletier, the young poet Jacques Tahureau appended an "Avis au lecteur" to his *Sonnets, Odes, et Mignardises à l'Admirée*. In this he cautions his contemporaries against the excesses of their language reforms, which sometimes lead to obscurity:

> comme plusieurs du jourd'huy, qui ne penseroyent pas avoir rien faict de bon, si a tous propos ils ne farcissoient leurs livres d'une infinité de termes nouveaux, rudes et du tout eslongnez du vulgaire; se faisans, par ce moyen et par telles autres quint'essences estimer grands seulement de ceux qui n'admirent rien plus que ce qu'ilz entendent le moins.[37]

Pasquier, in his *Recherches de la France*, begun as early as 1560, applies to such obscure writers as Scève the "non vis intelligi nec ego te volo intelligere" of Saint Jerome, which

[35] For Ronsard on Lucretius, see the 1587 preface to the *Franciade* (VII, 83).

[36] In his notes, Boulanger says that Peletier is here mindful of the declaration of Lucretius: "Nec me animi fallit Graiorum obscura reperta difficile illustrare Latinis versibus esse."

[37] Quoted in Raymond, *Influence de Ronsard* (Paris: Champion, 1927), I, 199.

Peletier and Guillaume des Autelz had quoted before him.[38] Scève is said to write "avec un sens si ténébreux et obscur, que le lisant je disois estre trèscontent de ne l'entendre puis qu'il ne vouloit estre entendu." [39] (Several decades later Pierre Deimier will use the same wording as this in his *Académie de l'art poétique.*) [40]

Moreover, the "non te volo intelligere" part of Saint Jerome's statement is emphasised by d'Aubigné in a prefatory stanza to the *Printemps*:

> Ces périphrases obscures
> Sont subjectes aux injures.
> Et on leur peut répliquer
> En les réduisant en cendre:
> Tu ne veux te faire entendre,
> Je ne veux pas t'expliquer.[41]

Even the neo-Latins, who were scarcely models of perspicuity themselves, joined in the condemnation of obscure writers. Buchanan, friend and correspondent of the Pléiade, questions Dolet sarcastically regarding some contemporary versifier, "Carmina quod sensu careant, mirare, Doleti? Quando qui scripsit carmina, mente caret." [42] Earlier, Vulteius had written an epigram entitled "Ad Piscem Poetam," beginning "Conscribis versus quos vix intelligat ullus," and which begs the author to be the interpreter of his own works if he would be read and understood.[43]

As has been intimated, not all of the remarks will deal with conscious obscuration. Sometimes, for example, it may be the brevity of the author which makes him unintelligible. This possibility is pointed out by Vauquelin, evidently recalling

[38] *Vide infra*, notes 67 and 68.

[39] Pasquier, *Recherches*, Bk. VII, chap. vii.

[40] See L. H. Gay, "Sources of Deimier's *Académie de l'art poétique*," PMLA, XXVII (1912), 404.

[41] Theodore Agrippa d'Aubigné, *Œuvres*, ed. by Réaume and de Caussade (Paris: Lemerre, 1873–92), III, 6.

[42] Buchanan, *Poemata quae extant* (Lugduni, 1628), p. 339.

[43] Vulteius, *Libri epigrammatum iv* (Lugduni, 1537), p. 66.

Horace's verse in the *Ad Pisones*: "Car l'un pour estre bref importunant la Muse, trop obscur il devient."[44] Excessive brevity may be the inevitable result of an ill-chosen genre. Either the enigma, as Du Bellay and Sébilet indicate, or the epigram, as Peletier states, may involve the author in difficulty by reason of their brevity.[45] As a matter of fact, Sébilet devotes a chapter of his poetics to enigma and finds it a superfluous genre. "If one doesn't wish to be understood, it becomes quite useless; if one wishes to be understood, then its obscurity is a great vice." Prolixity can lead to obscurity just as brevity can, as the Greek grammarians had shown. Vauquelin suggests that in didactic poetry one must always be clear and brief, employing no obscure and lengthy discourse.[46]

In 1598 the poetic manual of Laudun condemns the unintelligibility of the earlier poets of the century. Laudun objects to the contention of the ivory tower dwellers that to be hermetic is to remain above the profane crowd. "And as they said to Du Monin who took pride in being understood only by the learned, one had best give this writing to the fire to understand: for first of all there must be clarity in one's writings. . . . If clarity is an ornament of poetry, then obscurity is a vice. Furthermore, it's better not to talk at all than to talk without being understood."[47] One will note a similarity here between Laudun and Peletier. The former follows Peletier also in observing that unintelligibility may be the reader's fault, especially if the passage concerns some fable, philosophy, science, or history that the reader ought to know. To close a page on the Cinquecento, we might add that Deimier's *Académie de l'art poétique* contains similar borrowings from the two chapters of Peletier. His section entitled "De la clarté"[48] derives

[44] Vauquelin, *Art poétique* (Paris, 1885), p. 14.

[45] Sébilet, *Art poétique*, Bk. II, chap. xi: "De l'énigme"; Peletier, *Art poétique*, *ed. cit.*, p. 161.

[46] Vauquelin, *op. cit.*, p. 157.

[47] Quoted in Patterson, *French Poetic Theory* (Ann Arbor, 1935), I, 762, 763.

[48] Deimier, *Académie de l'art poétique* (Paris, 1610), p. 258.

largely from the chapter on ornament in Peletier, as both Boulanger and Gay have affirmed, but one reservation may be made. The notion that silence is better than incomprehensibility reflects not merely Peletier's *Art poétique*, but a conviction that had become almost a commonplace in the century and which may be encountered, as we have demonstrated, in the *Solitaire premier* of Tyard, the epigram of Peletier directed at the obscure poet, the poetics of Pierre de Laudun, and in Du Bellay's ode to Caracciolo as well (*vide infra*).

⚜ ⚜ ⚜

As there are no judgments on the clarity of the Hellenic *Ursänger* (except the tribute paid them in Du Bellay's "A Bertran Bergier") [49] the remarks begin with the second generation bards, Homer and Hesiod. For J.-C. Scaliger, by the way, these writers constituted the third generation of early poets. Both of these epicists illustrate the process of intentional obscuration which their oracular rôle made necessary. In his "Hymne de l'hyver," Ronsard cites them as his authorities for this process described in the *Abbrégé* and elsewhere.[50] Like Du Bellay, he deems this a function of the pictorial as well as the literary art:

> Puis à fin que le peuple ignorant ne mesprise
> La vérité cognue après l'avoir apprise,
> D'un voile bien subtil (comme les peintres font
> Aux tableaux bien portraits) luy couvre tout le front,
> Et laisse seulement tout au travers du voile
> Paroistre ses rayons comme une belle estoile,
> A fin que le vulgaire ait désir de chercher
> La couverte beauté dont il n'ose approcher.
> Tel j'ay tracé cest Hymne, immitant l'exemplaire
> Des fables d'Hésiode & de celles d'Homère.[51]

[49] Du Bellay, V, 119.
[50] *Vide supra*, Chapter I.
[51] Ronsard, IV, 327.

But if Homer is covert in this sense, there is a later writer who surpasses him by far. This is Lycophron, the author of the hermetic *Cassandra*, whom Ronsard audaciously included in the ode to Michel de l'Hospital as one of the outstanding Hellenic poets.[52] One should not infer from this greater obscurity that Lycophron was a more excellent artist than Homer, cautions Du Bellay, any more than one could judge one language superior to another because it was more difficult.[53]

The obscurity found in Pindar was of the type that a complex, involved order of ideas brings about. Pindar, wishing to celebrate an event or to congratulate some eminent person, would "wander about on a thousand topics" in order to give dignity and breadth to his ode, serving only to render the result more obscure. This habit Du Bellay eschews, and his "Ode au Prince de Melphe" contains a probable inference of censure against the Pindaric odes of Ronsard and his imitators:

> Si je voulois suyvre Pindare,
> Qui en mille discours s'esgare
> Devant que venir à son poinct,
> Obscur je brouillerois ceste Ode
> De cent propos: mais telle mode
> De louange ne me plaict point.[54]

The date of this reaction against Pindarism, by the way, Chamard sets at 1555 or 1556. These dates seem logical enough, for the revolt against Pindarism had already set in.

The obscurity of Plato, as Héroët saw it, was identical with that of Homer and Hesiod. Obscurantism was practised by Plato in the *Symposium*, when Plato had Aristophanes retell the story of the man-woman:

[52] On the diffusion of Lycophron's reputation for obscurity at this time, see H. Chamard, *Joachim du Bellay* (Lille, 1900), p. 56: "C'est une chose curieuse d'entendre un contemporain qui signe I. M. P. dans sa *Brève exposition de quelques passages du premier livre des Odes de Ronsard* (1550) louer Dorat d'avoir 'demellé les plus désespérés passages de l'obscur Lycophron, que nul de nostre age n'avoit encores osé dénouer.' "

[53] *Deffence*, ed. by Chamard, p. 158; on Lycophron, see also pp. 276–277.

[54] Du Bellay, V, 350.

. . . les ung parlent par signes,
Autres sous fable une verité cachent
Et peu souvent aux ignorants s'attachent;
Comme il advint à l'autheur de ce compte,
Lequel amy de sagesse n'eut honte,
Pour les secrets de nous dissimuler,
Entre les Grecs ainsi confabuler.[55]

That Plato is included as a practitioner of this art emphasises again the contemporary idea that the first Hellenic poets, as oracular singers, were philosophers of sorts. This type of identification had existed in classic literature. Protagoras, in Plato's dialogue,[56] had affirmed that the early poets were sophists in disguise, who concealed their doctrines because the time was not yet ripe for disclosure; so the stoics declared poetry "a kind of elementary philosophy." [57] Cleanthes even held the view that poetry was superior to philosophic discourse as a vehicle for expressing the highest truths of philosophy.[58] To the sixteenth-century poets the line between poets and philosophers could be finely drawn, and several of the criteria by which they judge poets they apply to philosophers as well. The Platonic distinction so rigidly kept by Socrates in the *Ion* was never completely adopted by the Pléiade, even by such Platonists as Héroët. The Pléiade had no scruples about referring to the "confabulations" of Plato or Aristotle, or the philosophical truths in Homer and Hesiod.

Belleau's translations from Anacreon won him praises in Ronsard's piece to Christofle de Choiseul. Ronsard congratulated the translator for not having selected some Greek author "obscur, masqué, brouillé d'un tas d'inventions." That this is another criticism of Pindar he almost immediately reveals, openly stating his preference for the sweet and simple Anacreon:

[55] Héroët, *Œuvres poétiques* (Paris, 1909), pp. 90–91.
[56] Plato, *Protagoras*, 317b.
[57] Strabo, i, 1, 10.
[58] J. Tate, "Horace and the Moral Function of Poetry," *Classical Quarterly* (April, 1928), p. 66.

> Me loue qui voudra les replis recourbez
> Des torrens de Pindare à nos yeux desrobez,
> Obscurs, rudes, fascheux, & ses chansons cognues
> Que je ne sçay comment par songes et par nues,
> Que le peuple n'entend: le doux Anacréon
> Me plaist. . . .[59]

These verses first appeared at the beginning of the odes of Anacreon which Belleau dedicated to Choiseul in August, 1556. Just as Du Bellay had censured the neo-Pindarism of Ronsard in his ode to Caracciolo (*c.* 1555–56), here Ronsard himself, in a palinode composed at the same period, condemns Pindaric unintelligibility.

If Ronsard progressed to an admiration of Anacreontic simplicity, his colleague Tahureau found little of simplicity and clarity in the Greek singers to Bacchus. Throughout the unbroken and unrelieved dialectic of Tahureau's *Dialogues*, his two colloquists, the Democritic and the Cosmophile, appear to agree only on this one score:

> Le Democritic: Mais cuidés-vous que ces anciens autheurs qui sont allé chercher les choses de si loing, les traittant d'un stile si obscur & si difficile qu'eus mesmes ne les entendoient pas, sont bien plus à louer que ceus qui parlent un langage entendu de chascun? Il me semble que je voi encores de ces vineuses Thiades de Bacchus qui enfoncèrent les matières si hautement qu'elles ne sçavoient pas elles mesmes ce qu'elles pensoient.
> Le Cosmophile: Quand est de moy je ne veus point estre si affecté à telle lourderie que je n'estime davantage ceus qui parlent entendiblement, que ces enfonceurs de matières, qui vont querir les choses si superliquoquentieusement . . . car tels yvrongnes ainsi comme tu as fort bien dit ne s'entendent pas eus-mesmes.[60]

This insistence upon the possibility that the author may not understand his own works is evocative of Browning's quip about one of his productions: "When I composed this only God and I knew what it meant; now God alone knows."

[59] Ronsard, V, 186.
[60] Tahureau, *Les Dialogues* (Paris: Lemerre, 1870), p. 168.

An elaboration which results from artifice rather than art may well lead to obscurity. That Pindar was chosen as the most flagrant illustration of this weakness among the Greek writers is not surprising. More unexpected is the inclusion of Vergil and Statius among the Romans who were unclear for reason of their artifice. Du Bellay, in his "A Bertran Bergier," laments that the lucid, natural style of Orpheus, Homer, Hesiod, and Musaeus had disappeared by the time of Latinity:

> De là vindrent ces *Énéides*,
> Et ces fascheuses *Thebaïdes*,
> Où n'y a vers sur qui ses dois
> On n'ayt rongé plus de cent fois.[61]

Although this pleasant piece ends on an obvious note of badinage, the quatrain above is quite consistent with the Pléiade's belief that the Latins did not write with the spontaneity of the Greeks. Moreover, these verses are taken seriously by Chamard, both in his notes to the poem and in his biography of Du Bellay. They are accepted as a general "profession de foi" on art and nature and as a palinode on Vergil and Statius.[62]

Just as Homer was far outstripped in obscurity by Lycophron, so was Vergil outdone by Lucretius, his contemporary, whose Epicureanism displeased Ronsard,[63] but of whose works Du Bellay made fragmentary translations.[64] Again the reservation must be made that greater difficulty does not make Lucretius the greater artist, a possibility which had possibly entered their minds during their student days at Coqueret, and one which found its way into the *Essays* of Montaigne.[65]

Jacques Peletier selects a different prototype of obscurity from among the Latin writers. The abstrusity which he dis-

[61] Du Bellay, V, 120.

[62] *Ibid.*, n. 1, and Chamard's life of Du Bellay (Lille, 1900), p. 402.

[63] Ronsard, VII, 82–83.

[64] Du Bellay, VI, 403.

[65] *Essays*, Bk. II, chap. x: "Ceulx des temps voysins à Virgile se plaignoyent dequoy aulcuns luy comparoient Lucrèce; je suis d'opinion que c'est à la vérité une comparaison ineguale, *etc.*"

cerns in Seneca is apparently that of the philosophically discursive type, which Peletier finds cumbrous or pedestrian. Seneca's is stylistic or syntactical obscuration. "Des Latins nous n'avons que Sénèque, qui n'est pas guère magnifique; ençois pesant et obscur, et tenant beaucoup du changement de la Latinité." [66]

One Latin whose obscurity became almost proverbial was the young satirist Persius. In the *Réplique aux furieuses défences de Louis Meigret*, Guillaume des Autels draws an inferential parallel between the incomprehensibility of Maurice Scève and that of Persius.[67] Des Autels says that his initial impression of Scève could be summed up in that judgment on the works of Persius: "Non vis intelligi nec ego te volo intelligere." This pronouncement Peletier lifted and inserted into his *Art poétique*: "Comme lon dit de S. Gerome: lequel après avoer long tans demeuré sus la lecture de Perse, sans le pouvoer comprandre, geta le livre dedans le feu." [68] Even Boileau recalled the obscurity of Persius, following, as he often did, in the wake of the Pléiade.[69]

Du Bellay, flaying some of his contemporaries for their ignorance, points out that what may seem obscurity on the part of the author may be only the effect of that ignorance, an idea entertained by Peletier in 1555. Du Bellay excoriates those who understand only the poetic fictions of Marot (Marot and Anacreon seem to be the modern and ancient prototypes of clarity in these discussions) and assures those who find him, Du Bellay, obscure that the Greeks and Romans and Italians did not write like Marot.[70]

⚜ ⚜ ⚜

[66] Peletier, *Art poétique*, *ed. cit.*, p. 192.

[67] Des Autels, *Réplique aux furieuses défences de Louis Meigret* (Lyon, 1551), pp. 71–73.

[68] Peletier, *Art poétique*, *ed. cit.*, p. 139.

[69] Boileau, *Art poétique*, Bk. II, vss. 155–156: "Perse, en ses vers obscurs, mais serrés et pressans, affecta d'enfermer moins de mots que de sens."

[70] *Deffence*, ed. by Chamard, pp. 315–316.

In the ranks of the poets of the Renaissance whom the Pléiade judged obscure, one unknown writer, like an unknown soldier, stands out as typical of his fellows. This is the individual against whom Jacques Peletier directed his bitter epigram, "A un poète escrivant obscurement." Perhaps, like an unknown soldier's tomb, the poem encompasses a real person; perhaps, like a cenotaph, it contains only a symbolic emptiness.

> Tes vers obscurs donnent a maintz espriz
> En les lisant, fascherie et torment:
> Pour ce qu'on croit que tu les as escriz
> Pour paraprès y faire le comment,
> Ou bien affin, et je ne sçay s'on ment,
> Qu'en eux ne soit ta pensée choisie:
> Or s'il y a fruit en ta Poésie,
> On le deust lire à clair sans commentaire:
> Mais si tu veux cacher ta fantaisie,
> Il ne faudroit seulement que te taire.[71]

From this epigram, combatting pedantic or esoteric obscurity which demands commentaries, one of the basic prejudices of the Pléiade becomes apparent. The Pléiade writers, imbued with the *doctus poeta* ideal, believed themselves learned, the most learned scholars of their century, and from a humanistic viewpoint they very nearly fitted that description. Each one of them might have enjoyed appearing in annotated volumes like the reëditions of classic authors beginning to issue from the presses of Paris, Lyons, Venice, and elsewhere, and the fact that the 1553 edition of Ronsard appeared with the Muret commentary probably did more to foster this wish than to discourage it. However, it was perhaps these inhibited ambitions of their own which made them quick to criticise others for confusing erudition and unintelligibility. Thus, a new type is added to the *Begriffsgeschichte* of literary obscurity, use or misuse of erudition. This is generally a willful, rather than an unintentional type of unintelligibility, although it might conceivably be of either type.

[71] Peletier, *Œuvres poétiques*, ed. by Séché (Paris, 1904), p. 119.

This early penchant of the Pléiade poets for displaying their learning in their verse and being intolerant of those who found them difficult is evident in such writings of the early 1550's as Du Bellay's preface to the *Olive*, where he states that the only audience he needs is a dozen or so of his learned friends. Also from this early period dates the conviction that Italian poetry was great because learned men, even prelates and cardinals, practiced verse.[72] Claiming that Caliban deemed everything obscure that exceeded his understanding, Joachim dismissed the uncomprehending and unsympathetic masses with an abrupt, "je les laisse avecq' ceulx qui, après l'invention du bled, vouloient encores vivre de glan." [73] Such was the haughty attitude of the Pléiade's spokesman at the half-way mark of the century. This was when they themselves were the most obscure poets of the time, excepting certain neo-Latins, if judged by standards of erudition and complexity. Yet even before they had corrected their own excesses, the *chefs d'école* scolded Scève and Tyard for their incomprehensibility. Moreover, they never rid themselves completely of their tendencies toward showy and obfuscated erudition, and the most honest and outspoken critics of the period toward their own contemporaries remained, beyond Peletier, poets outside the inner circle of the Pléiade: Tahureau, Fontaine, Des Autels, Aneau, and others.

In later years the Pléiade leaders perceived more clearly how extreme erudition could cause obscurity. Ronsard's judgment on Du Bartas, whose learning made Ronsard somewhat jealous and whose Protestantism displeased him, is based on the seeming lack of organisation and the encyclopedic knowledge found in the *Semaines*:

> Bartas voulant desbrouiller l'univers
> Et luy donner une meilleure forme

[72] Mentioned in two places: *Deffence*, ed. by Chamard, pp. 328–329; the second preface to the *Olive* (Chamard edition of the poems, I, 16).

[73] Du Bellay, I, 9.

Luy mesme a faict un grand cahos de vers
Qui plus que l'autre est confus et difforme.[74]

One of the contemporary authors whom Du Bellay praised as a campaigner against obscurity was Giovanni Caracciolo, a seneschal of the Kingdom of Naples who gave his allegiance to the French crown. Du Bellay is heartened by the knowledge that this poet does not seek to emulate his vain and incomprehensible contemporaries: "My Caracciolo, who aspires not to those meaningless writings that people admire only for their obscurity." [75] His *Mirouer de vraye religion* Du Bellay commends as avoiding the misty perplexities of so many theological works.

Il nous dénoura les passages
Qui geinent les plus doctes sages,
Sans que pour la facilité
Qui rend la chose moins obscure
La majesté de l'Escriture
Perd rien de sa gravité.

Et que sert d'une obscure nue
Rendre une lumière incognue
Sans jamais arriver au poinct?
Que sert il de se vouloir faire
Esmerveillable au populaire
Par les choses qu'il n'entend point?

Whereupon Du Bellay echoes the advice which Peletier had given "A un Poète escrivant obscurement," that is, if one would hide his meaning, he has only to cease writing. Joachim gives his strophe the same *pointe* that Peletier had given his dizain.

Ou s'il veut cacher son dire,
Sans prendre peine à l'escrire,
Qu'il le cache en se taisant.

The efforts of some of these unintelligible contemporaries to "esmerveiller le populaire" (a phrase now reminiscent of Bau-

[74] Ronsard, VI, 488.

[75] Du Bellay, V, 358.

delaire) [76] to which Du Bellay refers in his ode calls to mind the familiar sonnet of Ronsard to Tyard opening the second book of the *Amours*. Ronsard complains that the popular throng which had found him obscure in his Pindarism now finds fault with his Anacreontic simplicity. This sonnet is included in the *Continuation des Amours* of 1555.

> Tyard, on me blasmoit à mon commencement
> Dequoy j'estois obscur au simple populaire:
> Mais on dit aujourd'huy que je suis au contraire.
> Toy, de qui le labeur enfante doctement
> Des livres immortels, dy-moy, que doy-je faire? [77]

As we have suggested, chief among those who blamed Scève, Tyard, and Ronsard in the latter's obscure period were Tahureau, Fontaine, and Aneau. Jacques Tahureau, whom Ronsard lists in the "Isles fortunées" as one of the astral bodies circling about the constellation of the Pléiade, objects in two passages to the excessively learned authors of his day. The highly refined obscurity of the neo-Pindarists and the imitators of Scève makes him describe their works in both passages as "quintessences." The first of these objections in which he ridicules the readers of obscure writers as well as the writers themselves, we have already quoted above.[78] The other text, at the end of the *Admirée* (1554) is a thrust at those

> qui tirent de si loin
> Un tas de si hautes sentences
> Qu'eux-mesmes ilz auroyent besoin
> D'interprète à leurs quintessences.[79]

Another of those who blamed Ronsard's Pindarism was Charles Fontaine, whose extreme clarity placed him in a better position to make accusations of incomprehensibility than some of his contemporaries. Noting that familiar, "sweet" pieces

[76] *Cf.* the *Olive* xxxix: "éblouir les yeulx du populaire" (I, 60).
[77] Ronsard, I, 131.
[78] *Vide supra*, note 37.
[79] *Revue de la Renaissance*, I (1901), 256.

were published alongside the heavily formal ones in Ronsard's *Continuation* and *Nouvelle continuation*, he encourages the author,

> Ne creins, ne creins, Ronsard, ce dous stile poursuivre,
> Stile qui te fera, non moins que l'autre, vivre:
> Autre, obscur et scabreux, s'il ne fait à blâmer,
> Si se fait-il pourtant trop plus creindre qu'aymer.[80]

Mellin de Saint-Gelays, in a poem apparently addressed to Ronsard, decries the "choses confuses en son style ou invention," and Belleau recalls the obfuscation of Ronsard's initial style.[81] Still another critic of Ronsard, weary of the pedantic incomprehensibility of certain of his verses to Cassandre, addressed him, "Croyez-vous que votre Cassandre, pour qui vous aviez fait ce sonnet, en eût une pensée si avantageuse?" [82]

It is the same Charles Fontaine who levels an accusation of obscurity at Du Bellay. This takes the form of a play on words possible in French, if not in the classic languages as well,[83] and is a rebuttal to the play on words by which Du Bellay had attacked him in the *Deffence*:

> Jamais si tost ne tarira
> Claire eau de ma fontaine vive,
> Que legier feu estainct sera,
> De l'huile obscur de ton olive.[84]

The same pun is encountered in the *Quintil Horatian* of Barthélemy Aneau, who defends Fontaine against Du Bellay: "la

[80] Quoted in Marcel Raymond, *Influence de Ronsard*, I, 33.

[81] Saint-Gelays, *Œuvres poétiques* (Paris, 1873), II, 262; Ronsard, STFM, X, xxii.

[82] In P. de Nolhac, *Ronsard et l'humanisme* (Paris: Champion, 1921), p. 93.

[83] These puns on the double meanings of *clair* and *obscur* could not exist in Latin or Greek, according to Scaliger's discussion of perspicuity: "Perspicuum autem non est idem quod lucidum. Namque lux est actus superficiei visi[bi]lis, hoc est *φωεινόν* [*sic*]. At perspicuum idem quod pellucidum: vulgus transparens vocat: Graeci *διαφανές*; quod superiori contrarium est: transmittit enim visibilem, *etc.*," *Poetices libri* (Heidelberg: Commeliano, 1617), Bk. IV, chap. i, p. 404.

[84] Cited by Baur, *Maurice Scève et la Renaissance lyonnaise* (Paris, 1906), p. 112.

Fontaine aussi purement coulante et claire, que l'huile de ton Olive est crasseux et faisant obscure lumière."[85]

It might be added in passing that despite all their arguments aimed against the neo-Latins, the Pléiade did not rail at the obscure compositions of the latter. Yet the style of the neo-Latins was often involved and unclear. As a sample of the difference between the possible complexity of Renaissance Latin and the simplicity of classic Latin, one need only compare an epigram of J.-C. Scaliger with one of Martial.

⚜ ⚜ ⚜

Just as Petrarch dominated the discussions of literary sincerity in the writings of the Pléiade, Maurice Scève actuates much of their discussion of obscurity. Although the *Microcosme* is heavily learned, it is of course the *Délie*, with its Platonic abstractions and its highly refined imagery borrowed from Serafino, Tebaldeo, Chariteo, and others, which confused and irritated Scève's contemporaries. So many and varied were the reactions to his obscurantism that an attempt will be made to enumerate them in a partially chronological order.

As early as 1545 Pernette du Guillet noted the obscurity of her fellow townsman, but her friendship for Scève would not permit her to call his style anything more than *sévère*, obviously a pun.[86]

That Du Bellay was somewhat in sympathy with Scève as the outsanding representative of the break with the Marotic tradition is evidenced by the haughty first preface to the *Olive* and by the following excerpt from the *Deffence*: "Je m'attends bien qu'il s'en trouverra beaucoup de ceux qui ne treuvent rien bon, si non ce qu'ilz entendent et pensent pouvoir immiter, aux quelz nostre poète ne sera pas agréable."[87] But Du Bellay,

[85] Aneau, *Quintil Horatian*, ed. by Person (1878), pp. 210–211.
[86] Pernette du Guillet, *Poésies* (Lyon: Perrin, 1830), p. 60.
[87] Du Bellay, *Deffence*, *ed. cit.*, pp. 315–316.

for all his impatience with the general reader of his century, discovered that he could not stomach the distilled concepts of the *Délie*. "Quelque autre, voulant trop s'éloigner du vulgaire, est tumbé en obscurité aussi difficile à esclersir en ses escriz aux plus sçavans comme aux plus ignares." [88] The palinode which Du Bellay included in his *Musagnœomachie* reverses this opinion in one respect. He still objects to the incomprehensibility of Scève, but the notoriety (perhaps a more appropriate word than fame) of the Lyonese poet was increasing among the more critical of his contemporaries, even if not among the average readers. In 1550, then, Du Bellay realised that Maurice Scève was a figure to be reckoned with, and amends his former statement by affirming that Scève is no longer so unintelligible to the learned reader:

> Scève, dont la gloire noüe
> En la Saone, qui te loüe
> Docte aux doctes éclerci.[89]

In 1552, Jean-Antoine de Baïf refers to a poet who is so obscure that he is incomprehensible even to himself. Guégan suggests that Baïf had Scève in mind while penning these lines from the *Amours de Méline*:

> Autre que moy s'esgare en ses discours
> Non entendu, ny s'entandant luy-mesme.[90]

Scève's greatest defender within the Pléiade, as is to be expected, was Pontus de Tyard. Tyard, not an exemplar of perspicuity himself, is Scève's apologist in both the "Chant en faveur de quelques excellens poètes de ce temps" and the *Premier solitaire*. In his register of the leading poets of the age, Tyard adheres to the *doctus poeta* ideal which Du Bellay formulated in the first preface to the *Olive*, realising that there is a reaction against the transcendental dizains of Scève, but choosing to ignore it. "Que luy peut en murmurant nuire le

[88] *Ibid.*, pp. 182–183.
[89] Du Bellay, IV, 13.
[90] Baïf, M.-L., I, 52.

vil ignorant? Premier emporte le pris. . . ."[91] The same disdain or pity for the unschooled who cannot understand learned literature underlies the extravagant defence in the *Premier solitaire:*

"Vous souvient-il point (repliqua elle) de celuy qui un jour arrivant icy, me trouva une *Délie* en main: & de quelle grace, l'ayant prinse & encor non leu le second vers entier, il se rida le front & la jetta sus la table à demy courroucé? Oh, si fais deà (respondy-je) & ay bien memoire qu'entre autres choses, quand je le vy autant nouveau & incapable d'entendre la raison, que les doctes vers du Seigneur Maurice Scaeve (lequel vous sçavez, Pasithée, que je nomme tousjours avec honneur) je luy respondis, qu'aussi se soucioit bien peu le Seigneur Maurice que sa *Délie* fust veue, ny maniée des veaux."[92]

Guillaume des Autels echoes this belief circulated by all the apologists for Scève that the obscurity of the latter's style is not the fault of the writer, but of the reader. But Des Autels continues with the affirmation that the epidemic of enigmatic poets following in the wake of Scève has counterbalanced any of the good the Lyonese poet did for French verse; just as mediocre Petrarchists, one might add, undid the good that Petrarch had done Renaissance poetry.

"Donc nous sommes bien tenuz à la *Délie,* laquelle (combien qu'elle ait quelques ans demeuré sans crédit sus le vulgaire) a enhardy tant de bons esprits à nous purger de telle peste. Mais (comme la vertu au milieu des vices) je desirerois la fin d'un autre avis contraire et plus pernicieux, que je vois pulluler entre ce peuple, voyre s'enraciner au cerveau de ceux qui se meslent d'aristarquiser: c'est de n'estimer rien bon et digne d'un poète qui soit propre, et vouloir partout avoir des tropes, voire des ainigmes."[93]

Two others who will neither condemn Scève unreservedly for his unintelligibility, nor yet defend him, are Jacques Peletier and Charles Fontaine. Having at some length described clarity as the greatest virtue and obscurity as the greatest vice of

[91] Pontus de Tyard, M.-L., p. 124.

[92] Pontus de Tyard, *Discours philosophiques*, L'Angelier edition (Paris, 1587), fol. 33.

[93] *Amoureux Repos de Guillaume des Autels* (Lyon: Temporal, 1553), fol. 8.

literature, Peletier will say no more of Scève and Tyard than to call them respectively "parfond en inventions" and "net et subtil." [94] Fontaine takes the second position of Du Bellay, that Scève's poetry is clear only to a scholar, and adds that one derives little or no pleasure from reading it.

> Tes vers sont beaux, et bien luysants,
> Graves et pleins de majesté,
> Mais pour leur haulteur moins plaisants:
> Car certes la difficulté
> Le grand plaisir en a osté.
> Brief ils ne quierent un Lecteur,
> Mais la commune autorité
> Dit qu'ils requierent un Docteur.[95]

Although Pasquier was not a member of the greater Pléiade group, the admiration in which the Pléiade held him [96] and the late-century opinion which he represents may justify our quoting him here. In his chapter of the *Recherches de la France* entitled "De la grande flotte de poètes que produisit le règne du Roy Henry deuxiesme," Pasquier has the last word in the matter and testifies that Scève is no longer a literary figure to be reckoned with:

> Ceux-cy du commencement firent profession de plus contenter leurs esprits, que l'opinion du commun peuple. Le premier qui franchit le pas fut Maurice Scève Lionnois, lequel ores qu'en sa jeunesse eust suivy la piste des autres, si est-ce qu'arrivant sur l'aage, il voulut prendre autre train. Se mettant en butte, à l'imitation des Italiens, une Maistresse qu'il celebra sous le nom de Délie . . . avecques un sens si tenebreux et obscur, que le lisant, je disois estre très-content de ne l'entendre, puis qu'il ne vouloit estre entendu . . . et toutesfois la vérité est qu'il affecta une obscurité sans raison. Qui est cause que son livre mourut avec luy, au moins ne vois-je point que depuis il ait couru par nos mains.[97]

[94] Peletier, *Art poétique*, *ed. cit.*, p. 77.
[95] Cited in the Guégan edition of Scève, pp. liii–liv.
[96] On the admiration of the Pléiade for Pasquier, see Belleau, M.-L., I, 117–119; Ronsard, II, 364.
[97] Pasquier, *Recherches* (Paris: Menard, 1643), Bk. VII, chap. vii.

Regarding Scève, then, the many criticisms of his mystification were aimed at one weakness or *desmesure*, an unfair disregard for his perplexed reader. Criticism among the classic rhetoricians and philosophers had seldom bothered to take this idea into consideration, one notable exception being Quintilian, whose mention of it was inspired by Livy.

Strangely enough, none of the Pléiade, even those who made a practice of defending and praising Scève, realised that he was the outstanding contemporary illustration of the art of *feintise* (Guégan calls it cabalism),[98] whereby a poet disguises truths as a regular function of his craft. Brunetière wrote of the Pléiade: "Si on leur eût dit que Scève était quelquefois difficile à comprendre, je crains qu'ils n'eussent répondu qu'aucun mérite . . . n'était plus conforme à la définition du poète."[99] But in their written applied judgments they censured this obscurity and saw in it no philosophical function. They selected Ronsard's neo-Pindarism, instead, as the archetype of *feintise* during the Valois-Orléans reigns. One gathers from this that the amount of disguising or *feintise* a poet might indulge in was limited. As compared with the dizains of the *Délie*, Ronsard's early sonnets and odes were relatively clear. What difficulties they did present could at least be solved by a consultation of the *Magnus Elucidarius* or the *Dictionarium* of Robert Estienne, as M. de Nolhac has suggested. With these guides Ronsard became, to reiterate the phrase applied to a recent writer, "un obscur que tout le monde peut comprendre."[100] And yet this Pindarism was held by him and his associates to represent oracular cloaking. In practice, then, they apparently limited *feintise* to conscious obscuration through ornamentation and elaboration; its object became not incomprehensibility, but merely rewording of eternal truths or principles padded with elegant amplifications and illustrations

[98] Scève, *Œuvres poétiques complètes*, ed. by Guégan (Paris: Garnier, 1927), p. xxiii.

[99] F. Brunetière, *Revue des deux mondes* (December 15, 1900), p. 908.

[100] Pablo Picasso's reported observation on James Joyce.

("mille discours," as Ronsard had said). The complexity of Scève, on the other hand, did not appear to the Pléiade to have the eventual purpose of communication. This is the reason they did not call his unintelligibility *feintise*. It was, as they viewed it, an early manifestation of symbolism and expressionism, a form of literature whose obscuration depends more upon incoherence of the ideas involved than on syntactic irregularities. With Scève, the problem was principally semantic. The words were there in clear grammatical order. The problem was to know just what meaning and value the words held, words such as *le Naturant*, *le cerf de François*, *souffrir non souffrir*, and the like. Scève cared not whether the reader understood these terms, or so it appeared to the Pléiade. In Ronsard the symbols were relatively clear, for their classic derivation was plain to the Hellenists of his age. In Scève, the symbols were not clear and most of them have remained hermetic down to the present day. Had the others of the Plèiade been as thoroughly versed as the Lyonese in the symbolism of the minor Petrarchists such as Chariteo, Serafino, Tebaldeo, and others from whom Scève borrowed his conceits, they might have judged him a less obscure and incidentally a somewhat less original poet. Thanks to the competent source studies of Parturier and others, the present-day student of the Pléiade is better able to measure the perspicuity and originality of Scève than were his contemporaries.

It is quite possible that the Pléiade poets in their incomprehension were missing what may have been the real motive behind the transcendental presentation of Scève's love verse.[101] Perhaps the Pléiade failed to realise sufficiently that Scève was trying to ascribe to his love definite mystic and esoteric qualities through his almost ritualistic endeavor to guard it from the profane and the common. Just as the mediaeval priest screened certain religious offices in holy mystery, just as a

[101] This possible interpretation of Scève's obscurity was suggested to us by Professor Louis Cons.

hierophant of the pagan goddess Aphrodite exercised certain devotions of the cult which remained unintelligible to the uninitiate, Scève wishes to hallow his idealised passion for his Délie. Like certain hermetic verses of the troubadours, his dizains are enveloped in a holy, quasi-religious "mystery."

Referring again to the matter of conceits, it might be added here that clear foreign words could be admitted into the literary language, even if foreign conceits could not. Such intrusion was a necessary method of enriching the French language, as both Du Bellay and Ronsard wrote. Peletier, too, approved Bonaventure's adopting Provençal words in his *Vandange.* But this was not considered a form of willful obscuration, comparable to Scève's importation of concetti.

To illustrate further the distinction between the obscuration of Ronsard and that of Scève, one may draw a comparison from the pictorial arts, following the lead of Du Bellay. In his "Discours au Roy sur la poésie" he points out that the prototype of Pindaric obscurity in poetry is Ronsard, and in painting, Michelangelo. If one would carry this *pictura poesis* to a logical conclusion, one would have to pair Maurice Scève with some modern symbolist like a Matisse. Later on, when obscurantism became popular again with the Decadents and Symbolists, it was taken up by the painters and even the sculptors. In the sixteenth century, however, it remained solely a literary phenomenon.

⚜ ⚜ ⚜

From these foregoing remarks, it becomes apparent that the Pléiade evinced a definite interest in the problem of obscurity in literature.[102] As we have noted, two types, conscious and

[102] Professor S. F. Will's recent bibliography of American studies on the French Renaissance which we have lately examined mentions a dissertation on the subject of literary obscurity in French literature of the sixteenth century, submitted to the University of North Carolina in 1927. We have not seen this

unconscious, were recognised by them. In his history of French clarity, Mornet distinguishes between these two types.[103] He observes of the most unintelligible works of the century, the *Délie*, the *Cabinet de Minerve*, the *Cymbalum Mundi*, and some of the imitations of Colonna's *Hypnerotomachia Poliphili*: "Tout cela est obscurités volontaires, procédés d'art ou légitimes précautions." But there was also a need to combat syntactical abstrusity. The general style, sometimes the grammar itself, of the century was bad, even granting the immaturity of the French language. For example, we have found in the *Dialogues* of Tahureau a sentence of 383 words.[104] Mornet may justifiably conclude: "Longtemps ainsi, surtout chez les moins habiles, la phrase française du XVIe siècle reste une période maladroite, disloquée, qui ne sait trouver ni l'ordre savamment équilibré de la phrase complexe, ni la simplicité et la succession logique des phrases coupées." [105]

Although the Pléiade was aware of both types, their critical practices reveal that they were more interested in intentional

---

unpublished thesis. Although it came to our attention after some pages of the present volume had already been submitted to the press, we have found a brief abstract of it in the *University of North Carolina Record*, and shall note a few interesting points which will supplement our own study.

Professor Lyons's history of obscurity starts with the early Middle Ages, shows how Vergil was allegorised by the Christian theologians, provides examples of obscure poems occurring in mediaeval Celtic and Icelandic literature. He shows that in Spain Juan Manuel and Juan de Mena preceded the obscurity of Góngora. He declares that the philosophic group around Marguerite de Navarre encouraged obscurity as did the Lyonese school. He points out the position of Ronsard and several of his contemporaries on the subject. He shows that obscurity was no longer a live issue by the time of the *Première Sepmaine* of Du Bartas and the *Phoenix* of Du Monin. Although our approaches to the problem do not appear to be quite the same, the abstract of the research of Professor Lyons indicates that our conclusions are apparently in harmony. Two references to this abstract have been inserted above (notes 23 and 26) and appropriate acknowledgment has been made. The present author has already expressed publicly his esteem for the scholarship of Professor Lyons (in a review of the Holmes-Lyons-Linker edition of Du Bartas: *Modern Philology*, May, 1939, pp. 441–445).

[103] D. Mornet, *Histoire de la clarté française* (Paris: Payot, 1929), p. 264.

[104] Tahureau, *Dialogues* (Paris: Lemerre, 1870), pp. 24–25.

[105] D. Mornet, *op. cit.*, p. 265.

than in unintentional obscuration. It is true that their works emphasise stylistic clarity to some extent. Their treatises give instructions in prosody which have the aim of clarity. If one would read a solid lesson on concise, clear style, let him read Ronsard's detailed analysis of the sonnet by the young poetaster in the "Epistre au lecteur" of the *Recueil des Nouvelles poésies* (1564). However, this preoccupation with stylistic clarity remained for the most part an unarticulated principle. The spelling reforms which Peletier adopted in his prose, and Baïf in his *Étrénes*, were manifestations of the Pléiade's striving for clarity which were not accepted by the Renaissance. Consequently, it has not been generally suspected that the Pléiade group was as critical about obscurity as was the generation of Malherbe. This statement must be qualified. From the foregoing pages one gathers that they were as concerned about clarity as was the publicised reform of Malherbe, but with three differences. First was their endorsement of oracular obscurantism which Malherbe could only reject as sophistry and nonsense. Second, they were greatly concerned with the ethical intention of the poet to be communicative and honest with his reader. Third, the *doctus poeta* convictions of the Pléiade and their disregard for the unschooled reader caused them to admire complexity and learned paraphrase. That they succeeded in being as critical regarding obscurity as they were could only result from a sort of psychomachy, for it meant overcoming two of their inherent weaknesses, pedantry and exclusivity.

Had the Pléiade taken the advice of their own Peletier, they would have been more critical about syntactical and logical clarity. As it was, the remarks of Malherbe on this subject far exceed anything that any one of them had to say. In his *Commentaire sur Desportes* alone, declares Brunot, there are twenty questions involving obscurity, with such typical notations as "Je ne vous entends point," "Qu'est-ce?" "Que veut-il dire?" "Je crois qu'il a intention de dire quelque chose de bon, mais il faut deviner."[106] Vaugelas was as strict as Malherbe:

> C'est peu qu'on puisse nous comprendre, il faut qu'on ne puisse pas ne pas nous comprendre. . . . C'est à faire aux paroles de faire entendre le sens et non pas au sens de faire entendre les paroles, et c'est renverser la nature des choses que d'en user autrement.[107]

The common belief ("enfin Malherbe vint . . . et de son tour heureux imitez la clarté") that Malherbe and his disciples corrected the excesses of the Pléiade and inaugurated a new era of verse is true, of course, to some extent. As we have intended to demonstrate in these pages, however, the all-important issue of clarity was one of which the Pléiade was already cognisant, and one which became a criterion of judgment used rather widely by them. If they were unable to stop the excesses of some of their contemporaries, if Malherbe could find such ambiguous passages as Desportes's "Si vous voyez mon cœur ainsi que mon visage meurdry, couvert de sang . . ." it is nevertheless true that in their later years, in the post-Pindaric period, the Pléiade began to write with greater clarity, the result of their increasing recognition of the necessity of communicability in art.

The moment for a brief recapitulation is now at hand. The Pléiade poets were caught in two opposing currents regarding obscurity. The Hellenic or oracular tradition, later supported by the *trobar clus* of the troubadours and the *difficulté vaincue* notions of the mediaeval and pre-Renaissance *rhétoriqueurs*, required that truths be veiled. This same tradition was revived in the nineteenth century, when Mallarmé theorised, "Nommer un objet, c'est supprimer les trois quarts de la jouissance du poème, qui est faite du bonheur de deviner peu à peu." The tradition of the ancient grammarians and rhetoricians, buttressed by the commonsensible conviction that art must communicate, demanded simplicity and clarity in literature. The

[106] F. Brunot, *La Doctrine de Malherbe d'après son Commentaire sur Desportes* (Paris: Masson, 1891), pp. 185–187.

[107] *Ibid.*, p. 187.

classic rhetors and philosophers attacked abstruseness as an unconscious evil based on syntactic or logical difficulties; Quintilian was one of the very few to mention the condemnable indulgence in willful obscurantism. The syntactic obscurity against which the ancients cautioned resulted from lexical, logical, phraseological mistakes, prolixity and brevity, ambiguous and mixed figures, and asyndeta. Peletier, Tyard, Du Bellay, and others who attack or defend obscurity in their treatises or polemics are cognisant of stylistic difficulties, but are especially interested in conscious obscuration. Pindar is cited as the most flagrant example of unintelligibility among the Hellenic, or Latin authors, even more than Lycophron, Heraclitus, and Persius, because of his complex, involved style. In censuring Pindar, the Pléiade is also aiming at the neo-Pindarism of Ronsard and his imitators. Three stock criticisms were leveled at contemporaries who wrote unintelligibly; the second of these was the comment of Saint Jerome on Persius:

I. You are so incomprehensible that you don't understand yourself.
II. "Non vis intelligi nec ego te volo intelligere."
III. If you are so desirous of not being understood, then you have only to cease writing.

Their early ideal of erudition made the Pléiade poets reticent about condemning learned complexity and tempted them to disregard the chief object of literary communication: the reader. Their exclusivity had two facets. First, they wrote for a limited and learned audience. Second, many of their productions were little more than personal communications, composed for the specific interest or enjoyment of a mistress, monarch, courtier, or friend, and containing allusions which the general public could only fail to understand.

Maurice Scève's obscurity was a counterpart of the contemporary neo-Pindarism. Scève became the scapegoat for all obscure authors just as Petrarch had been for insincere authors. His unfamiliar symbolism and Italianate conceits would have proved more intelligible had his century known better Scève's Italian sources.[108] Finally, as has been noted above, although the Pléiade left much for the reform of Malherbe to correct, they did succeed during their later years toward mending some of their own ways. Born to an age when the complex style and rimes of the Floral Games of Toulouse and the Puy de Rouen were the rule, the Pléiade poets made a greater contribution to the development of French literary clarity than Malherbe or Boileau realised.

[108] For the student of Scève's unfamiliar symbolism two domains remain yet to be explored. The vast literature of alchemy which sprang up in France and Italy in the sixteenth century contains symbolism akin to Scève's. Also, the symbols frequent in the contemporary emblematic literature quite possibly will serve as a further clue toward the solution of the riddle of Scève.

The Function of Poetry . . .

IV

POETIC SWEETNESS AND UTILITY

> A heresy which, in the brief period it has already endured, may be said to have accomplished more in the corruption of our Poetical Literature than all its other enemies combined: I allude to the heresy of the Didactic.
> — Edgar Allan Poe, *The Poetic Principle*

> A poem appeals to the mass through the individual; a slogan, a political speech appeals to the individual through the mass. Poetry is of its nature more personal than "straight" propaganda: the latter is heavy artillery, the former is hand-to-hand fighting.
> — C. D. Lewis, *Revolution in Writing*

In their amoristic manner, the young Pléiade poets attempted to introduce a "sweet new style" into France. One might expect any group of poets admittedly nurtured on Petrarch to fill their sonnets with *doulx, doulceur*, and their cognates. Witness Baïf, for example:

> Doux dédain, douce paix qu'un doux courroux ameine,
> Doux regard, doux maintien, doux parler, beauté douce,
> Doux trait, que dans mon cœur amour doucement pousse.
> Douceur du doux brazier de l'amour toute plaine.[1]

These words were so freely used by Petrarch (*dolce* alone being employed at least two hundred and seventy-seven times in the *Rime*) [2] that they lost not only much of their expressive,

[1] Baïf, M.-L., I, 193. This entire sonnet is a plagiarism of Petrarch's sonnet, "Dolci ire, dolci sdegni e dolci paci."

[2] *Cf.*, K. McKenzie, *Concordanza delle Rime di Petrarca* (New Haven, 1912), *s. v.: dolce.*

but their semantic value as well. It is understandable, then, why the concept of sweetness is so indiscriminately used by the Pléiade in their love sonnets.

Less to be expected, however, are the frequent allusions to sweetness in the critical writings of the Pléiade, allusions that are sustained throughout their entire literary or critical evolution. "Le doux" is one of the most common epithets used in their judgments on other writers. The question immediately arises concerning its value as a critical standard, and its possibilities of meaning. When one finds the term applied to authors with almost nothing in common, such as Sappho and Rabelais, or Anacreon and Pindar, one wonders whether it was not used as a critical concept fully as indiscriminately as an amatory conceit.

The motif of poetic sweetness was no idle matter to the Pléiade. When the chief of this movement describes his favorite type of poems as "douces et doucement coulantes d'un doux stile,"[3] the content of this word so readily used becomes a significant matter.

This chapter will devote itself to three aims. It will attempt to determine the several meanings of the concept of sweetness, and secondarily, of utility, as used by the Pléiade in their critical observations. It will investigate whether the Pléiade considered the hedonistic or the didactic use of literature the more important. It will study the poetic imagery or motifs which derived from the notion of poetic sweetness. The principal sources of information for all facets of his problem will remain, as in the previous chapters, the observations and judgments on other writers.

It must be granted at the outset that whereas the Pléiade's remarks on a writer often center upon his sweetness, they almost never treat of his "utility." Therefore, this chapter will of necessity include a catalogue of the "sweet" authors, without a corresponding list of "useful" writers, except for those

[3] Ronsard, V, 186.

classed as "douxutile." As we shall be obliged to repeat later whatever unity, coherence, and proportion this chapter contains will be the inevitable result not of our own planning, but of the nature and amount of working materials or copy furnished us by the Pléiade poets.

A few words may be said about the first of our aims. There are of course various meanings which may be given sweetness as a critical term. This chapter will try to determine which are the most frequent general senses in which it is used. A piece of poetry may be sweet because of its euphony, because of its thought content, or because of its cadence. To the Pléiade who were trying to revive the musical ode, it might be sweet because of its melody, or even, if presented as a recitative because of the melody which accompanied it. Even some of Ronsard's post-Tridentine fulminations might seem sweet if set to music or declaimed to the lyre of Ferabosco or Roland de Lassus.

Again, the poet or poem might be "sweet" according to Horatian definition. The poet is sweet because he aims to please rather than instruct. The poem is sweet because of what it does rather than what it is. In this sense *le doux* was contrasted, in the Renaissance, with such adjectives as *l'utile l'industrieux*, *le profitable*, and the like. This type of contrast simplifies our task considerably, clearly showing that one of the major incentives and authorities for the frequent use of "le doux" is the *Ad Pisones* of Horace, or, by extension, the conflict between ψυχαγωγία and διδασκαλία with which the Greek grammarians (Eratosthenes, Dionysius of Halicarnassus, and others) had preceded Horace's remarks. The rôle of Horace, described by Du Bellay in the *Deffence* as having "le cerveau mieus purgé et le nez meilleur" than any other in critical matters, was a paramount one here, as further proved by the Pléiade's invention of the adjectives "utiledoux" and "douxutile," which dictionaries from Cotgrave to Littré have rejected.

Other considerations in the attempt to give "sweetness" it

specific meanings will involve: the parallel the Pléiade set up between sweetness and gravity, as distinguished from sweetness and utility; the specific uses of the term as applied to Greek, Latin, and Renaissance writers; and, finally, its place in the poetic imagery of the musical ode.

Something may be prefaced here concerning the third aim of this chapter, a study of the special vocabulary or motifs which arose in connection with the Pléiade's interest in literary sweetness. There are three major motifs which will be investigated: the Swan, the Bee, and Distillation. The Swan concept, like that of the Bee, was classical in origin. The fact that poets sing sweet songs led the Pléiade to consider poets as Swans, whose song (with that of the nightingale) [4] was reputedly the sweetest of all nature. This comparison was a commonplace, however, even among the Greeks. The swan legend is a pretty fiction, but any group of poets who believed that the elephant carries its young nine years would certainly have little difficulty believing that swans break out in sublime song just before dying. For all their wide humanistic interests and their love of external nature, the Pléiade poets were not ornithologists. Sweetness of content gave rise to imagery (some stereotyped and some original) centering upon bees, and the inevitable concomitants of honey, gardens, flowers. If the motifs of the Bee and the Swan dated from antiquity, that of *alambiquage* was more or less their own invention. We shall return to these motifs in due course.

That literature should be pleasing is an idea which traverses all lands and all ages.[5] It can best please by being sweet, either in thought or expression. As it does not please if it is not sweet (in the broad Horatian sense of *dulcis*), a distinction between sweetness as the nature of literature and sweetness as its function may become an invalid distinction.

Similarly, that literature should sometimes be labeled either

[4] *Ibid.*, III, 417.

[5] This applies even to those decadent and *scapigliati* groups to whom unorthodox conceptions of sweetness create an unorthodox idea of pleasure.

sweet or useful because of its intention or function may be another questionable distinction. For both sweet and philosophical or didactic literature can teach. Many before us have reached this conclusion. "Lasciamo stare," wrote Giacomo Leopardi in the *Preambolo allo Spettatore*, "che lo scopo finale di ogni cosa essendo il piacere, il quale poi all' ultimo si ottiene rarissime volte, la nostra privata opinione è che il dilettevole sia più utile che l'utile." Both sweet and useful literature may attempt to teach the same lessons. It is only their means which differ. As most readers will prefer the sweet way to the grave or hard way, sweet literature may even accomplish what the utilitarian types cannot. This is the reason Philip Sydney presents in his *Apology for Poetrie* for holding that the Poet is the monarch of all sciences: "For he dooth not only show the way, but giveth so sweete a prospect into the way, as will entice any man to enter into it."[6] And in a piece entitled "Poetae utiles," Julius-Caesar Scaliger recognises the utilitarian value of such enticement (*lenocinium*).[7]

This very sweetness made poetry dangerous in the opinion of its opponents, the *μισόμουσοι*. For the question of poetic sweetness, like that of poetic mendacity, is intimately related to the old problem of the moral justification of verse. Sydney declared that this sweetness was one of the three specific objections of these poet-haters. "Poetry infects us with desires, with a syrens sweetness, drawing the mind to the serpents tayle of fancy."[8] This Renaissance attitude is representative of both the classic antipathy to poetry articulated by Plato, and the Christian antipathy voiced by Boethius, who held that the Muses, being "sweet with deadly sweetness," should be cast out of society with the poets themselves.[9] This objection kept

[6] Sir Philip Sydney, *Apology for Poetrie*, ed. by Gregory Smith (1904), p. 172.
[7] J.-C. Scaliger, *Poemata* (1591), II, 237.
[8] Sir Philip Sydney, *Apology for Poetrie*, *ed. cit.*, p. 181.
[9] Quoted and refuted by Boccaccio, *Genealogia Deorum Gentilium*, XIV, v. See also, XIV, ix, on the utility of fables.

the apologists for poetry, from Aristotle down, busy explaining that poetry had compensatory utilitarian values.

At this point our attention is drawn to the long history of the debate on the function of poetry, the controversy over hedonism and didacticism. Although the outstanding name in this lengthy history is that of Horace, one cannot enter upon a discussion of the Horatian pronouncements on sweetness and utility unless one first weighs the meaning of the Horatian precepts in the light of their Hellenic origins. To begin, then, a few observations on the pre-Horatian currents of this debate, to be followed by a summary of the position of the *Ad Pisones* itself, that little epistle which exerted such a powerful influence upon France of the sixteenth and seventeenth centuries.

⚜ ⚜ ⚜

The focal point on which the Aristotelian and Platonic disagreements about the moral worth of literature centered was none other than this opposition of sweetness and utility, or as Croce tagged them, the Arte-meretrice and Arte-pedagogo tendencies.[10] Plato, of course, saw in poetry principally hedonistic purpose, which became the basis for his condemnation of poets. Others to share the view that pleasure (ἡδονή) was poetry's sole reason for being, although not joining in the condemnation, were such grammarians as Heracleodorus and Eratosthenes, whom Strabo quoted as holding the exaggerated opinion: ποιητὴν ἔφη πάντα στοχάζεσθαι ψυχαγωγίας, οὐ διδασκαλίας.[11] Critics before Eratosthenes had held that poetry should charm, but his is the earliest known proposal that this was its exclusive function. In Dionysius of Halicarnassus, Herodotus is said to conjoin the καλόν and the ἡδονή as the twin purposes of coupling words with metre.[12]

For those of the Arte-pedagogo persuasion, the interest of

[10] Benedetto Croce, *Estetica* (Palermo, 1902), p. 165. [11] Strabo, i, 2, 3.
[12] Dionysius of Halicarnassus, *De Compos. Verb.* 10–11.

poetry lay in the content, with its historical, natural, or ethical lessons. To them, as to Ruskin in the *Aratra Pentelici*, "the great representative and imaginative arts are to teach what is noble in past history and lovely in existing human life." This is the position held by the Stoics. It is found in the *Poetry* of Philodemus.[13] It is the assumption posited by Aristophanes in the *Frogs*.[14] So firmly did the Stoics believe that literature should teach and not entertain that they virtually turned the poets into Stoic philosophers.[15]

Aristotle was, of course, especially interested in the didactic, utilitarian side of poetry. As a champion of the moral justification of literature, he was obliged to be. But, partly because of a clinical interest in the effects of poetry on the body, he was drawn into hedonistic considerations of art.[16] He posited as the purpose of art the commotion (συμπαθεῖα) of our senses. For this reason he treated of the ἡδονή of a work of art, a word with all the force of the Latin *voluptas*, and of its ψυχαγωγία, the psychological thrill which courses through one's being in the appreciation of a work of art (*cf.* the *animum agunto* of Horace).

The disciples of Aristotle, the Peripatetics, studied in verse the instruments of pleasure (ψυχαγωγικά) and the literary devices producing pleasing effects (ἡδύσματα). They maintained that content and manner of presentation had an equal importance. From this they concluded that the aims of profit and delight were of equal value, that literature should err neither by delighting to excess nor by teaching to excess. The Alexandrian Neoptolemus was one of the earliest to maintain that literature had a two-fold aim, admitting the charm of psychagogy and yet contending that there should be a didascalic purpose as well.[17]

[13] Jensen, *Philodemus über die Gedichte* (Berlin, 1923), Bk. V.

[14] Aristophanes, *Frogs*, 1054–55: "Children and boys are given teachers, but the poet is the master of the man."

[15] *Cf.*, Cicero, *De Nat. Deorum* i, 15, 41.

[16] Aristotle, *Poetics* xiv.

[17] See J. Tate, "Horace and the Moral Function of Poetry," *Classical*

The roster of Hellenic authors who espoused didacticism in art includes Aeschylus, Isocrates, Strabo, Xenophon, and other names familiar to the Pléiade.[18] It is interesting to note that the adjective used by these pre-Horatian writers, διδασκαλικός, was known to the sixteenth-century poets and used by them. Ronsard, in the 1587 preface to his *Franciade*,[19] declares that both tragedy and comedy are entirely "didascaliques et enseignantes." Du Bartas claims that his *Sepmaines* are not a heroic or epic, but rather a "didascalique" work.[20] One wonders from the uses of this adjective how well the sixteenth-century poets knew the treatises of Neoptolemus, Eratosthenes, Dionysius of Halicarnassus, or Heracleodorus. None of the leaders of the Pléiade mentioned them, to our knowledge. The adjective may have come to the Pléiade through one of the creative writers, or may possibly have been recalled to them by Leo the Jew.[21]

The prominence of the concept of sweetness in Horace's poetics can be accorded no more than a summary treatment here. It has been fully discussed by many competent scholars. Three passages in the *Ad Pisones* present the essential points of the doctrine:

> Non satis est pulchra esse poemata; dulcia sunto
> Et quocumque volent animum auditoris agunto.[22]
>
> Aut prodesse volunt aut delectare poetae,
> Aut simul et iucunda et idonea dicere vitae.[23]
>
> Omne tulit punctum qui miscuit utile dulci,
> Lectorem delectando pariterque monendo.[24]

Quarterly (April, 1928), p. 66. For classical theory on the function of verse, see D. L. Clark, *Rhetoric and Poetry in the Renaissance* (New York: Columbia University, 1922), Part II, chap. i.

[18] See D. L. Clark, *Rhetoric and Poetry in the Renaissance, ed. cit.*, Part II, chap. i: "The Classical Conception of the Purpose of Poetry."

[19] Ronsard, VII, 79.

[20] In the "advertissement" to the first *Sepmaine*.

[21] Leo the Jew, *Etymologiae* ix.

[22] Horace, *Ad Pisones*, vss. 99–100.

[23] *Ibid.*, vss. 333–334.

[24] *Ibid.*, vss. 343–344.

That literature conforms to aesthetic standards of beauty is not enough. It must have ethical values which it imparts to the reader. Both the words "sweet" and "useful" have here very broad connotations. "Sweetness" does not refer to melody, rhythm, or syntactic qualities specifically. It refers rather to the aim of the poet to be pleasant and to have delight as his principal object. Boileau, for example, translates *dulce* as "le plaisant," stating that satire more than any other poetic form should combine the sweet and the useful, a Horatian idea in which Ronsard had preceded him.[25] The Horatian meaning of *utile* is ethical, deriving from the original classic contention, found in Aristotle and elsewhere, that literature, to justify its existence, must improve the reader.

Beyond being formally beautiful, poetry must also have a pleasing subjective quality which produces that spiritual commotion which is the purpose of all literature, didactic or other. This commotion may result in two changes in the reader or hearer. It may leave him a better man or it may leave him a wiser man, like the spiritually moved Wedding Guest after the Ancient Mariner's tale; it may make both of him. This is the exact sense of the Horatian precepts which Du Bellay reproduced in his *Regrets*. Whereas Ronsard emphasised the psychagogy ("doucement enchanter") of sweet poetry in his ode to De l'Hospital,[26] Du Bellay congratulates the chancellor for raising the level of French poetry. He celebrates the dignitary "qui nous monstres seul, d'un art Horacien, comme il fault chastier le vice et l'ignorance." [27]

Of the three excerpts from the *Ad Pisones* quoted above, it is the last one which produced the deepest impression upon the Pléiade. A proof of this is the number of translations and paraphrases of the "utile dulci" opposition which one finds in their writings, and particularly in their judgments on other writers. Rémy Belleau renders the Latin as "industrieus" and

[25] Boileau, Satire IX; for Ronsard, *vide infra*, note 90.

[26] Ronsard, II, 120.

[27] Du Bellay, II, 185.

"dous," applying one adjective to the brush of Nicolas Denisot and the other to his pen: "Ce double trait, dont l'un industrieus ravist nostre œil, l'autre dous, nostre oreille." [28] Another translation is met at the close of Ronsard's *Abbrégé de l'Art poëtique,* where the humble poet hopes that posterity will find his meagre counsel "aggréable et utile." [29]

Du Bellay adheres still closer to the Latin in his translations of these adjectives. They are rendered literally in his "Ode au Seigneur des Essars" and in his "Lyre Chrestienne":

> Des poétiques espris
> L'utile et doulce escriture
> Comprent ce qui est compris
> Au ciel et en la nature.[30]
>
> Cestuy là qui dict que ces vers
> Gastent le naïf de mon style,
> Il a l'estomac de travers
> Préférant le doulx à l'utile.[31]

In other passages he translates the *dulce* as "le plaisir." His "Discours au Roy sur la poésie" declares that the poet and historian are moved with a common desire, "de profiter et de donner plaisir." [32] In the ode to the Prince de Melphe, he congratulates Caracciolo as one having a Horatian purpose in his verses, as one who "sçait mesler en sa doctrine le plaisir à l'utilité." [33] Still another version is found in the *Deffence,* where the poet is advised to avoid triviality and banality; Martial is cited as one who composed epigrams to please, but having another deeper purpose: "A l'imitation d'un Martial, ou de quelque autre bien approuvé, si la lascivité ne te plaist, mesle le profitable avecques le doulx." [34]

It might be noted parenthetically that the royal privilege to the Third Book of Rabelais acknowledged that the two

[28] Belleau, M.-L., II, 455.
[29] Ronsard, VII, 65.
[30] Du Bellay, IV, 174.
[31] *Ibid.*, IV, 139.
[32] *Ibid.*, VI, 164.
[33] *Ibid.*, V, 359.
[34] *Deffence, ed. cit.*, pp. 206–207.

published books of Pantagruel were "non moins utiles que delectables." Although the utility of these particular works might be hard to establish, it would seem that public utility was a practical advantage for the author who was petitioning for a publishing patent.

Another reminiscence of the *utile dulci* is the opposition of "plaisant" and "docte" which one encounters twice in the *Deffence*. As students of the classics demonstrate,[35] this Horatian phrase has an inevitable connotation of wisdom, for if any poetry is to teach, the poet himself must be better instructed or more experienced than his readers. As Du Bellay wrote to De l'Hospital, the "Horatian art" overcomes ignorance as well as vice. Thus, when Joachim refers to the *Coltivazione* of Alamanni as "non moins docte que plaisante,"[36] or to the sonnet as being a "non moins docte que plaisante" invention of the Italians,[37] he is adopting Horatian terminology.

It is not surprising to meet translations of the *utile dulci* in Vauquelin's handbook of neo-classical counsel. Recalling that youngsters dislike severe poetry as much as their elders like it, he concludes that "qui sçait entremesler l'utile avec le dous, l'honneur facilement remportera sur tous."[38] And again, "enseigner, profiter, ou bien donner plaisir, ou faire tous les deux, le Poète a désir."[39]

The neo-Latinity of the Renaissance led to a curious paradox. Nothing would seem more futile than to paraphrase Horace in his own language, but the neo-Latin Utenhove did just this. His version was included in the *Bellaicae Musae et Latinae et Gallicae carmina*:

> Utile iucundo doctus miscere, Poetas,
> Omne ferens punctum, maximus inter eris, *etc.*[40]

[35] See J. Tate, *loc. cit.*
[36] *Deffence, ed. cit.*, pp. 265–266.
[37] *Ibid.*, p. 222.
[38] Vauquelin, *Art poétique, ed. cit.*, p. 158.
[39] *Ibid.*, p. 157.
[40] Du Bellay, *Poésies françaises et latines* (Paris: Garnier, 1918), I, 534.

An interesting fabrication by the members of the Pléiade was the term "utiledoux." The meaning of this word seems to arise directly from the text of the *Ad Pisones,* if not from the earlier Peripatetic view of literature. A poet may aim both to delight and teach ("simul et iucunda et idonea dicere vitae"). As well as calling a writer "le doux" or "l'utile," the Pléiade could, taking the last precept of Horace and the Peripatetics, call him both by coining through mere juxtaposition of the Horatian components, "l'utiledoux." This compound word they must have considered a higher compliment than either of its components used alone. After all, as Horace had written, he who mixes profit and pleasure takes the prize.

It is not surprising to learn that it was Du Bellay who invented and exploited this coinage when one considers the praises Joachim heaped upon Lazare de Baïf for inventing [*sic*] the term "aigredoulx." [41] Du Bellay applies "utiledoux" to Rabelais in the *Musagnœomachie*, listing him as one of the contemporary authors combatting ignorance.[42] The adjective is transposed to "doulx-utile" in the "Discours à Salmon Macrin," but Du Bellay is still applying it to Rabelais, the new Democritus,[43] recognised for his utility, as we have demonstrated, by royal patent. Jean Morel describes Du Bellay as the "doux-utile Angevin translateur, qui ses thresors tirez de maint aucteur nous jecte icy d'une main plantureuse." [44]

These, then, are the various ways in which the Pléiade interpreted the Horatian doctrine of the function of poetry.[45] The Pléiade was not split into two factions on this question, as was Italy, where Robortelli and Castelvetro held that literature's first aim was to delight, whereas Minturno and others took the

[41] *Deffence*, ed. by Chamard, p. 335.

[42] Du Bellay, IV, 12–13.

[43] *Ibid.*, IV, 145.

[44] At the head of Du Bellay's translation of the fourth book of the *Aeneid. Ibid.*, VI, 245.

[45] In the preface of his *Œuvres* (1579), Pierre Larivey translates Horace in his advice, "par un honnête plaisir apporter, suyvant le précepte d'Horace, quelque profit et contentement ensemble."

opposite stand. The Pléiade took the position that Philip Sydney, Webbe, and others were taking in England, namely, that poetry had a dual aim.[46] To the Pléiade the solution of the "iucunda et idonea dicere" was a way out which satisfied both their pagan hedonism and their Christian morality.

If these writers decided on a compromise between utility and pleasure, this was a largely theoretical conviction and not one borne out by actual practice. First of all, a great proportion of their production consisted of love sonnets and must be classed as hedonistic. Most of their odes must come into this same category, as must the majority of their eclogues, epigrams, chansons, blasons, epistles, baisers, and even many of their elegies and epitaphs. Furthermore, their ivory tower tendencies and their concern with only the "happy few" were not characteristic of didacticism, which aims to serve the greatest social number. Those works of the Pléiade which had as their purpose the moral, educational, or social betterment of the reader were few, indeed. Among them one might include their vulgarisations and translations of the classics, the allegories and "temples," which they adopted from earlier writers, the orisons and psalms, the social satires, a few of their discourses, and an occasional piece like the "Enseignements de vertu" of Peletier.

What little utility did exist in the Pléiade's compositions was of an educative order; it was moralistic rather than political utility, useful to the individual rather than the state. True, the Pléiade poet sometimes reminded a king or treasurer that he had served the monarchy in his writings. Yet these writings were merely encomiums and commemorative pieces celebrating individuals; any references to statecraft were normally couched in the most general phrases. They were not writings justifying or defining the policies or doctrines of the state. The propa-

[46] Philip Sydney, *Apology for Poetrie* (1583): "Poesy therefore is an art of imitation . . . with this end, to teach and delight." W. Webbe, *A Discourse on English Poetry* (1586): "The right use of poetry is to mingle profit with pleasure, *etc.*" Both quoted in R. P. Cowl, *The Theory of Poetry in England* (London, 1914), pp. 298, 302.

gandistic use to which literature was later put under totalitarian governments was never envisioned by the authoritative French state of the Renaissance, even though that state did perceive that certain dissident (Protestant) literature could be harmful. In other words, the French crown recognised the negative, but not the positive uses of literature in wielding public opinion. If one were to accept the emphatic view of Lenin that every book must further a cause, "must be a cog in the social mechanism," then the only utilitarian books of the century were by Jean Bodin, Étienne de la Boétie, Henri Estienne, Montaigne, and the authors of the *Satire Ménippée*. The Pléiade would not be represented in the list.

⚜ ⚜ ⚜

A common practice of the Pléiade was to contrast sweetness with gravity rather than utility. This does not mean, of course, that gravity was held to have a semantic value equal to that of utility. Maurice Scève, for example, was as grave as any mortal poet should be, but one would not turn to him for profit or ethical betterment. When a comparison is drawn between "et l'un et l'autre stile du grave Scève et du doux Saingelais," [47] grave has something of the same meaning as the epithet "hautement sévère," applied to Scève by Pernette du Guillet, implying a lofty and serious tone. A "grave" poet may write either to please or to instruct.

Generally, however, the word connotes a seriousness of purpose, as well. This may be discerned in either the thought content or the form of expression (tragedies, elegies, Pindaric odes, as opposed to comedies, epithalamiums, Anacreontic verse, *etc.*). Such a contrast between sweetness and gravity is established in the case of Pontus de Tyard. When Du Bellay perceived the new Platonic tendencies of the *Discours philo-*

[47] Pontus de Tyard, M.-L., p. 59.

sophiques, he charged Tyard with shifting his style from the sweetness of a Petrarch to the gravity of a Plato.[48] Quite the contrary shift of manner was visible in Ronsard, whose grave style was displaced by a sweet one. Ronsard was conscious of this evolution himself:

> Or si quelqu'un après me vient blasmer de quoy
> Je ne suis plus si grave en mes vers que j'estoy,
> Dy luy que les amours ne se souspirent pas
> D'un vers haultement grave . . .
> Il suffist qu'on luy chante au vray ses passions
> Sans enflure ny fard, d'un mignard et doux stile.[49]

Here Ronsard posits sweetness as the *sine qua non* of erotic verse and seems to infer that there is little room for gravity in a love poem. Those who attempt to overload their love sonnets with gravity, he concludes, are guilty of an offense against Venus and her son Cupid. This change of manner on the part of Ronsard is also noted in the *Amours* of Baïf. Jean-Antoine is glad that Ronsard "va modérer en plus douce chanson son brave cœur sous un moins grave son." [50]

Several writers combine both of these attributes. Ronsard describes the chronicles of Macé as sweet and grave.[51] Du Bellay affirms that he cannot praise the gravity of Caracciolo without praising his sweetness as well.[52] Even as early as 1537, Vulteius, in his "Ad poetas Gallos pro Doleto," calls upon his contemporaries to succor the bard "qui de more graves versus dulcesque canebat." [53] In his epithalamium for Marie de Lorraine, Jean Dorat hails the troupe of Apollo which is hastening to celebrate her marriage:

> Ia Déportes le doux, et Baïf le nombreux,
> Et ton grave Ronsard le père aisné des deux.[54]

[48] Du Bellay, II, 176.
[49] Ronsard, I, 130–131.
[50] Baïf, M.-L., I, 8–9.
[51] Ronsard, STFM, I, 267.
[52] Du Bellay, V, 354.
[53] Vulteius, *Epigrammatum libri iiii* (Lugduni, 1537), p. 231.
[54] Dorat, M.-L., p. 22.

Du Bellay records a similar contrast in his "De poetarum amoribus," where "Ronsardus gravis & gravis Thyardus" are compared with "mollis Baifius." [55]

Just as the Pléiade members were wont to juxtapose the two opposite attributes of sweetness and utility in a single expression ("utiledoux" and "douxutile"), so one might expect to find them conciliating the two opposites of sweetness and gravity and making a single concept of them. To complete the parallel, one should expect to encounter a coinage of "sweet gravity" and "grave sweetness" as well. This is precisely what one finds. Beginning with those uses where sweetness is the first named of the two complements, we may recall Du Bellay's approval of the sweet gravity of the Cardinal de Guyse [56] or divine Pasithea, one of the Graces.[57] In his ode to Des Essars he praises the sweet gravity of the language in the *Amadis* translations.[58] Similarly, Jean-Antoine de Baïf was stirred by the dignified qualities of Du Bellay's translation of the fourth book of the *Aeneid*; he found that his friend had captured so well the "doulce gravité" of Vergil that Vergil would have been astonished at these natural graces.[59] Vauquelin, by the way, used the expression "sweet gravity" in two places. He decrees that this is one of the requisites of good satire; again, he opines that the "doucement grave" eloquence of Garnier has acted as a tonic on French tragedy.[60] Magny finds that the subject of a love poem as well as the poem itself may express a sweet gravity.[61]

The converse of this expression is not infrequent. Magny admitted a desire to ornament his ode to François de Revergat with "les plus graves douceurs." [62] In a posthumous sonnet of

[55] Du Bellay, *Poésies* (Paris: Garnier, 1918), I, 499.
[56] Du Bellay, III, 102.
[57] *Ibid.*, V, 286.
[58] *Ibid.*, IV, 173.
[59] Baïf, M.-L., V, 231.
[60] Vauquelin, *Art poétique*, ed. by Pellissier, pp. 104, 121.
[61] Magny, *Soupirs*, Courbet edition, p. 26.
[62] Magny, *Dernières poésies*, Courbet edition, p. 50.

Ronsard, one finds him relating to his old master Jean Dorat that the nine Muses "trempèrent mes vers dans leurs graves douceurs."[63] And, finally, La Borderie congratulated Jean de la Péruse on "tes graves-doux vers liriques."[64]

Other passages where the grave is contrasted with the sweet are not rare. One finds them even in Boileau.[65] In a whimsical stanza referred to in another chapter, Ronsard wished that the sweet works of Bacchylides, Simonides, Alcman, and others might be resuscitated from oblivion. Should these works be found, conjectured Ronsard, he and his friends would read them for their "douces paroles, et les graves seroyent pour les maistres d'escoles."[66] Most of the references to sweetness and gravity, however, apply to the contemporaries of the Pléiade, as the preceding paragraphs indicate. Du Bellay presents an amusing variation in describing Héroët as surpassing honey in sweetness and Stoic brows in gravity.[67] Belleau contrasts the sweet grace and "sentences graves" of Garnier.[68] In his "Complainte d'une nymphe sur la mort de Du Bellay," Belleau again mentions these attributes, "Fortunate Loire to have received the sweet accents and grave accords of the Vendomois hand."[69] In his elegy "A son livre," Ronsard contrasts the grave and high style of the tragic Muse with the sweetness of the Muse of amoristic verse.[70] Other identifications of high and grave style with low and sweet style may be encountered in the works of the Pléiade.[71] Similarly, Maurice Scève evokes the gravity of Aeschylus and the pleasantness of Menippus as examples from antiquity.[72] Du Bellay adds a third attribute in his *Sonnets divers*, characterising Jodelle as "grave, doulx, et copieux," a stylistic combination of which any author of the period might be proud.[73]

[63] Ronsard, VI, 457.

[64] *Le Trésor des pièces angoumoisines inédites et rares* (Angoulême, 1866), p. 116.

[65] Boileau, *Art poétique*, I, 75–79.

[66] Ronsard, V, 187.

[67] Du Bellay, III, 136.

[68] Belleau, M.-L., I, 159.

[69] *Ibid.*, II, 134.

[70] Ronsard, I, 131.

[71] *Ibid.*, II, 183; Jodelle, M.-L., I, 260.

[72] Guégan edition, p. 240.

[73] Du Bellay, II, 285.

As a probable result of the lexical influence of the Pléiade, Cotgrave's dictionary contains an entry of "douxgrave," although none of "utiledoux" or "douxamer."

Gravity had two meanings in the Pléiade's critical terminology. In the first place, it was synonymous with sublimity or loftiness of style, the quality which the Pléiade theorists called the "altiloque." As such, "grave" was contrasted with "doux," meaning informal, familiar, pleasant, or possibly frivolous of purpose. When gravity refers to the manner of writing it conforms to the definition of Confucius, who said that gravity was merely the bark of wisdom but that it preserved wisdom. The pejorative sense which the word sometimes had in common usage disappeared when it became part of the Pléiade's vocabulary. Authors thought it a compliment to be considered "grave," even though Montaigne was suggesting that no living being was more grave or serious than an ass. In short, gravity was one of the attributes the Pléiade encouraged in the campaign to establish "quelque plus haut et meilleur style" in French literature. In the second place, gravity could refer to more than mere manner or tone. It could apply to the subject matter of a literary work. Thus, the Pléiade could call Tyard grave because of the serious erudition he displayed in his *Discours philosophiques*, treating of music, astrology, and other learned matters. Scève earned the title of grave as much for his erudite *Microcosme* as for his cabalistic dizains. An artist who created grave works had already something as serious about him as a frankly utilitarian artist. By the same token, one would never call the authors of *nugae* or Petrarchian verse grave any more than one could call them utilitarian. Such authors were "sweet."

⚜ ⚜ ⚜

We have already called attention to the lack of observations by the Pléiade on the utilitarian or didactic qualities of individual authors, save those regarded as "douxutile." On "sweet" writers, however, the Pléiade poets have left us an abundance of remarks. Too many of these, unfortunately, are mere mentions rather than critical appreciations. The following chronological catalogue of writers will nevertheless enable us to see the broad connotations which the word "sweet" held in the Pléiade's lexicology.

The first Hellenic writer whose sweetness the Pléiade mentioned was Hesiod (excepting the specific mentions to be included below in our treatment of the motifs of the Swan, the Bee, and Distillation). Wherever it may be, the sweetness of Hesiod is certainly not in his dianoia, for there is little sweet about the following thoughts:

> "Le Potier hait le Potier,
> "Le Feuvre le Charpentier,
> "Le Poète tout ainsi
> "Hayt celuy qui l'est aussi,"
> (Comme a dit la voix sucrée
> Du vieil habitant d'Ascrée.)[74]

Certainly, Hesiod's *Theogony* and the *Works and Days*, from which these lines were taken, were not sweet with the lyric sweetness of the melic love poets. But Hesiod was one of the second generation of Helladic *Ursänger* which had lost little of the primal sweetness of the first generation's singers, Orpheus, Linus, Amphion, and Eumolpus. As such, he could have discoursed upon any grave or didactic subject and still have been called sweet. The use of the image of the sugary voice here coupled with the accumulation of hate is a capital stylistic device.

Taking these passages in the chronological order of the Greeks mentioned, one arrives next at Pindar, whose works Ronsard judged anything but sweet in his "A Christophle de Choiseul" (1556). In this piece, dating from a period of waning Pindarism, he called them obscure, rough, "fascheux"

[74] Ronsard, II, 156.

torrents. But in 1552, the date of the "Voyage d'Hercueil," Ronsard's Pindarism permitted him to see all good virtues in the Theban poet and to praise the "sweet nectar" of Pindar's verse.[75] As early then as 1550 and 1552, Hesiod and Pindar were given attributes of sweetness, largely because of a belief that all Hellenic poetry possessed some Orphic sweetness, Attic honey. In the "Discours à Salmon Macrin," for which Chamard proposes the date 1551, Du Bellay shares the early enthusiasms of his friend and admires "les douces Thébaines odes." [76]

Sweetness related to the love poets is always more understandable. In his "Ode à la Contesse de Tonnerre," Du Bellay seems to hold that the Sapphic odes possessed more of this quality than the Pindaric. Listing the most accomplished women of antiquity, he cannot omit Corinna of Thebes and Sappho of Lesbos.

> Sur toy, Pindare, mordoit
> La doulce lyre ancienne,
> Que la fille Lesbienne
> Si doctement accordoit.[77]

Ronsard, like Du Bellay, saw Sappho as a prototype of Hymettic sweetness, but he would propose Anacreon as her peer, or even her superior in this respect:

> le doux Anacréon
> Me plaist, et je voudrois que la douce Saphon
> Qui si bien resveilloit la lyre Lesbienne,
> En France accompagnast la Muse Téïenne.[78]

As a matter of fact, on the following page he calls Anacreon the sweetest Greek of all. But the sweetness of Anacreon is tinged with bitterness, just as the amatory passion itself is accompanied by pain. Ronsard congratulates Choiseul on his choice of the Anacreontic ode as a poetic form, for Anacreon

[75] *Vide infra*, note 286.
[76] Du Bellay, IV, 146.
[77] *Ibid.*, III, 146.
[78] Ronsard, V, 186.

is an excellent model to follow, and adds that his sweet words portray the bittersweet of love:

> Tu as daigné tenter d'exprimer la faconde
> Des Grecs en nostre langue, et as pour ton patron
> Choisi le doux archet du vieil Anacréon,
> Qui monstre comme il faut d'une parolle douce
> Plaindre nos passions, lors que Venus nous pousse
> Sa flèche dans le cœur.[79]

Many are the Greeks of the fifth century B.C. whom the Pléiade register for their sweetness. Among those mentioned in the *Deffence*, for example, Du Bellay lists "la véhémence de Démosthène et la joyeuse douceur d'Isocrate." [80] Isocrates had, then, what Philip Sydney termed a "syrens sweetness" of argument, a mellifluous speech capable of beguiling the listener to his cause of Panhellenism.

On one occasion Ronsard reflects upon all the sweet and grave poetry of those Greeks whose compositions are lost to posterity. The sweetness of "le doux Simonide" is of a sentimental sort, and Ronsard would wish him resuscitated only "pourveu qu'il ne pleurast." [81] Philosophers may be sweet as well as poets. In an elegy to Hélène [82] Ronsard tells how he lived a life of study before being imprisoned by love, much in the manner of the narrator of the *Prisons* of Marguerite d'Angoulême. The favorite cicerones whom he had "toujours ès mains" were Aristotle, Plato, and the learned Euripides: "O douce compaignie et utile et honneste." The last Greek writer in this roster is the Alexandrian Callimachus, who diffused a sweetness and an intimate pleasure that captured the heart, particularly in his *Hymn to Delos*.[83]

The allusions to Roman authors were fewer.

Sweetness could involve cadence, as was the case when a poem's measure was regular and lyric. In his "Second Curieux,"

[79] *Ibid.*, V, 186.
[80] *Deffence*, *ed. cit.*, p. 100.
[81] Ronsard, V, 187.
[82] *Ibid.*, I, 337.
[83] *Ibid.*, VI, 29.

Pontus de Tyard stated that Cicero, Caesar, Vergil, Horace, Ovid (all of whom wrote in Latin although they were versed in Greek) improved the style of their age with a sweeter cadence. "Ils haussèrent vrayment et eslevèrent les façons de parler, ils s'enrichirent de mots bien choisis, et balancèrent leurs paroles de mieux mesurée, plus aggréable, et plus douce cadence." [84] To this sweetness and other qualities Vergil added Latin majesty, a property caught by Des Masures in his translation of the *Aeneid*.[85] The image of the sugared voice which Ronsard had applied to Hesiod is called into play by Du Bellay in his "Hymne de santé." He celebrates the delights of the Elysian fields:

Là est ta place éternelle
Près de celle
De Catule aux vers sucrez.[86]

Both Du Bellay and Ronsard mention the sweetness of Horace, the theorist from whom they derive their interest in the *dulce*. Twice the adjective is used in a stanza addressed by Du Bellay to Diane de Poitiers. He is introducing a fragment translated from Horace and wishes to recapture especially the euphony of the Roman poet:

Là des beaux vers d'Horace
Imitant les doulx sons,
Pour donner plus de grace
A mes humbles chansons,
J'empliray l'univers
Du doulx bruit de ces vers.[87]

In the preface to his *Odes* (1550), Ronsard relates how he invented the Gallic ode. Not finding competent poetry to imitate in the French idiom, he went to the classics and particularly to Horace. He does not specify that it was possibly Jacques Peletier who recalled the classic Horace to him, but the men-

[84] Pontus de Tyard, M.-L., p. 237.
[85] Du Bellay, II, 171.
[86] *Ibid.*, V, 276.
[87] *Ibid.*, V, 376.

tion of Peletier in the next sentence leads one to suppose that the latter's 1545 translation of the *Ad Pisones* may have been in the back of Ronsard's mind. "J'allai voir les étrangers, et me rendi familier d'Horace, contrefaisant sa naïve douceur." [88] It was Horace who understood the secret of writing the most effective satire. Juvenal was bitter, but Horace realised that one must be sweet. It is here, in the *Bocage royal*, that Ronsard proposes the formula for satire which Boileau was to echo in his ninth *Satire*: [89]

> Il faut la préparer si douce et si à point,
> Qu'à l'heure qu'on avalle on ne la sente point.[90]
>
> La satire en leçons, en nouveautés fertile,
> Sait seule assaisonner le plaisant et l'utile, *etc.*[91]

Ovid becomes the sweet Ovid in "Le satyre" of Ronsard.[92] The adjective here evidently refers to the Roman poet's subject matter as well as to his expression. Additional references to specific types of sweetness noted in the writers of antiquity will be recorded below in our discussion of the three poetic motifs contingent upon sweetness.

⚜ ⚜ ⚜

Further aspects of the conceit of sweetness become apparent in the judgments on the writers of the Renaissance. Sometimes, for example, the sweetness lies in the inspiration itself. The expressions "sweet fire" and "sweet madness" were not uncommon to describe poetic inspiration. This is particularly true of amatory verse. Ronsard recalls to Du Bellay the latter's

[88] Ronsard, VII, 4.
[89] The general idea, of course, had come from Horace, *Satire*, I, 23–24: ". . . quanquam ridentem dicere verum quid vetat?" Peletier paraphrased it in 1555 in his *Art poétique*, II, vi.
[90] Ronsard, III, 208.
[91] Boileau, *Satire* IX.
[92] Ronsard, V, 70.

days of penning sonnets to his Olive, asking whether that sweet fire which once burned in Joachim's breast is still alive.[93] This literary inspiration is called a sweet madness by Du Bellay.[94] Ronsard echoes the phrase, opining that the *Erreurs* of Pontus de Tyard can only be the vagaries of a sweet madness.[95]

As we endeavor to catalogue these many tributes paid by the Pléiade to their contemporaries, we become lost in a "wilderness of sweets," to crib a phrase from Milton. Some of the following are indiscriminate uses which flattery would engender, possessing little of semantic interest. Ronsard claims that if others found his compositions sweet (as did Baïf, for example, in his "Amymone") [96] they have rendered unto him the honor that Clotho had spun for him.[97] Baïf finds that Belot's poetry has sweet graces.[98] Des Autels admires most in Scève his "douceur," native grace, and propriety.[99] Magny compares the dulcet style of Paschal to that of the best Roman writers.[100] Ronsard resorts to the image of the sweet mouth to praise the sweet wind of Paschal's tongue.[101] The two tributes which Ronsard paid the chancellor Michel de l'Hospital have a humble echo in the "Épître-préface à Jean de Morel" of Du Bellay,[102] who characterises this dignitary as "that incomparable luminary of sweetest laws and letters." That his contemporaries awarded Herberay des Essars the flattering title of French Homer was attributable to his "douceur alléchante," according to Du Bellay.[103]

Pontus de Tyard considers many of these new and promising poets together and predicts a brilliant future for them.

[93] *Ibid.*, I, 28.
[94] Du Bellay, III, 100.
[95] Ronsard, VI, 199.
[96] Baïf, II, 129.
[97] Ronsard, II, 226.
[98] Baïf, II, 71.
[99] *Réplique*, quoted in the Guégan edition of Scève, p. lxiii.
[100] Magny, *Soupirs*, *ed. cit.*, p. 102.
[101] Ronsard, II, 299.
[102] Du Bellay, VI, 254.
[103] *Ibid.*, IV, 177.

They will be read, he is sure, when their rivals are forgotten:

> Le doux fruit de vos travaux
> Soit cueilli en la louange
> Immortelle. . . .[104]

The sweetness may be the effect poetry creates in the reader's soul rather than an inherent quality of the verse. This sweetness may be a spell or a general feeling of spiritual well-being. Such an enchantment is cast by the lyre and voice of Ferabosco.[105] Not only do the music and voice of the poet serve to create this *ψυχαγωγία*, but the very gestures of the poet serve as well.

The watchword of Paul Verlaine, "Music above all else," was taken as seriously by the Pléiade as by any succeeding group of French poets. Did not the word Ode mean song, and was this not the age when the "ode was married to the lyre"? To at least two of his colleagues, Baïf and Jean de la Péruse, Ronsard claimed to have been the first to set poetry to musical cadence.[106] The poets began to congratulate one another on the sweetness of their voices, their lyres, lutes, reeds, and pipes, even though the poet congratulated could neither sing nor play a note. This figurative language, therefore, is more pertinent to a study of literary sweetness than to a study of Renaissance musical practices. To say that a writer had a fine voice or a dulcet flageolet simply meant that his verse had a fine lyric quality.[107]

The sweetest of these figurative instruments, if one is to judge by the frequency of its appearance, was the lyre. We have already referred to the sweet lyre of Sappho, in Du Bellay's "Ode à la Contesse de Tonnerre,"[108] a sweetness which

[104] Pontus de Tyard, M.-L., p. 122.

[105] Ronsard, IV, 240–241.

[106] *Ibid.*, II, 161, and V, 34–35.

[107] Use of the lyre served not only to augment the sweetness of the verse, but its gravity as well. Ronsard, recalling the Italian revival of the lyre (by the strambottists), adds "laquelle lyre seule doit et peut animer les vers et leur donner le juste poix de leur gravité." (VII, 7.)

[108] Du Bellay, III, 146.

piqued Pindar. Du Bellay praises equally that of Orpheus.[109] However, the lyre of Pindar was sweet as well, and Ronsard was proud to have revived this sweetness in the musical ode.[110] The third Hellenic writer to possess a sweet lyre was Anacreon, and Henri Estienne was generally recognised as the scholar who had rediscovered the "douce lyre Téienne." [111] Anacreon, by the way, was also mentioned for his sistrum, but here for once was an instrument which the Pléiade could not very easily call sweet.[112]

Among Renaissance writers who were musical there was Saint-Gelays, whose sweet lyre and voice charmed the ears of kings.[113] There was Macrin, whose dulcet lyre was the favorite of the gods.[114] Then there was Ferabosco, the musician, mentioned above. Ferabosco, like Mellin, combined the voice and lyre:

> Mon Dieu, que de douceur, que d'aise et de plaisir
> L'ame reçoit alors qu'elle se sent saisir
> Et du geste et du son, et de la voix ensemble
> Que ton Ferabosco sur troys lyres assemble, *etc.*[115]

Ronsard, explaining the origin of the *Olive* to Jean de la Péruse, avers that Du Bellay won an eternal glory through his sweet playing of an ivory lyre; [116] and Du Bellay will admit that his own lyre is sweet.[117]

Other instruments are attributed to other sweet writers. Both Ronsard and Du Bellay agree that pastoral poets perform appropriately on sweet reed shawms.[118] Jacques Grévin claims that he plays a sweet flageolet and Nicolas Denisot a sweet musette.[119] Tahureau records that Ronsard (who termed himself "Harpeur Françoys éleu" in his ode "A sa lire") has taught them all to "animate the sweet harp." [120] The lute, according

[109] *Ibid.*, V, 256.
[110] Ronsard, IV, 146.
[111] *Ibid.*, II, 434.
[112] *Ibid.*, V, 161.
[113] *Ibid.*, III, 274.
[114] Du Bellay, IV, 32.
[115] Ronsard, IV, 240.
[116] *Ibid.*, V, 35.
[117] Du Bellay, IV, 136.
[118] Ronsard, I, 170; Du Bellay, IV, 187.
[119] Grévin, *ed. cit.*, p. 226.
[120] Tahureau, *ed. cit.*, I, 27.

to Du Bellay, combines epic qualities and sugared sweetness.[121] He himself combined the lute and the sweet voice.[122] And the lute playing of Dorat was even sweeter than that of Alcaeus, at least to his pupils.[123]

The human voice was often conjectured as the medium by which the particular authors expressed the musical sweetness of their creations. One such formalised reference to the voice is found in the *Regrets.* Both the Quercinois poets, Magny and Hugues Salel, are judged sweet singers, but Magny was the sweeter and therefore the greater.[124] Du Bellay records that a sweet enchantment makes him sing his verses.[125] Baïf opines that the sweetness of Aubert's song would make honey seem bitter.[126] Again in the *Regrets,* Du Bellay wishes that Apollo had given him as sweet a voice in his own tongue as Buchanan, the Scotch humanist and playwright, possessed in Greek and Latin.[127] The ancients had this sweetness of voice, of course, and in his "Hymne de santé" Du Bellay speaks of Hesiod, Linus, Pindar, Stesichorus, and others as the Aonian choir.[128] To this august personnel of the Aonian choir he adds Ronsard, in his Latin poem "In Francinam I. A. Baifii." [129]

However, passages about sugary voices need not always be symbolic; they need not always refer to a harmonious or lyric written style. They may refer to the actual singing voice. Such was the intention of Ronsard's reminiscence of Dorat in the "Voyage d'Hercueil," already quoted above. The old humanist sang to his pupils, literally. The colorful setting to this singing of Dorat has been recreated by various biographers of the Pléiade in a most engaging manner.[130]

If the critic endeavors to interpret the reasons behind this conglomeration of excerpts which we have been quoting, if he

[121] Du Bellay, III, 83; II, 261.
[122] Ronsard, V, 35.
[123] *Ibid.*, II, 160.
[124] Du Bellay, II, 180.
[125] *Ibid.*, II, 289.
[126] Baïf, I, 147.
[127] Du Bellay, II, 200.
[128] *Ibid.*, V, 275.
[129] Du Bellay, *Poésies* (Paris: Garnier, 1918), I, 459.
[130] See P. Champion, *Ronsard et son temps* (Paris, 1925), pp. 49–55, and Gustave Cohen, *Ronsard, sa vie et son œuvre* (Paris, 1932), pp. 57–60.

is unwilling to accept them as merely conventional imagery without critical meaning, he will probably discover that there were three convictions underlying all this seemingly indiscriminate talk involving hypothetical voices and imaginary instruments. All three concern the innermost nature of lyric poetry. (The reader may have noticed that none of those authors cited for their sweet voices or instruments was a prosaist; each was a poet.) All three underline the hedonistic rather than utilitarian purpose of poetry.

I. Lyric poetry must offer a psychagogic experience; it has or should have the function of thrilling the soul and the senses; beyond satisfying the mind it must appeal to the senses of sight (*cf.* the "gestes" of Ferabosco) and hearing, and for this latter function music is indispensable. The poet who can satisfy our sense of hearing will be perforce a musician.

II. Among the ancients, lyric poetry was either song or recitative. The soul of poetry was music and the writer became a musical composer, so to speak. The sixteenth century, which saw dramatic poets draw upon Hellenic theory to create musical drama (*i.e.*, *opera*), witnessed also lyric poets drawing upon Hellenic practice to create musical poetry. Musical poetry was an inevitable consequence of humanism. If poetry was to be musical, the creator could be considered, with some license of the imagination, a musician.

III. To the Pléiade, poetry was no longer written to be read in the silence of the study or the chamber; it was written to be heard. When Ronsard tells Corydon that he is going to lock himself in his room for three days and read the *Iliad* of Homer, he is speaking as a humanist rather than a poet; furthermore, he is making a distinction between the purposes of epic and lyric poetry. The verse of the preceding generations, the *rhétoriqueurs* and the specialists in *difficulté vaincue*, had to be read, followed on the printed page, in order that one might notice and appreciate the tricks of prosody, the tours de force of metrics and versification. With the Pléiade, however, the printed page became as mechanically incidental to poetry as the printed stave and notes are to music.

These then were the principal reasons why the poets wrote glibly of one another's sweet voice and sweet shawm, and why they so readily accepted the allegory of the Swan poet and the Bee poet, to be discussed immediately below. Thus, just as the imagery which the Pléiade evolved about inspiration emphasised the function of nature to the exclusion of art (see below, Chapter V), the imagery of the Swan and Bee will emphasise the sweetness or hedonistic purpose of poetry to the exclusion of its utilitarian values.

⚜ ⚜ ⚜

The Pléiade, then, could praise the lyric qualities of a writer by referring to his golden voice or to some imaginative musical instrument in his employ. There was another forceful way to praise him. One could call him a Swan, whose song (with that of the nightingale) [131] was reputedly the sweetest of all nature. This motif will be considered as the first of the three major motifs of sweetness adopted by the Pléiade, for it is closely identified with musical sweetness.

The frequency of the figure of the Swan entitles it to a place in our study of poetic sweetness, for no research has apparently been undertaken on the Pléiade's conception of the Swan-poet.[132] Yet no critical imagery of theirs had a more substantial classical antecedence. One might posit three reasons why the ancients had accepted the swan as the incarnation of the poet:

I. The swan was sacred to Apollo.
II. The swan possessed a beautiful voice.
III. The swan had prophetic powers.

[131] Ronsard, III, 417.

[132] For brief mentions of the swan motif, see Alice Cameron, *Influence of Ariosto on Ronsard and his Group* (Baltimore, 1930), p. xvi; and R. V. Merrill, *Platonism of Joachim du Bellay* (Chicago, 1925), pp. 87–90.

The white swan and the dark raven were sacred to Apollo. For this reason the swan became the Bird of Apollo and Bird of Orpheus in the ancients' nomenclature. Just as the swan was sacred to Brahma in India, writes D'Arcy Thompson, so was it sacred to Apollo in Greece.[133] One of the earliest passages establishing Phoebus as the eponym of this bird is in the *Phaedo* of Plato. This is an especially noteworthy passage, for it illustrates not only the sacredness of the swan, but his singing ability and what is more important, his prophetic powers. For this reason we quote it fully. Socrates is discussing the immortality of the human soul,

> Will you not allow that I have as much of the spirit of prophecy in me as the swans? For they, when they perceive that they must die, having sung all their life long, do then sing more than ever, rejoicing in the thought that they are about to go to the god Apollo whose ministers they are. But men, because they themselves are afraid of death, slanderously affirm of the swans that they sing a lament to the last, not considering that no bird sings when cold or hungry. . . . But because they are sacred to Apollo, and have the right of prophecy, and anticipate the good things of another world, therefore they sing and rejoice in that day more than they ever did before.[134]

Others among the ancients recorded the fact that the swan sang particularly to Apollo. Aristophanes, in the *Birds*, writes of the Bacchic cry of the birds of Apollo.[135] Callimachus, in his *Hymn to Delos*, speaks at some length of the singing and divine powers of swans, whom he describes as "the god's own minstrels," and the most musical of all birds that fly.[136]

Among the Latins, Cicero also emphasises that swans are birds of Apollo and pays tribute to their powers of divination: "Itaque commemorat ut cygni qui non sine causa Apollini dicati sint, sed quod ab eo divinationem habere videantur, qua provi-

[133] D'Arcy Thompson, *A Glossary of Greek Birds* (London, 1936), p. 184. This and Paulus Cassel. *Der Schwan in Sage und Leben* (Berlin, 1863), are the best treatments of the swan legend among the ancients.

[134] Jowett, *Works of Plato* (New York, 1936), p. 225.

[135] Aristophanes, *The Birds*, vs. 769.

[136] Callimachus, *Hymn IV*, vss. 249–250.

dentes quid in morte boni sit, cum cantu et voluptate moriantur." [137] That this eponymy was familiar to the members of the Pléiade is gathered from passages of the two leaders. Ronsard notes in the preface to the *Franciade* that swans are birds "dedicated to Phoebus Apollo," [138] and Du Bellay described them as "the sacred covey of Phoebus" in his *Vers lyriques*.[139] These are the principal writers who establish the Apollinic divinity of the swans. There are further references of this nature in Pindar, the *Homeric Hymns*, and Sappho.[140]

The low musical notes of the swan (the whistling swan or *cycnus musicus*), which it makes in flight either by singing or with its wings, were part of the poetic imagery of many of the ancients, although there were some doubters like Pliny and Claudian who denied that swans sang at all. The very earliest writers of Hellas, those whom the Pléiade called the second generation of Helladic bards, spoke of this phenomenon. Hesiod alludes to the loud cry of the high-soaring swans,[141] and the *Homeric Hymns* mention the singing of the swan as clear-toned (λίγ'ἀείδει).[142] Aeschylus, in his *Agamemnon*, compares a human being to a swan who has chanted her last strain, a dirge of death and now lies dead.[143] Apollonius of Rhodes, in his *Argonautica*, tells how the river banks echo with the notes of the swan's song.[144] And Polybius, in his histories, speaks of a swan's song as the plaintive plea of someone whose life or purpose is frustrated.[145]

The references in Latin literature are no less numerous. The sweetness of the swan's song is indicated by the "cycnea mele" of Lucretius.[146] Vergil employs the image in both the

[137] Cicero, *Tusculan Disput.* i, 30. This passage recalls the *Phaedo*.
[138] Ronsard, VII, 98.
[139] Du Bellay, III, 88.
[140] D'Arcy Thompson, *op. cit.*, p. 184.
[141] Hesiod, *Shield of Herakles* 316.
[142] *Homeric Hymns* xxi.
[143] Aeschylus, *Agamemnon*, vss. 1443–46.
[144] Apollonius of Rhodes, *Argonautica* iv, vss. 1300 ff.
[145] Polybius, *Histories* xxx, 12; (London, 1927), VI, 183.
[146] Lucretius, ii, 505; also, iii, 7; iv, 181, 545–546.

Eclogues and the *Aeneid*: "Cum sese a pastu referunt et longa canoros dant per colla modos, sonat amnis et Asia longe pulsa palus." [147] Others to record that the swan sang were Horace, Statius, Martial, and Ovid.[148] Ovid in the *Metamorphoses* relates that "carmina iam moriens canit exsequialia cygnus." [149]

Having established, then, the similarities between the swan and the sweet-singing poet, the ancients went one inevitable step further. This step is of especial interest to the student of the Pléiade. The ancients carried the analogy to the logical conclusion of calling their contemporaries swans, just as the poets of the Renaissance were to do later. Pindar, for example, becomes the "Dircaean swan" in Horace,[150] and the "Heliconian swan" in Christodorus.[151] A popular legend in ancient times relates that Socrates called the youthful Plato his swan.[152] Zeno was named *ὁ σοφὸς κύκνος* by Posidippus.[153] The likening of the swan, not to the poet, but to the aged poet specifically, proposed by Du Bellay in his *Poemata* (the piece "Ad Gordium"),[154] was also an image encountered in classical antiquity. It occurs in Horapollo [155] and in the *Hercules* of Euripides: "So will I raise the paean-lay, swan song of singer hoary grey." [156] Vergil is called by Christodorus *λιγύθροος κύκνος . . . φίλος Αὐσονίοισι*.[157] And just as the poet will immortalise his contemporaries in song, so will the swans render eternal glory to their friends. An interesting parallel is offered by a passage from the ninth eclogue of Vergil and one from the odes of Magny:

[147] *Aeneid* vii, 700.

[148] Horace, *Odes* ii, 20; Ovid, *Tristia* v, i, 11; Statius, *Silvae* ii, 4, 10; Martial, i, 53; xiii, 77.

[149] Ovid, *Metamorphoses* xiv, 430.

[150] Horace, *Odes* iv, 2, 25.

[151] Christodorus, *Ekphrasis* 382.

[152] Apuleius, *De Doctrina Plat.* i; (Paris, 1891), II, 170.

[153] Posidippus, *Epigrammata* v, 134.

[154] Du Bellay, *Poésies* (Paris: Garnier, 1918), I, 467.

[155] Horapollo, *Hieroglyphics* ii, 39.

[156] Euripides, *Hercules Mainomenos* (London: Heinemann, 1912), vss. 691–692.

[157] Christodorus, *Ekphrasis* 414.

Vare, tuum nomen. . . .
Cantantes sublime ferent ad sidera cycni.[158]

Car soubdain que ces sacrez Cygnes
Ont prins dans leurs bouches divines
Quelques uns des noms precieux
Ilz montent haut jusques aux cieux.[159]

It was a fundamental part of the Pléiade's creed of glory that they should render immortality unto those they celebrated in their verse, even as much as they rendered to themselves. That Vergil should speak of the swans as immortalising individuals of whom they sing was, so to speak, playing right into the hands of the Pléiade. To conclude our register, there was Horace, who spoke of himself as a swan; [160] and Lucretius, whom the Pléiade read but disagreed on, who adopted the same metaphor: "Parvus ut est cycni melior canor, ille gruum quam Clamor." [161]

We have proposed, then, three reasons why the poets were likened to swans. Swans were sacred to the god of poesy, Phoebus Apollo. They possessed sweet voices. They had powers of prophecy and communication with the gods,[162] just as we found the ancient poets themselves considered divine and theoleptic. There is yet another reason why poets, especially poets like those of the Pléiade, should be personifications of swans. This reason involves the swan's affinity with love, the greatest poetic inspiration. The bird was sacred not only to Apollo, but some later (Roman) phases of the swan legend linked it with the goddess of love and her son Eros. A competent treatment of this phase of the myth is to be found in *Der Schwan in Sage und Leben* of Paulus Cassel. Annotating

[158] *Eclogue* ix, vs. 27.
[159] Magny, *Odes*, *ed. cit.*, I, 97.
[160] Horace, *Odes* ii, 20.
[161] Lucretius, iv, 181–182.
[162] This prophetic power of the swans as regards their own death is recorded by Rabelais (III, 21), who voices the opinion that until they see death approaching, they never sing. He likens them to prophetic poets.

his statements with references to the standard Latin authors, Cassel concludes:

Darum sind es römische Dichter, die Venus mit Schwänen besingen; und Horaz verleiht ihr unter den Ersten das Gespann der glänzenden Vögel. Mannigfaltig stellen auch Kunstwerke dies dar. Auf einem römischen Amethyst fährt Eros mit Schwänen. Auf einem Gemälde, das Philostratus schildert, halten die Liebesgötter mit Schwänen ein Wettrennen, *etc.*[163]

To quote only a few instances, there is the statement of Ovid that swans draw the cart of Venus,[164] the declaration of Statius in the *Silvae* that "molles agitat Venus aurea cycnos," [165] and two mentions of this affinity in Horace.[166]

⚜ ⚜ ⚜

The Pléiade applied the Swan epithet to the ancients less frequently than they applied it to their contemporaries. Pindar is pictured by Du Bellay as a swan soaring high in the empyrean, looking down upon the clouds beneath him. This is an interesting passage, for it illustrates how the image was coordinated with the Pléiade's ideas on poetic altitude, that is, lofty as opposed to low (*rampant*) style. The poet, as Plato had written, was a winged thing, soaring above his fellow mortals. This is perhaps a reason for the ancients' considering poets in the image of bees and swans. In the reference of Du Bellay, it is apparently to Pindar metamorphosed into a swan rather than to the human Pindar that Du Bellay alludes,

Où est celuy qui tant s'abuse
De cuider encores voler
Où par régions incongnues,

[163] P. Cassel, *Der Schwan in Sage und Leben* (Berlin, 1863), p. 4.
[164] Ovid, *Ars Amatoria* iii, 809–810, and *Metamorphoses* x, 708.
[165] Statius, *Silvae* iii, 4, 22.
[166] Horace, *Carm.* iii, 28, and iv, 1. See also Kalkmann, *Aphrodite auf dem Schwan*, Jb. d. k. d. Arch. Inst., I (1886).

Le cygne Thébain si souvent
Dessoubs luy regarde les nues.[167]

Horace, too, is viewed as having undergone metempsychosis and as soaring about heaven as a swan.[168] This soaring about, this meteorisis, naturally became a goal and a reward to which the Pléiade poets themselves aspired. Du Bellay, for example, expresses such a hope in his *Sonnets à la Royne de Navarre*:

C'est maintenant (ô Carles) que mes vers
Egaleront l'une et l'autre buccine:
C'est maintenant que transformé en cygne
Je voleray par ce grand univers.[169]

And Ronsard augured such a metamorphosis in his tutor Jean Dorat:

Tu fus en ton vivant des Muses le soustien:
Et pour ce après ta mort tu deviendras un Cygne.[170]

Completing the register of ancients viewed as swans, one might add that both Passerat and Vauquelin called Vergil the "swan of Mantua," Vauquelin also baptising him the "Ausonian swan." [171]

This conception of the Greek and Roman authors as swans engendered a picturesque trope of imitation which has failed to be recorded in the textbooks on the Pléiade. The basis of the image is in the fact that quills from swans' feathers were used as pens, that the word "plume" had the double meaning of pen and feather. Thus, when one wrote with the plume of a classical swan, one was imitating that classical author. This mimetic procedure is first mentioned in the second preface to the *Olive*, where Du Bellay includes both the ancients and

[167] Du Bellay, III, 98.
[168] Ronsard, VI, 157.
[169] Du Bellay, II, 231.
[170] Ronsard, I, 140.
[171] Passerat, *Poésies* (Paris, 1880), I, 59; Vauquelin, *ed. cit.*, pp. 57, 80. Du Bartas, in his *Uranie* (verse 129) speaks of the psalmodists of the Bible as "hundreds of swans."

the Italians as swans to be imitated: "des anciens Romains et des modernes Italiens, leur arrachant ces belles plumes empruntées dont ilz volent si haultement, ilz seroient en hazard d'estre accoutrez en corneille Horacienne." [172] A second reference to this type of imitation is contained in Sébilet's *Art poétique*, where the ancients are described as "the Swans from whose wings one plucks the quills with which one writes correctly." [173]

Among these "modern Italians" identified with swans, it was Petrarch especially whom Du Bellay was classing with the ancients. In his "Complainte du désespéré," Du Bellay calls Petrarch the "beautiful swan of Florence." [174] In an elegy, Ronsard characterises him as "that Florentine who as a swan surmounted Destiny." [175] His good friend, Del Bene, Ronsard calls "second Cygne après le Florentin qui de près suit son vol et sa vois." [176]

Many are the Pléiade's references to living poets as swans, not poets transformed into swans by Pythagorean metempsychosis, of course, but poets possessing cygneous characteristics during their natural lifetimes. Du Bellay referred to his friends as "the new swans who are now singing throughout France." [177] On Du Bellay's return from Italy, Jean Dorat penned him an affectionate Latin welcome, hoping that Joachim would compose French verse, after rivaling the ancients with his poemata: "Idcirco patria est oblitus carmina voce cantare, emeritus qualia cantat olor." [178] In what is evidently his only reference to English literature, Ronsard predicts that one day many swans, white swans, will gather on the shores of the Thames to sing the glories of the royal family.[179]

[172] Du Bellay, I, 19.
[173] Sébilet, Gaiffe edition, p. 28.
[174] Du Bellay, IV, 90.
[175] Ronsard, IV, 104.
[176] *Ibid.*, VI, 26.
[177] Du Bellay, IV, 51.
[178] H. Chamard, *Joachim du Bellay* (Lille, 1900), p. 389; image found also in Vauquelin, *Art poétique*, *ed. cit.*, p. 30.
[179] Ronsard, III, 249.

An interesting phenomenon which becomes apparent at this point is the prevalence of the term "new swan" applied by these poets to their contemporaries. In the previous paragraph we have found it used by Du Bellay. We shall first record its many occurrences and then investigate its meaning. In the *Olive*, Du Bellay overcomes his earlier reserve regarding Scève and calls him "new Swan, who soars singing from the warm river bank to the cold hyperborean regions."[180] Ronsard's fondness for this epithet was such that he applies it to himself in at least four places.[181] Du Bellay, half as modest, applies it to himself only twice.[182] Ronsard describes Magny as a new swan in 1553,[183] and Magny himself, in a passage reminiscent of Du Bellay's use of the expression (note 177), celebrates in his *Gayetez* the new swans winging to immortality.[184] The significance of this expression becomes clear when it is contrasted with the *vieils Cygnes* mentioned in the introduction of the *Franciade*.[185] The Old Swans are merely the renowned Greek and Roman and Trecento Italian poets. The New Swans are their spiritual descendants, those who pattern their verse on the classical models. But the word *nouveau* implies the whole revival of culture and enthusiasm implicit in the word Renaissance itself. The Pléiade writers were conscious of the fact that they were living in a Renaissance, even though the word itself did not occur to them as it did to Vasari in Italy, speaking of the *rinascita* in his country. This time-consciousness on the part of the Pléiade tends to support the Burckhardt rather than the Burdach theory of the Renaissance. Just as the sixteenth century marked the beginnings of geographical nationalism, it also engendered a sort of chronological nationalism, if you allow the expression. The idea of

[180] Du Bellay, I, 116.
[181] Ronsard, I, 42; III, 349; IV, 304; VI, 86.
[182] Du Bellay, II, 201; IV, 53.
[183] Ronsard, VI, 395.
[184] Magny, *Gayetez*, ed. by Courbet, p. 92.
[185] Ronsard, VII, 98.

spiritual awakening which *nouveau* carries is discerned in Magny's piece commemorating the birth of Princess Marguerite (1553), where the poet invokes the "nouveaus Cynes,"

> Metez à part Homère pour un peu,
> Vous enflammant d'un autre *nouveau* feu,

and concludes that he is going to celebrate the honor, welfare, and fame of the new princess "d'une *nouvelle* trompe." [186]

As there are many other references to contemporary poets as swans,[187] we shall select only a few more of particular interest. In a disconsolate sonnet written from Rome (presumably to Ronsard, according to Chamard), Du Bellay likens himself, Panjas, and Magny to three swans lamenting their approaching death. This is one of the few references where the image has undertones of imminent death, and one of the few where the swan's song is pictured as melancholy.[188] Most of the Pléiade accepted Plato's contention that it was a joyful song.

A picturesque variant of this image is encountered in sonnet CXV of the *Olive*, where Du Bellay is marveling at the virtuosity of his colleague Ronsard:

> Quel cigne encor' des cignes le plus beau
> Te prêta l'aele? et quel vent jusqu'aux cieulx
> Te balança le vol audacieux,
> Sans que la mer te fust large tombeau? [189]

Not all of the references to these wings of the poet mention specifically that they are swan's wings. In the works of Du Bellay, there are several instances of the poet's soaring into space which are quite evidently part of the swan motif.[190]

[186] Magny, *Dernières poésies*, ed. by Courbet, pp. 4, 12, 13.

[187] Du Bellay, I, 33; Ronsard, I, 72, 323; Magny, I, 109; also *Gayetez*, p. 81; *etc.*

[188] Quoted in H. Chamard, *Joachim du Bellay* (Lille, 1900), p. 351.

[189] Du Bellay, I, 124.

[190] See R. V. Merrill, *Platonism of Joachim du Bellay* (Chicago, 1925), pp. 87–89, for a discussion of these "wings."

As we have remarked above, Horapollo and Euripides both adopted the swan image to apply, not to all poets in general, but to aged poets particularly. That an ageing author's white hair might be compared to the white plumage of the swan was proposed again in the poemata of Du Bellay, in the piece with the cheery title, "Ad Gordium, ut laetus vivat":

> Iam mea Cygnaeis sparguntur tempora plumis,
> Inficit & flavas cana senecta comas.
> Sic nobis perit ante diem decus omne iuventae,
> Et faciunt septem lustra peracta senem.
> Quis Deus hoc, Gordi? num formam vertit Apollo,
> Et Cygnum vatem sic iubet esse suum? [191]

Whereupon he describes poets as the sweet brood of the Muses ("dulces foetus Musarum") and concludes with the contrast of swans and crows:

> Hinc mihi canities, Gordi, & properata senectus,
> Hinc iuveni frontem ruga senilis arat.
> Vive igitur laetus, ne te quoque noxia cura
> Efficiat Cygnum, qui modo Corvus eras.

The two birds of inferior song with whom the Pléiade confronted their swans were crows and geese. But in each of these contrasts they were merely following the pattern established by the classic poets. Vergil, Martial, and Propertius all contrasted the sweet notes of the swan to the raucous honking of the goose or jay.[192] Martial carried this same contrast to the crow, to the obvious advantage of the swan, of course.[193]

In a canto of the *Orlando Furioso* familiar to most of the Pléiade, good poets were likened to swans who bestow immortality, and poetasters to crows and vultures, whose songs are as short-lived as they themselves. With a Horatian haughtiness which must have pleased the Pléiade, Ariosto had concluded that "Son, come i cigni, anco i poeti rari, poeti che non sian

[191] Du Bellay, *Poésies françaises et latines* (Paris: Garnier, 1918), I, 467.
[192] Vergil, *Eclogues* ix, 35; Martial, i, 53; Propertius, II, xxxiv, 83.
[193] Martial, i, 53.

del nome indegni," and that poetasters, like crows, are unfortunately found in abundance.[194] It is quite conceivable that the Pléiade's adoption of the swan-crow contrast may be traced to Ariosto, as Miss Cameron surmises,[195] but one must not forget that the Pléiade had ample opportunity to learn this contrast from classical literature as well.

One of the earliest appearances of this image in sixteenth-century France was in Marot's epistle purportedly composed by Fripelipes. The worthy Fripelipes is not content to brand Sagon and other adversaries of Marot with the stinging sobriquet of geese. To diminish their stature further, he calls them goslings.[196]

This contrast with geese and crows made numerous appearances in the Pléiade's works. In the "Chant en faveur de quelques excellens poëtes" of 1551, Tyard reassures his friends that the future will bring them eternal kudos after the noise of the jealous crows has long since died away.[197] Du Bellay, in his second preface to the *Olive* (1550), retells the circumstances of the composition of the *Deffence* and states that his purpose has been to rouse the swans from their overlong silence and to hush the importunate croaking of the crows.[198] Rémy Belleau, too, warns these crows, or slanderous rhymers, that sweet singers like Nicolas Denisot have a certain divinity, and advises the former to seek prey elsewhere.[199] Both Jacques Grévin and Ronsard describe the poetasters as unwanted crows crowding into the temple of Minerva.[200] We have already noted how Ronsard, like Henri Becque, employed the term crow with the meaning of plundering hypocrite in the *Bocage royal*.[201] Du

[194] *Orlando Furioso*, XXXV, 23.

[195] Alice Cameron, *Influence of Ariosto on Ronsard and his Group* (Baltimore, 1930), p. xvi.

[196] Clément Marot, *Fripelipes, valet de Marot, à Sagon* (1537).

[197] Pontus de Tyard, M.-L., pp. 122–123.

[198] Du Bellay, I, 14–15.

[199] Belleau, M.-L., II, 453.

[200] Grévin, ed. by Pinvert (Paris: Garnier, 1922), p. 220; Ronsard, IV, 153.

[201] Ronsard, VII, 382.

Bellay, in a moment of humility, wonders how he, a mere Crow, dare hope to sing with the beauty of a Swan like Petrarch. This sonnet of the *Amours*, probably composed about 1559, is a fairly late manifestation of the cult of Petrarch.[202] But no such self-effacement is found in Joachim's "Contre les envieux poètes." These enemies he characterised as a "thousand envious crows, come from the bank of oblivion and the hot Moorish strand" to trouble the swans of France.[203] This passage was obviously inspired by Ariosto, as was the description of Lethe in the *Vers lyriques*. [204] Here again he pictures the black flock of crows hovering over the swans and compares himself to one of the swans.[205] In his "Aux dames Angevines," Du Bellay gives the contrast a gallant turn. Recalling the Querelle des Femmes, he calls such misogynists as Gratien du Pont crows and adds that he himself is a swan whose plumage is turning white as that of the birds of Apollo.[206] For the edification of Diane de Poitiers, he distinguishes such swans as himself from greedy crows.[207] In his introduction to the *Franciade*, Ronsard cautions his friends against composing Latin verse. No matter how well you may write, it will seem no more than the cry of a goose; you cannot possibly aspire to the golden notes of the swans of Apollo, the classic poets.[208] Macrin also compares raucous geese with the "Apollineos olores" in his Latin ode on Du Bellay's *Olive*.[209] Baïf lends some variety to this figure by contrasting harmonious swans with "geays criards" in one of his eclogues.[210] Olivier de Magny

[202] Du Bellay, II, 241.

[203] *Ibid.*, IV, 51.

[204] *Ibid.*, III, 88.

[205] The crowd of new poets beginning to write in France were also branded as crows in his poem, "In turbam poetarum Gallicè scribentium," Garnier edition, I, 460.

[206] Du Bellay, IV, 38–39.

[207] *Ibid.*, V, 372.

[208] Ronsard, VII, 98. To Du Bartas, great poets were nightingales, and poor rimers became crows and frogs (1584 "Avertissement sur sa première et seconde Semaine").

[209] Du Bellay, I, 5.

[210] Baïf, M.-L., III, 23.

borrows copiously from the allegory of the swans and crows in the *Orlando Furioso*, without mentioning Ariosto, in his "Ode à Jean Bertrand, en faveur de Pierre de Paschal."[211] This, to illustrate again the *locus communis* of the Pléiade that the swan-poet wins everlasting glory for those whom he celebrates in song.[212]

In sum, we have noted numerous and varied reasons why the swan rather than the nightingale or some other melodious bird was chosen as the symbol of the poet. The reasons we have cited were not original lucubrations of the Pléiade, but dated from classical antiquity. Beyond those which were actually set down by the ancients, there may have been further contributory explanations such as the swan's dignity, gravity, beauty, and perhaps even his ivory-tower attitude about society. Heine once wrote that the swan, like the soul of the poet, is misunderstood by the insensate world. However, the paramount reason for the selection of the swan was that he sang sweet songs and that the poet emulated him by creating a melodic sweetness. This was one of the principal functions of poetry and was a strictly hedonistic one. And since the swan has no utilitarian incentive or purpose in his singing, since his unique aim is to create sheer beauty (for such the swan's song was held to be), this should also be the exclusive purpose of the lyrist.

⚜ ⚜ ⚜

That the sweetness and productivity of the poet are akin to those of the bee is a notion which the Pléiade discovered in the classics and which they adapted to their own use. Not only in the familiar "Hylas" of Ronsard, but throughout the

[211] Magny, *ed. cit.*, I, 97–98.

[212] W. B. Cornelia, *Classical Sources of the Nature References in Ronsard's Poetry* (New York, 1934) includes one reference by Ronsard to the swan song, p. 158, and three references of this poet to honey as eloquence, p. 162.

works of the Pléiade one encounters the image of the poet as a bee creating mellifluous harmonies. The ancients held that bees had three functions or characteristics in common with the poets. As will be shown, the Renaissance theorists accepted these three, but added three more of their own. We have already pointed out on several occasions that the Pléiade poets set out to exhaust all conceivable possibilities of any imagery or conceits they adopted.

From antiquity, the foremost and most obvious reason for this analogy is that both bee and bard create a superlative sweetness. Each culls the beauties of nature. That the human voice was early compared to honey is shown by the use of μελίφωνος by Sappho [213] and μελίφθογγος by Pindar. The second reason for the analogy is that poets cull and store ideas in the manner of the honey-bee. The third reason embraces the fact that bees were considered sacred to the Muses, being identified by some with the Muses themselves.

Reviewing the reasoning of the ancients, one may start with Aristophanes's statement in the *Birds* (vs. 750) that a honeyed sweetness likens the poet to a bee. "There it was that, just like a bee, Phrynicus would go and cull the ambrosia of his verses." But the most significant passage is in the *Ion*, where Socrates discusses poetic inspiration and says of competent writers:

For all good poets, epic as well as lyric, compose their beautiful poems not as works of art, but because they are inspired and possessed. And as Corybantian revellers when they dance are not in their right mind, so the lyric poets are not in their right mind when they are composing their beautiful strains: but when falling under the power of music and metre they are inspired and possessed; like Bacchic maidens who draw milk and honey from the rivers, when they are under the influence of Dionysus, but not when they are in their right mind. And the soul of the lyric poet does the same, as they themselves tell us; for they tell us that they gather their strains from honeyed fountains out of the gardens and dells of the Muses; thither,

[213] Sappho, *Lyrica* 195.

like bees, they wing their way. . . . For the poet is a light and winged and holy thing.[214]

Theocritus, whom the Pléiade knew and imitated, has two references of this order in his epigrams. In the one he states that singing is to the ear as honey to the lip; [215] in the other, that the voice issuing from the singer's mouth is as sweet as honeycomb.[216] The comparison between μέλι and μέλος was not, then, uncommon among the Greeks.[217] Its imaginative possibilities were not lost to Hebrew literature, a literature of rich imagery. Typical is the Vulgate text from the *Liber Psalmorum*, "Quam dulcia faucibus meis eloquia tua, super mel ori meo." [218]

Among the Romans it had become traditional that poetry and eloquence embodied honeyed sweetness. Cicero, for example, employs the image in his *De Senectute* (X): "ex eius lingua melle dulcior fluebat oratio." And Ciceronian eloquence itself is called "mel Tullianum" by later Latins.[219] Just as the Greeks applied the word bee to the poet directly,[220] so one finds Horace describing himself as "ego, apis Matinae." [221] Claudian defines poets as pious bees of the mount of Helicon.[222] Of his own creations Lucretius writes,

> Floriferis ut apes in saltibus omnia libant,
> Omnia nos itidem depascimur aurea dicta,
> Aurea, perpetua semper dignissima vita.[223]

The second facet of the ancient analogy between bard and bee concerns the process of imitation which the culling action

[214] Plato, *Ion*, Jowett translation (New York, 1936), V, i, 533d.
[215] Theocritus, *Epigrams* (London: Heinemann, 1928), p. 119.
[216] *Ibid.*, p. 241.
[217] For the mythology of the bee in Greek and Roman times, see W. Robert-Tornow, *De Apium mellisque apud veteres* (Berlin, 1893). The passages quoted are most interesting, although bibliographical indications are occasionally incorrect.
[218] *Liber Psalmorum* 119: 103.
[219] Symmachus, *Epistolae* I, 25.
[220] Anthologia Palatina (Jacobs) 580.
[221] Horace, *Odes* iv, 2, 27.
[222] Claudian, *Laus Serenae*, vss. 9–10.
[223] Lucretius iii, 11–13.

represents. Although this resemblance is hinted in the *Ion*, it is best expressed by Seneca. The Roman author says that one must neither read all the time nor write all the time. It is better to commerge the two pursuits, so that the best fruits of the reading may be reproduced by the pen. "We should follow, men say, the example of the bees, who flit about and cull the flowers that are suitable for producing honey, and then arrange and assort in their cells all they have brought in." [224] Needless to say, this mimetic idea was to catch the fancy of the Pléiade.

The third facet of the honey-bee legend in antiquity pertains to the bee's particular vocation as minister to the Muses. Hesiod, in the *Theogony*, termed honey the liquid of the Muses.[225] Varro wrote that bees "musarum esse dicuntur volucres, quod et, si quando displicatae sunt, cymbalis et plausibus numero redducunt in locum unum." [226] Trimalchio, in Petronius, calls bees "divinae bestiae." [227] The passages in classic literature which recall the divinity of bees are legion.[228] Of even greater interest are those texts which identify the bees with the Muses themselves. In his *Deipnosophists*, for example, Athenaeus describes the *μέλεα μελιπτέρωτα* Μουσᾶν.[229] Thus, in his historical study of the bee, Robert-Tornow was able to conclude that the bees were finally viewed as both Muses and poets. "Apes igitur sapientes, Musarum volucres, vel Musae ipsae, pueris, ut philosophi, vel poetae fierent, mel eloquentiae artisque poeticae instillare putabantur." [230] It is interesting to

[224] Seneca, *Epist. ad Luc.* lxxxiv, 2–3, English translation from Loeb edition (London: Heinemann, 1920), p. 277.

[225] Lenz shows that the classics believed bees to be both "Demeter's Sonderngeschöpfe" and the "Vögel der Musen" in *Zoologie der alten Griechen und Römer*, quoted in Folklore Fellows, XXVIII (1928), pp. 29–30. Hesiod, *Theogony*, vss. 81, 83, 84, 86.

[226] Varro, *De Re Rustica* 16, 7.

[227] Petronius, *Satyricon* 56.

[228] Vergil, *Georgics* iv, 64, 150 ff.; Ovid *Fasti* iii, 741–762; Lucan, *Bell. Civ.* ix, 283–292; Pliny, *Historia Naturalis* xi, 22.

[229] Athenaeus, *Deipnosophists* (Cambridge, U. S. A., 1937), vi, 415.

[230] W. Robert-Tornow, *op. cit.*, p. 105.

note that it was not only their sweetness, but their wisdom as well which earned the poets this double distinction.

We have discerned in these paragraphs that there were three reasons why the ancients likened bees to poets. These were their common sweetness, mimetic activity, and inspired divinity. The additional reasons which the Pléiade poets were to contribute were quite simple.

One merely proposed that bard and bee sing a song, and more particularly, a sweet song. Witness a couplet in the *Passetemps* of Baïf, pointing out how "les ménagères avètes font ça et là un doux bruit." [231] A second reason for the trope was that poets were as industrious at their trade as bees. We have noted how the Pléiade translated the *utile* of Horace as industrious. When the Pléiade treated of the industrious bees, then, it was attributing to them both the *utile* and the *dulce*. Baïf, in his *Poèmes*, likens himself to an industrious bee: "Moy laborieux je volète comme une industrieuse avète." [232] This combination of sweetness and industry is again ascribed to the bee, and to himself, by Baïf in the *Amours de Méline*:

> J'ay sucé la fleur doucète
> Du buissonnier chèvre-fueil
> Et de la soigneuse avète
> Le laborieux recueil.[233]

Vauquelin de la Fresnaye ventures still another reason why poets are like bees. This is the very reason for which swans were sometimes likened to poets, and arises from their relations with love. The passage is doubly interesting for the image of sweetness it contains:

> L'Avette, pour aimer la douceur savoureuse
> De toute plante douce, est tousjours amoureuse:
> L'homme aussi de luy mesme estant ingénieux
> Aime, embrasse et chérit tout œuvre industrieux.[234]

[231] Baïf, M.-L., IV, 211.
[232] *Ibid.*, II, 351.
[233] *Ibid.*, I, 60.
[234] Vauquelin, *Art poétique*, Pellissier edition, p. 69.

Earlier, Ronsard had twice written of bees kissing roses,[235] and Passerat had drawn an unmistakable parallel between the bee and the ravishing lover; the analogy between the soft-speaking lover and the amoristic poet is clear:

> Comme on vit l'Abeilole murmurer
> Autour du Thym qu'elle vient défleurer.

⚜ ⚜ ⚜

With these various aspects of the bee motif in mind, one may proceed to the observations of the Pléiade on individual writers. A few of these, like the selections from Baïf quoted immediately above, are autodiagnostic; the writer discerns one or several of these apian characteristics in himself.

Ronsard twice refers to himself as a bee, since he culls from ancient writers and produces new sweetness. The dates of these admissions are 1556 and 1569. The "Hylas" is the better known of these two pieces, in so far as the bee imagery is concerned, but it was published thirteen years after the "Épistre à Charles Cardinal de Lorraine," which opened the second book of the *Hymnes*. In a passage of the latter poem very evidently derived from the *Ion*, Ronsard announces that the nine Muses will admit him into their grottoes and valleys ("gardens and dells" in Plato), where he will learn the art of poetry and "choisir, ravir, et desrober" the beauty which he finds there:

> Tout ainsi que l'abeille, animal né du ciel,
> Choisist les belles fleurs pour en faire du miel,
> Honorant son logis de ces liqueurs infuses:
> Ainsy je choisiray les belles fleurs des Muses
> A fin d'en esmailler un livre en vostre nom.[236]

The exordium of the "Hylas" is very similar to this, but is

[235] Ronsard, III, 359; 370.
[236] *Ibid.*, VI, 296.

more specific and detailed about the actual borrowing from classic authors:

> Mon Passerat, je resemble à l'abeille
> Qui va cueillant tantost la fleur vermeille,
> Tantost la jaune: errant de pré en pré
> Où plus les fleurs fleurissent à son gré,
> Contre l'Hyver amassant force vivres.
> Ainsi lisant et fueilletant mes livres,
> J'amasse, trie et choisis le plus beau,
> Qu'en cent couleurs je peints en un tableau.[237]

No mention is made here of sweetness. Sweetness had earlier been explicit in this concept, but by now was barely implicit. We believe, nevertheless, that there was a transfer of imagery, and that the bee existed as an image of sweetness before it became the image of imitation in the Pléiade's imagination. Supporting this contention are the numerous references to the honeyed sweetness of authors in the Pléiade's poetry composed before 1556.

This classic trope of imitation based upon apiculture made a deep impression not only upon the Pléiade, but on their Italian contemporaries as well. In his study of plagiarism and imitation, Professor Bullock shows that Minturno, Cammillo, and others had adopted it in their treatises.[238]

Others than Ronsard were struck by the beauty of this trope identifying verses and flowers, the trope which gave us our English word "posy" from "poesy." In his *Dernières poésies*, Magny addresses a sonnet to the king telling how he has learned to "gather the flowers of the most accomplished Greeks" and imitate from them.[239] Belleau begins a sonnet "Au Sieur Salomon," "Ainsi tu vas triant au jardin des neuf sœurs d'industrieuse main, les mieux fleurantes fleurs, pour te ceindre le front d'une couronne torte."[240] Ronsard, however, remained the

[237] *Ibid.*, V, 132.

[238] W. L. Bullock, "Precept of Plagiarism in the Cinquecento," *Modern Philology*, XXV (1928), 307.

[239] Magny, *Dernières poésies*, ed. by Courbet, p. 2.

[240] Belleau, M.-L., I, 162–163.

fondest of this image. Ronsard it was who called poesy a "vast multicolored field of flowers" and a "meadow all spangled with flowers." [241] Similarly inspired by the *Ion*, and perhaps a penchant for punning as well, is the bucolic picture of Simon Bouquet in the garden of the Muses, selecting the choicest poems.[242]

This figure was applied even to musical compositions and to translations. Ronsard illustrates by the example of the musician Orlando di Lasso (Lassus) that the mimetic processes adopted by the poet can be identical with those of the musician. Orlando is said to have culled the beautiful flowers of the ancients, like a "mouche à miel," to compose his divine harmonies.[243] Morel calls upon the figure to praise Du Bellay, not as a creative poet, but rather as a translator of selections from the *Aeneid*. Recalling Hybla, the ancient town of Sicily famous for its apiaries, Morel pens:

> Comme lon voit l'abeille industrieuse
> Aux champs d'Hybla sucer de mainte fleur
> L'emmiellée et celeste liqueur,
> Dont nous succrons l'amertume odieuse.
> Telle est aussi la Muse ingénieuse
> Du doulx-utile Angevin translateur,
> Qui ses thésors tirez de maint aucteur
> Nous jecte icy d'une main planteureuse.[244]

How this culling was performed upon the Greek classics is the burden of Jamyn's remarks upon the composition and argument of Ronsard's *Franciade*.[245] Jamyn writes that Ronsard derived the early part of his epic from Homer, Vergil, and Apollonius of Rhodes. By extracting his honey from many flowers he is not indebted to any single one, but to all in general. These observations of Jamyn are apparently a paraphrase of the "Hylas." Once again one perceives what a fine line of distinction existed between creation and imitation.

[241] Ronsard, VI, 42; 326.
[242] *Ibid.*, VI, 425.
[243] *Ibid.*, VII, 20.
[244] Du Bellay, VI, 245.
[245] Ronsard, III, 3.

IV. PIERRE DE RONSARD

Poème & Poésie ont grande différence.
Poésie est un pré de diverse apparence,
Orgueilleux de ses biens, & riche de ses fleurs,
Diapré, peinturé de cent mille couleurs. . . .

(see page 170)

Sébilet, by the way, approved of all this culling. He opined that it enriched the language, but his *Art poétique* infers that all such borrowings should be of sweet words exclusively. Let the future poet pattern himself after the "mouche à miel," which will never alight on thorns or nettles when he can find thyme. As long as the poet encounters sweet words to cull, let him eschew the harsh and the bitter.[246]

Let us turn now to the Pléiade's remarks upon the mellifluence of the writers of Hellas. The Hellenic sweetness which the Renaissance was endeavoring to recapture became known as "Attic honey." Before listing references to individual writers centering upon the honey-bee conceit, we shall note how popular this expression became. In his *Dernières poésies*, Magny says that the writings of François de Revergat "drip with Attic honey." [247] This is the very tribute which Du Bellay paid Magny and De Mesmes.[248] Ronsard lists such varied possessors of "miel attic" as Demosthenes, Michel de l'Hospital, the neo-Latin Secundus, and the Muses in as many poems.[249] Passerat employs the phrase "attique miel" in two different works.[250] A variant of this expression, "Hymettian honey," from Mount Hymettus south of Athens, was used by Ronsard in the first book of *Hymnes*, the second of the *Amours*, and a posthumous sonnet to D'Urfé.[251] Although the expressions "Attic wit" and "Attic salt" are more familiar to us, the meaning of "Attic honey" is clear. It meant refined, simple, dignified, lyrical sweetness.

We have already found Demosthenes mentioned as an embodiment of Hellenic sweetness. Another was the philosopher Plato, and Du Bellay repeats the old myth about the bees foretelling Plato's great eloquence by swarming at his lips as

[246] Gaiffe edition, p. 30.
[247] Magny, *Dernières poésies*, *ed. cit.*, p. 53.
[248] Du Bellay V, 65; 263.
[249] Ronsard, STFM, V, 186; Laumonier-Lemerre edition, II, 120, 146, 422.
[250] Passerat, *ed. cit.*, I, 96; 189.
[251] Ronsard, I, 140; VI, 455; VIII, 94.

he lay in his crib.[252] A third Greek possessing this merit was Socrates. Ronsard praises both Socrates and his own contemporary Jean Belot in the same breath in "La lyre":

> Lors de ta voix distile l'eloquence
> Un vray Socrate, & ton docte parler
> Fait le doux miel de tes lèvres couler. . . .[253]

Pontus de Tyard decides that, among the Latins, Catullus expressed this Hellenic sweetness, a quality he is pleased to discern also in the *Méline* of Jean-Antoine de Baïf, a pun on *mel* and *Méline*. In fact, Baïf "renders even more honeyed the spirit of Catullus." [254] Belleau's ode congratulating Jamot on his translation of Demetrius provides another instance where the bee conceit is applied to translations as though they were creative works embodying style and ornamentation. Belleau praises his friend for having culled from the Attic flowers honey "that the Greek bee stored for the French mouth." [255]

The remarks on the honeyed qualities of their contemporaries are more frequent than those on ancient writers, thanks to the Pléiade's penchant for solicitous adulation. Poets could spread honey as well as store it. Tyard congratulated "Quelques excellens poètes de ce temps" for having bestrewn their honeyed sweetness not only throughout the courts of princes, but over the entire world as well.[256] Baïf recorded that the mouth of D'Asserac brimmed over with honey, liquid of the goddess of Persuasion.[257] Jean de la Péruse holds that Buchanan's song distills a style sweeter than honey.[258] Ronsard pays the same tribute to the chronicles of Macé.[259] And Du Bellay praises Ronsard in like wise, succumbing like the rest to the temptation

[252] Du Bellay, III, 136.
[253] Ronsard, V, 50.
[254] Pontus de Tyard, M.-L., 105.
[255] Belleau, M.-L., II, 463.
[256] Pontus de Tyard, M.-L., 122.
[257] Baïf, M.-L., II, 316.
[258] La Péruse, *Poésies* (Angoulême, 1866), p. 119.
[259] Ronsard, STFM, I, 267.

to rhyme *ciel* with *miel*,[260] a recidivism apparent also in his greeting to

> Héroët aux vers héroïques,
> (Subject vrayment digne du ciel)
> Qui en doulceur passent le miel,
> En gravité les fronts Stoiques.[261]

Toying with the idea of metempsychosis he had found in Pythagoras, Ronsard is not satisfied merely to state that Dorat's sweetness surpassed Hymettus. He further predicts to his old master,

> Tu deviendras Cigalle ou Mousche Limousine
> Qui fait un miel plus doux que n'est l'Hymettian;[262]

and in a questionable outburst of enthusiasm, adds that after Dorat's death the old pedagogue will become a beautiful pentamorphic being composed of a voice, swan, grasshopper, bee, and bird.

The idea of honey in the mouth, apparently derived from the legend of the bees circling the newborn Plato's lips, became common in the Renaissance, as these examples show. In the "Voyage d'Hercueil," Ronsard falls back on it to praise the singing of Dorat; in his *Hymnes*, he applies it to De l'Hospital.[263] In the "Hymne des astres," Ronsard identifies Mellin de Saint-Gelays with Plato and relates once again the cradle story. That Mellin should be chosen as the bee-mouthed duplicate of Plato proves of what inordinate flattery the Pléiade poets were capable. It is true, of course, that the name Mellin made some sort of analogy with honey inevitable.[264] These poets were never averse to indulging in a good pun, or even a bad one. Such a play on the name Mellin is encountered in Du Bellay's *Vers lyriques*, where Saint-Gelays's verses and his name are found sweet as the nectar of the Muses.[265] In sonnet

[260] Du Bellay, IV, 44.
[261] *Ibid.*, III, 136.
[262] Ronsard, I, 140.
[263] *Ibid.*, V, 225; IV, 245.
[264] *Ibid.*, VI, 276.
[265] Du Bellay, III, 93.

CXV of the *Olive*, Du Bellay pays homage to Ronsard in one of his finest inspirations. Borrowing three comparisons from external nature, he congratulates his colleague on the fluidity, the force, and the sweetness of his lyrics:

> De quel rocher vint l'éternelle source,
> De quel torrent vint la superbe course,
> De quele fleur vint le miel de tes vers? [266]

These passages summarise the adaptations of the honey-bee image as they occur in the Pléiade's works. Occasionally attaining beauty, particularly when they describe the garden or bower of the Muses, they often tend to become commonplace and repetitious. As they did with so many of these tropes, the Pléiade adopted this one with their customary immoderation. They did give evidence of some originality, however, in contributing three new reasons for identifying poets with bees. And when they borrowed this image from the ancients, in other words, when they culled the gardens of the past, they were only seconding precept with practice.

Looking back, then, we note that both bee and swan symbolised the literary artist in ancient times, but the image of the bee was not so directly arrived at as was that of the swan. The swan was a direct and dignified embodiment of a singer. The bee merely happened to become the symbol of the poet because of the universal cliché that sweet eloquence resembled nothing so much as honey. This notion was so widespread in the Renaissance that its reappearances were as frequent as in classic literature. In England, for example, Shakespeare was writing, "But for your words, they rob the Hybla bees and leave them honeyless," and Edmund Spenser was penning, "And when she spake, sweete words, like dripping honey, did she shed." These examples could be multiplied many times from contemporary authors in England and the other European countries. Once this basis for the bee image was established,

[266] *Ibid.*, I, 124.

both the ancients and the Pléiade supplied other similarities between poets and bees. But the basic reason remained that the bees and poets created sweetness. We are again dealing with a terminology of sweetness. We are back in the realm of the hedonistic function of literature.

⚜ ⚜ ⚜

The most original of the Pléiade's poetic images involving sweetness was that of distillation, *alambiquage*. It was apparently a distinct contribution to which the Pléiade held the first copyright. For the semantic values they gave the word "distillation" they were not indebted to the grammarians and critics of classical antiquity. The meaning which they gave it was to be corrupted in the following century. In the seventeenth century, *alambiquage* as applied to literature came to connote the excessive refinement which characterised Gongorism, Marinism, and the new preciosity.

In the sixteenth century, however, the word had no such pejorative sense as descriptive of literary style. It merely described a general mimetic process by which elements of former writers are distilled into a new style of one's own. Although this new style would be more highly refined than any of the component styles from which it was blended, it would not be overrefined or excessive.

What is most important for our purposes, the new style was a "sweet new style," sweeter than any of those placed into the literary alembic. That the notion of sweetness should be intimately identified with the motif of distillation requires some explanation. In order to understand how connotations of sweetness enveloped this alchemistic practice one must examine briefly the state of development which distillation had attained by the sixteenth century.

The word *alembic* moved about the linguistic atlas of Europe coincidentally with the art of distillation itself.[267] From the Greek ἄμβιξ, it became the Arabic *al-anbîq* and was reintroduced into Europe by the Arabic alchemists of the late Middle Ages. Jean de Meung's use of the word in the *Roman de la Rose* shows that it was generally accepted by the end of the thirteenth century. The process of distillation was already an ancient one by the time of the Renaissance.[268] To the alchemists it was more closely connected with the transmutation of metals into gold with the aid of the Philosopher's Stone than with the refinement of anything sweet. And when the alchemists were not working to capture the Philosopher's Stone and eternal happiness with their alembics, they were using them to brew volatile oils, valid waters, and lotions for medicinal purposes.[269] The distillation of sweet essences, however, became a widespread trade in the fifteenth century. The two principal products became spirituous liquors and perfumes. A great new industry started up toward the close of the fifteenth century in the manufacture of distilled wine, brandy, leading to distinct improvements in the distillation process.[270] As early as 1512, Brunschwygk's *Liber Distillandi* declared that distilled wine was a common product. One is tempted to cite as literary proof Rémy Belleau's

> Par toy l'humeur du vin nouveau distille
> Dedans la tonne, écumant jusqu'au bord.[271]

It is probable, however, that Belleau is misusing the verb to describe fermentation.

Nor should one forget the widespread distillation of perfumes

[267] See Bloch and von Wartburg, *Dictionnaire étymologique de la langue française* (Paris, 1932), vol. I; also W. von Wartburg, *Französisches Etymologisches Wörterbuch* (Bonn: Schroeder, 1922–), vol. I.

[268] J. M. Stillman, *Story of Early Chemistry* (New York, 1924), p. 70.

[269] These and other products are mentioned in Giovanni Battista Porta's treatise on distillation, published at Rome in 1608. See also, J. Read, *Prelude to Chemistry* (New York, 1937), p. 77.

[270] Ernst von Meyer, *History of Chemistry* (London, 1871), p. 87.

[271] Belleau, M.-L., I, 191.

which sprung up in the late fifteenth century while considering the background for the transfer of this chemical process into a literary image of sweetness. Just as blossoms and flowers furnished the raw materials of the bee motif, so may flowers have been a determining factor in the conception of this one. For as we shall note in the Pléiade's references to *alambiquage* or "Mercurial fire" (as they themselves called it), it is sweetness which characterises the residual product of poetic distillation.

Huguet, in his *Dictionnaire de la langue française au XVIe siècle*, explains that the verb *alambiquer* had three major definitions at the time of the Pléiade. These were "distiller; extraire, tirer; épuiser, vider." [272] The first two meanings will have an especial interest for us in this discussion, as they were applied to the doctrine of imitation. Moreover, Huguet could have included "imiter" itself as a fourth synonym.

Distillation as a poetic conceit the Pléiade found in Petrarch, where the poet speaks twice of his sorrow as distilling pure tears.[273] This expression was copied in the sixteenth century by many of the amoristic poets, but the distillation by sorrow remained only a minor facet of the image in this century.[274]

Distillation as a form of imitation consisted of taking the best elements of the ancients and refining them in a literary process duplicating that one described by the alchemist Glauber: "Dissolve the fixt, and make the fixed fly, the flying fix, and then live happily."

Having found at least three contemporary expositions of *alambiquage* as a literary practice, we shall start with the description by Vauquelin, the latest but also the lengthiest:

[272] Huguet, *s. v.: alambiquer*, in vol. I.

[273] K. McKenzie, *Concordanza delle Rime di Petrarca* (New Haven, 1912), *s. v.: distillare.*

[274] The idea of tears as distillations became such a commonplace in the works of the period that we shall attempt to give only a few representative examples: Du Bellay, *Olive* XXV and LXXII; *Regrets* LII; *Vers lyriques* IX; Garnier, *Les Juifves*, vs. 2020; Baïf, M.-L., I, 30; Tyard, M.-L., p. 30; Ronsard, I, 90; Saint-Gelays, *Sophonisba*, III, 237; Passerat, *Poésies*, II, 13.

Comme un Alambiqueur tire des mineraux
L'esprit, la quintessence et vertu des metaux,
Fait des eaux de parfum, des huiles salutaires,
Et sçait bien allier maintes choses contraires:
Tandis souventesfois de faux coin, faux alloy,
Il frape monnoyeur sur la face du Roy;
Tout ainsi maint poète ayant à gorge pleine
Beu de l'onde sacrée à la docte Neuvaine,
Fera mille beaux vers: Mais souvent orgueilleux
Il meslera des traits mutins et perilleux:
Et souvent contre Dieu superbe il outrepasse
Par folle opinion les loix du Saint-Parnasse;
Et puis il devient fol: car Dieu le veut punir.[275]

Thus does a poet, by imitating the creative processes of an *alambiqueur*, become visited by a sacred fury.

Another singular reference to *alambiquage* as a mimetic process is found in Jodelle's preface to his *Recueil des inscriptions*. Here, the poet may imitate either the wealth of examples in nature or those of previous writers:

J'en ay maintenant mile raisons & mile exemples au bout de ma plume, si je voulois, comme on dit en se raillant, alambiquer dans une familière épitre, les secrets et les belles quintes essences de la Nature, ou tirer avecque je ne sçay quelle friandise affectée, la mouëlle des profondes et abondantes histoires.[276]

The most specific mention of distillation as a mimetic or plagiaristic process, however, occurs in Du Bellay's *Deffence*. To distill an elegy, the pamphleteer advises, one borrows elements from Ovid, Tibullus, and Propertius, and adds occasionally from the ancient fables, no small ornament of poetry.[277] Later on, the verb is again used in this sense in the preamble to the *Recherches* of Étienne Pasquier (undertaken in 1560): "La plus grande partie de ceux qui par cy devant nous avoient enseigné d'escrire histoires, alambicquèrent de l'ancienneté tout ce qui leur avoit plû, pour puis le communiquer au peuple."

[275] Vauquelin, *Art poétique*, *ed. cit.*, pp. 181–182.
[276] Jodelle, M.-L., I, 232: "Épistre-préface du Recueil des inscriptions."
[277] *Deffence*, *ed. cit.*, pp. 207–208.

One of the reasons why distillation and sweetness were coupled was a current notion that honey itself could be distilled — either from flowers, trees, or the skies. The idea of arboreal honey seems to have originated as early as, or earlier than, Diodorus (XVII, 16) and was translated into French by Amyot: "Et si y a une sorte d'arbre semblable au chesne, des feuilles duquel distille continuellement le miel." This is echoed by Ronsard in his Eclogue I: "Le miel distillera de l'escorce des chesnes." [278] In his "Hymne de printemps," he pictures an airy Land of Cockaigne where milk flowed through the brooks and "le doux miel distila du haut des arbrisseaux." [279] Belleau's piece "Sur la mort d'une maistresse" evokes a land just as miraculous:

> Rien que douceur, rien que manne et que miel
> En ces beaux lieux ne distile du ciel.[280]

All this is reminiscent of the Biblical "land of milk and honey." [281] But sweetness can be distilled by other agents. Ronsard, paying tribute to Maclou de la Haye, asks the Muses to hallow the memory of Maclou and to distill his glory in the sweet sugar of their verses.[282] Pontus de Tyard indicates that the agent may be the pen itself. He praises the distilled sweetness of the honeyed pen of Saint-Gelays.[283] This should be compared with Marot's rondeau XV:

> Ainsi ma plume, en qui bourbe distile,
> Veult esclairsir l'onde claire et utile.

Because distillation was considered in connection with the creation of honey, of perfumes, and of sweet liqueurs, the conceit of distillation as applied to Renaissance writers has a definite place in this investigation of poetic sweetness. One finds Du Bellay, for example, writing several times of the distillation of a sweet style. There are his poems to Jacques

[278] Ronsard, III, 378.
[279] *Ibid.*, IV, 301.
[280] Belleau, M.-L., I, 126.
[281] *Numeri* XIV, 8 and *passim*.
[282] Ronsard, VI, 95–96.
[283] Pontus de Tyard, M.-L., p. 124.

Gohory[284] and the ironic verses to the courtier-poet.[285] The Bacchic "Voyage d'Hercueil" of Ronsard is a paean to the sweet style of Jean Dorat:

> Iô, iô, quel doux stile
> Se distile
> Parmy ses nombres divers.
> Nul miel tant ne me recrée
> Que m'agrée
> Le doux nectar de ses vers.[286]

The idea of culling sweetness from flowers as a mimetic procedure we have already noted in connection with the motif of the bee. It also becomes a part of the motif of distillation. In his *Petromachie*, Du Bellay refers to Pierre Galland's habit of refining his discourses out of quotations from Greek and Roman writers and orators:

> Son oraison tant bien parée
> Semble une juppe bigarée
> De plus de sortes de couleurs
> Que les prés ne portent de fleurs.
> Ha! je recognois bien le stile
> Que sa douce plume distile.[287]

Here the imitative process is given an extra dose of sweetness by the analogy with a field of multicolored flowers. Compare the rôle of flowers in this imitation (1552) with that in the "Hylas" (1569) and the poem to Simon Bouquet (1572).

Jean-Antoine de Baïf, who was quick to adopt the poetic imagery of his two friends and superiors, refers to distillation of style in his *Amours de Francine*. Baïf wishes that the fury of his passion could be converted into poetic fury: "si une fois mon stile pouvoit estre pareille à la belle fureur dont ta beauté m'ateint, mais ta rare valeur tariroit toute l'eau qui d'Hélicon distile."[288] Another analogy between sweet style

[284] Du Bellay, V, 259.
[285] *Ibid.*, VI, 134.
[286] Ronsard, V, 224.
[287] Du Bellay, V, 241.
[288] Baïf, M.-L., I, 94.

and distillation is brought up in Ronsard's description of the style of Tibullus, Ovid, and Catullus. In this case it is not wine or honey that is distilled, but apparently strong waters, *aquae validae*, a type of distillation not uncommon among the alchemists:

> Le fils de Venus hait ces ostentations:
> Il suffist qu'on luy chante au vray ses passions
> Sans enflure ni fard, d'un mignard et doux stile,
> Coulant d'un petit bruit, comme une eau qui distile.[289]

It is possible, of course, that in one or two of these latter cases, "distiller" may have been used in its etymological sense of dripping rather than condensing. But even in these cases the verb appears to refer to the dropping downward of the purified element after the condensation has been accomplished. Another contemporary passage, although not composed by a member of the Pléiade, might be regarded as an example of this familiar imagery:

> Et ont escript en si ample et beau stile
> Qu'on jugeroit que des cieulx il distille.[290]

Linguistically, the use of this new term, *alambiquage*, is an excellent demonstration of the Pléiade's practising what it preached. Ronsard, Du Bellay, Peletier, and the rest, urged their contemporaries to adopt new words from the trades and the sciences. Such a contribution was the word *alambiquage*, which remained in the language in an expanded meaning down to the present day. The word was either a borrowing from the distiller's trade, as we have seen, or it may have first come to their attention through the alchemists and the popular literature of alchemy. In the "Eurymedon and Callirée" of Ronsard,[291] as well as his *Amours de Cassandre*,[292] the poet employs

[289] Ronsard, I, 130–131.

[290] J. Fouchet, *La noble dame, à Éléonore d'Autriche*, quoted in Huguet, *Dictionnaire de la langue française au XVIe siècle* (Paris, 1935), fasc. 23.

[291] Ronsard, I, 230–231.

[292] *Ibid.*, I, 90.

the verb *alambiquer* to describe specifically the distillation of the alchemist's still. A similar use is the image, already mentioned, of the distiller in Vauquelin's *Art poétique*:

> Comme un alambiqueur tire des mineraux
> L'esprit, la quintessence et vertu des metaux.

The use of the term in the *Amours*, of course, dates from as early as 1552, but distillation as a concept of sweetness is met even earlier. Its occurrence in the "Chant en faveur de quelques excellens poètes" of Tyard, for example, dates from 1551. Whether the poets borrowed the word first from the wine distiller or from the alchemist, it matters little. What is more important is that the Pléiade enlarged their native vocabulary with a permanent contribution from the trades.

It must not be forgotten that alembication made a distinct contribution to the contemporary imagery of criticism. By advancing beyond the lachrymose conception of distillation which the Pléiade found in Petrarch and occasionally adopted in their love sonnets, they added a new figure to illustrate the process of imitation. After all, the doctrine of imitation was the alpha and omega of all Renaissance literary theory. That the graphic qualities of this portrayal of mimesis captured the fancy of the century is evident from its subsequent reappearance in the *Recherches* of Pasquier. The preceding paragraphs illustrate once again the Pléiade's versatility of ideation, to borrow a word from Alfieri, and their ability to exhaust all the possibilities of any poetic imagery which fell into their hands.

The seventeenth century, however, discarded the specific meaning which *alambiquage* had acquired under the Pléiade and employed it to designate the excesses of preciosity. Why the Age of Malherbe rejected the implications of sweetness and of mimesis which the term "distillation" held for the Pléiade is a problem to be explained by one of our modern semasiologists who combine lexicology with sociology and psychology. Perhaps the answer is that the new overrefinement of preciosity demanded a term with more vigor and graphic qualities than any word in common usage possessed. And as no refining process provided a more forceful term than the distillation of alchemy, with its *ascension* and *descension*, the seventeenth century appropriated it and gave it the single, exclusive meaning of overrefinement. Let this be remembered to the credit of the Pléiade. The seventeenth-century critics did not borrow the term from the arts and sciences. They borrowed it from the sixteenth century.

⚜ ⚜ ⚜

The preceding pages, as stated at the outset of this chapter, attempt to study the semantic values of the idea of sweetness and to investigate the expansion of these values into their broadest limits in certain specific poetic motifs. As we proceeded toward this end, we found of necessity that the concept of utility became quantitatively subordinate to that of sweetness. Sweetness of content or expression has been a desideratum of all poetry in every age, but to these poets creating a Sweet New Style in France and nurtured on the Petrarchian and Ariostean *dolce*, the concept became so important that it assumed a paramount position as a criterion of criticism. The second meaning of sweetness, concerning the function of poetry, they knew from Horace and probably the Greek grammarians. After weighing the Pléiade's exposition and translations of the *utile* and *dulce*, we reached the general conclusion that these poets believed in the Peripatetic and Horatian doctrine that literature must have utilitarian as well as hedonistic purpose, even though the poetry the Pléiade wrote seemed designed to lighten rather than enlighten. It was because of this belief that they invented the epithet, "utiledoux," considered a consummate compliment. However, we noted that even if the Pléiade's theoretical remarks showed them inclined toward a compromise between sweetness and utility, their literary practices and imagery showed them rather inclined toward the hedonistic function. Thereafter our attention turned almost exclusively to the matter of poetic sweetness. This was not of our own choosing. The unity of this chapter, like the unity of the entire volume, has been determined not by the author, but by the Pléiade poets themselves. And in this case these poets became more interested in the semantic possibilities of poetic sweetness than in its counterpart of utility.

Sweetness was such an integral part of the Pléiade's *dolce stil* that it inevitably pervaded their critical remarks. Two general concepts of sweetness, the Petrarchian and the Horatian, the first dealing with the sentiments and subject matter of verse, particularly love poems, and the second treating of the hedonistic function of literature, were accepted into their critical vocabulary. The distinction between them became at times so finely drawn that in some instances it disappeared entirely. This, as we have seen, resulted not merely from a lack of discrimination, but also from a conviction that the two concepts were in the last analysis two facets of a single idea.

The revival of the Pindaric ode and the seriousness with which the Pléiade took the trade of letters caused a frequent opposition of sweetness and gravity. Although gravity generally implied sublimity and solemnity of tone, in this contrast it came to mean also solemnity of purpose, just as sweetness meant hedonistic purpose. Thus gravity became germane to utility. But the *aurea mediocritas*, the Spirit of Compromise, operated upon this contrast just as it had on the previous one. Since a book or a poem may combine hedonism and didacticism, it may also combine seriousness of purpose with sweetness of expression, and the Pléiade's references to sweet gravity and grave sweetness are numerous.

Further aspects of the meaning of sweetness are revealed in the Pléiade's mentions of ancient and modern authors. From the remarks on individual writers one gathers that sweetness may stem from thought, wording, intention, sentiment, cadence, even delivery. It may be the less specific sweetness of Attic honey. It may lie in the harmony of the poem itself, or even the harmony of the musical arrangement, and these writers who "measured poetry to the lyre" imagined themselves sweet instrumentalists.

Equally important are the specialised meanings attributed to sweetness in the three poetic motifs which comprise over half of these mentions and judgments. Considerations of music turned the Pléiade's attention to the motif of the Swan, which they borrowed from classical mythology. As when treating of the Bee trope, they found reasons of their own why poets should be considered swans. They called themselves the New Swans, as the lineal descendants of the Old Swans of Greek and Roman and early Italian literature. This epithet expressed the epitome of spiritual revival and self-conscious enthusiasm which one naturally associates with the Renaissance. Writers who were not of their own literary persuasion the Pléiade characterised as geese, crows, or even jays, epithets derived from either Ariosto or classical literature itself.

The motif or myth of poets as Honeybees the Pléiade borrowed also from classical antiquity, contributing new reasons of their own for this identification. To the reasons of the past, that the bee creates sweetness, that he selects and culls, that he possesses divinity, the Pléiade posited further that bees and bards sing songs, are industrious, and fall continually in love.

The Pléiade borrowed the term *alambiquage* from the wine distiller, or possibly from the perfumer or alchemist, and made of it a critical concept. In doing so, they adhered to their own preachments about enriching the vernacular with words from the arts, crafts, and sciences. For several reasons they gave the term special connotations of sweetness and adopted it to describe a form of mimesis. The meaning they gave the word was replaced by a pejorative sense in the seventeenth century, when it served to describe the overrefinement of preciosity.

Ruminating on sweetness, the inventive and imaginative Pléiade created three new images of literary imitation, one from each of the three poetic motifs of sweetness:

I. The Renaissance writer composes best with the quills plucked from the Swans of antiquity.

II. Like a Bee, the Renaissance writer culls the sweet gardens of the past.

III. The Renaissance writer distills ever sweeter styles in the poetic alembic out of the *prima materia* of past writings.

The importance of these three motifs is evident from the frequency of their appearances throughout the *canzoniere* of the Pléiade. That they have not been investigated before indicates the value of consulting the Pléiade's practice as well as their theory to arrive at their most characteristic interests, theories, and prejudices.

The Inspiration of Poetry . . .

V

ART AND NATURE

> Ispirazione, estro, lirismo, entusiasmo, manìa: sono parole diverse con le quali ugualmente si denota il fenomeno primo che è all'origine dell'opera d'arte e senza del quale opera d'arte non c'è.
>
> Attuazione, esecuzione, espressione in senso empirico, o perfino tecnica, o lavoro artistico, o arte in senso stretto come subordinata e in qualche modo contrapposta alla poesia e al genio, o più comprensivamente creazione: con questi ed altri termini si suole indicare il secondo e decisivo momento dell'opera d'arte.
>
> — G. A. BORGESE, *Poetica dell' Unità*

THE final canon to be investigated upon which the Pléiade centered judgments and opinions is that of genius against art, of nature against nurture. Of the five major criteria which this study encompasses, this is the only one which the manifestoes and prefaces of the period treated at any length. Like all the others, this was a canon with roots extending deep into the subsoil of classical antiquity. Following a preliminary sketch of the general theory of art and genius in classic and Renaissance treatises, this chapter will present as heretofore the judgments and incidental imagery hinging upon art and nature which one encounters in the Pléiade's poetry.

One must not assume from the artificial and conventional language in which the ancients and Renaissance dealt with it that this problem was a specious one. Although the terminology of the Pléiade regarding genius and inspiration is now obsolete, the problem is not, and is still actively mooted. Like a twentieth-century Philosopher's Stone or *arcanum arcanorum*, it still resists exact formulation. Today, however, one basic weakness of the earlier discussions has been eliminated. In the Renaissance the point at issue was usually whether poets — as a class, not as individuals — owed more to native genius or to learned technique. Today the problem arises only for the individual, seldom if ever for the class. No one nowadays would affirm that an entire class, such as the poets of the Homeric era, possessed natural or spontaneous ability. Yet this statement was a commonplace in the works of the Pléiade and earlier writers as well.

The Renaissance approached the problem in two ways. Sometimes art was viewed as antagonistic to nature and the writer considered the exclusive product of one or the other. Again, art and nature were occasionally viewed as complementary factors in the making of a poet. In this case, the only question concerned which of the two complements, if either, contributed the larger share.

The contrast between art and nature, nature being accepted as defined by Jacques Peletier, "ce qui est imposé an nous, sans notre peine et notre premiere intancion," [1] is one presenting many lexical and conceptual variations. According to the Pléiade, a born poet had been favored by the nine Sisters, by the three Fates, by Apollo. The gods had visited him with a sacred frenzy; he had been touched by Corybantic madness; by the poetic Demon. The conjunction of the stars at his birth had exerted a benevolent influence. He had saddled the high soaring Pegasus. He had lunched on laurel leaves. He had supped atop Helicon; at the table of the Muses; at the board

[1] There is apparently no thorough study of this subject in the histories of Pléiade theory. There are several references to it, however. See H. Chamard, *De Jacobi Peletarij Cenomanensis Arte Poetica* (Lille: Bigot, 1900), pp. 11–12; P. Villey, *Les sources italiennes de la Deffence* (Paris: Champion, 1908), pp. 73–74; A. Boulanger, *L'Art poëtique de Jacques Peletier*, critical edition (Paris: les Belles Lettres, 1930), pp. 72–79, nn. 1–13; W. F. Patterson, *Three Centuries of French Poetic Theory* (Ann Arbor, 1935), II, 458; H. Franchet, *Le poète et son œuvre d'après Ronsard* (Paris: Champion, 1923), pp. 1–42, on poetic fury.

of Jupiter and Mnemosyne. He had drunk on Helicon; on Parnassus; at Hippocrene; at Aganippe; from the Permessus. These are some of the images of inspiration which will be considered in this chapter. Should an author have been so fortunate as to undergo one of these experiences, the matter of learned skill became relatively if not absolutely unimportant. If he has been so fortunate, he does not have to learn from others; it is the others who learn from him. Such, at times, was the wishful thinking of the Pléiade.

One must understand at the outset, however, that the Pléiade's doctrine of innate genius represented theoretics and wishful thinking rather than conviction. Trying to subscribe to the classic beliefs in ἐνθουσιασμός and *ingenium*, these poets were sobered by the disclosure that poetry was hard work. Because they were practitioners even more than theorists of poetry, they knew this from their own experience. Their precepts about a "higher and better style," their great campaign encouraging translation and imitation of the ancients and Italians, these were all part of the Pléiade's belief that one perfected one's art through labor and study. Not that this was an exclusive idea of the Pléiade, of course. Almost every poetics of sixteenth-century France included a final section on the genres and on the rules of versification — that is, on learned form and technique. All their theories of imitation and rules for composition were based on the assumption that any writer of the time, no matter how great his native talents, could learn to write better only through rules of art.

Two contradictory theories, then, arose coincidentally with the Pléiade's notions about art and nature. How the Pléiade dealt with these two contrasting theories will be the principal investigation of this chapter. Other contingent aims will be to examine what ideas about genius the Pléiade borrowed from classic literary criticism, and what they contributed of their own; to study the imagery regarding poetic inspiration in the vocabulary of the Pléiade academy.

⚜ ⚜ ⚜

A most interesting feature of this question of genius is the widespread attention it compelled from the very earliest times. In the true spirit of the Orphic poet, Pindar saw the real instigation of poetry in nature itself, nature as it is manifested in human nature. In the second Olympian ode, he affirmed that the genuine poet is the one whose knowledge comes as a gift of nature: *σοφὸς ὁ πολλὰ εἰδὼς φυᾶ*. Those poets whose wisdom comes only through learning are crows who caw in vain against the godlike bird of Zeus.[2] In a later ode he declares that "nothing is worth the natural endowments . . . ," things God does not share in pass away in silence.[3] Again, in the *Nemean Odes*, one reads that only strength inborn is effective strength; those who gain prowess only through training and drudgery will dwell forever in oblivion.[4]

Others familiar to the Pléiade followed in the Orphic tradition, although resolving the problem in less philosophical terms. In Homer it is God or the Muse herself who assumes the rôle of nature in inspiring the poet. There is, in the *Odyssey*, the minstrel Demodocus, to whom "the god has given minstrelsy as to no other," and whom "the Muse loved dearly."[5] In Book XXII, there is the son of Terpes, the minstrel, who tells Odysseus of the natural character of his inspiration: "Yet none has taught me but myself, and the god has put into my heart all manner of lays."[6] Hesiod, in the *Theogony*, is even more picturesque in his description of natural inspiration. The poet-singer relates how the nine Sisters selected him for natural endowment. "So said the ready-voiced daughters of the great Zeus, and they plucked and gave me a rod, a shoot of sturdy olive, a marvelous thing, and breathed into me a divine voice to celebrate things that shall be and things that were aforetime."[7]

[2] Pindar, *Olympian Odes* ii, 96 ff.

[3] *Ibid.*, ix, 100–102.

[4] Pindar, *Nemean Odes* iii, 40–42.

[5] *Odyssey*, trans. Butcher-Lang (London: Macmillan, 1925), pp. 64, 73.

[6] *Ibid.*, p. 347.

[7] *Theogony* 30–34, trans. Evelyn-White (London: Heinemann, 1914), p. 81.

It was Simylus, the comic poet, who first insisted upon the importance of learning in creative writing. In a remarkable passage quoted by Stobaeus (whom Ronsard used) [8] and later by Ben Jonson in his *Discoveries*,[9] Simylus voiced the compromise: *οὔτε φύσις ἱκανὴ γίνεται τέχνης ἄτερ.* "Neither is nature without art sufficient for anyone for any practical achievement, nor is art which has not nature with it. When both come together there are still needed a *χορηγία*, love of the task, practice, a happy occasion, time, a critic able to grasp what is said." Of this passage Saintsbury judiciously concludes, "it would be impossible to put the matter better after more than two thousand years of literary accumulation and critical experiment. It is the voice of Aristotle speaking with the experience of Quintilian." [10]

Most influential in forming the opinions of the Pléiade was Plato. It was Plato, wrote Richard Le Blanc in 1546, who proves "par subtiles raisons en ce présent dialogue intitulé *Io* que Poésie est ung don de Dieu." [11] The entire dialogue of the *Ion* is of course a development of this idea of natural genius and inspiration as the source of all poetry, independent of learned technique. It is begging the question to insist that Socrates is speaking in a mocking manner, as many have done. He is mocking, agreed, but he is nevertheless a philosopher presenting a widespread notion about poets. And a notion he heard from other philosophers as well, if one is to recall the *Apology*.[12] If in the *Ion* Plato's attitude is skeptical, in other dialogues he seems readier to accept the theory.[13] In so far as

[8] See Ronsard, STFM, VI, ix, on Ronsard and Stobaeus.

[9] See R. P. Cowl, *Theory of Poetry in England* (London: Macmillan, 1914), p. 7.

[10] George Saintsbury, *A History of Criticism* (London: Blackwood, 1922), I, 25–26.

[11] Preface to the Le Blanc translation of the *Ion* (1546), quoted in A. Lefranc, *Grands écrivains de la Renaissance* (Paris: Champion, 1914), p. 125.

[12] Plato's *Apology*: "That showed me in an instant that not by wisdom do poets write poetry, but by a sort of genius and inspiration, *etc.*," translated by Jowett (New York, 1936), III, 108.

[13] *Phaedrus* 238D; 244B; 245A; 265B; *Laws* 682A; 719C.

oratory is concerned, Plato seems to anticipate the later idea that poets are born, orators made. In the *Phaedrus,* Socrates states that good orators must add knowledge and practice to their natural endowments; at whatsoever point one is deficient in these, he will be incomplete.[14] The passages of Plato which left the deepest impression upon the Pléiade, however, were those where the imagery of natural genius was called into play. The most impressive remained that section of the *Ion* where the poet is called divine and mad.[15]

Even Aristotle, who placed such an emphasis on art and formula, adhered to the view that the poet is inspired.[16] In the *Poetics* he alludes to the two traditional ideas of natural genius and divine fury. Poetry demands either a favorable nature (*εὐφυία*) or a madman (*μανικός*).[17] Aristotle's theory of imitation would also seem to give the advantage to nature. Art imitates the creative processes of nature, of external nature or internal nature; the greatest gift that universal nature can grant an individual is an ability to adopt its own processes. No matter how skillful the poet may become at his imitating, his art remains secondary to the primary forces of nature.

Demetrius presented the notion that the earliest bards, the *ἀρχαῖοι* wrote with native genius and ingenuity, a statement which the Pléiade was to repeat seriatim.[18] He contributed another distinction to this question, asserting that poets write spontaneously and naturally when under the influence of their emotions; [19] he is no longer talking about divine fury, it appears, but about poetic enthusiasm, a phase of inspiration familiar to students of the Pléiade. Longinus, too, recognises that lofty emotions engender spontaneous or natural composition, but rather holds a brief for art.

Works of natural genius, so people think, are spoiled and utterly demeaned by being reduced to the dry bones of rule and precept.

[14] Plato, *Phaedrus* (London: Heinemann, 1933), p. 547.
[15] *Vide supra*, Chapter IV, note 214.
[16] Aristotle, *Rhetoric* III, vii, 11.
[17] Aristotle, *Poetics* xvii, 4.
[18] Demetrius, *On Style* 245.
[19] *Ibid.*, sec. 300.

For my part, I hold that the opposite may be proved, if we consider that while in lofty emotion Nature for the most part knows no law, yet it is not the way of Nature to work at random and wholly without system. . . . For genius needs the curb as often as the spur. . . . Nature fills the place of good fortune, Art that of good judgment.[20]

With the process of mimesis in mind, he concludes that in literature some effects patterned on nature can be learned only through art, and that "Art is only perfect when it looks like Nature, and Nature succeeds only by concealing Art about her person." [21]

That each side of this question had its proponents in Roman times is revealed by two Latin dicta familiar even today. The idea that native genius suffices to make a poet but not an orator is found in the "fiunt oratores, nascuntur poetae," which the Pléiade echoed so often. The implication of "ars coronat opus," on the other hand, is that perfection demands art. Both of these classical adages were known to the sixteenth century, and one finds reminiscences of them in various poems and treatises of the period (see below, Peletier, Vulteius, and others).

Although Seneca's "nullum magnum ingenium sine mixtura dementiae" [22] is representative of a belief which will exist in all ages, D'Alton states that the old Greek doctrine of divine madness disappeared from Roman literary theory, and that the issue became a simpler contrast between *ingenium* and *ars*.[23] In his *De Oratore*, Cicero explains what is meant by *ingenium*. This term includes natural faculties of sensitivity and imagination, an ability to receive deep impressions which may develop penetrating invention, a capacity for learning, and a retentive memory. These things are not acquired by art.[24] If in the

[20] Longinus, *On the Sublime*, trans. by W. H. Fyfe (London: Heinemann, 1932), p. 127.

[21] *Ibid.*, p. 193.

[22] Seneca, *Tranq. Animi* xvii, 10.

[23] J. F. D'Alton, *Roman Literary Theory and Criticism* (London: Longmans, 1931), p. 474.

[24] *De Oratore* i, 113 ff.

De Finibus one finds the compromise, "ars tamen est dux certior quam natura,"[25] it remains that Cicero accorded a greater rôle in literary creation to nature than Horace was willing to concede. Quintilian weighs the question in several passages and decrees that perfection is attained only when nature is assisted by art.[26] To this rhetorician, art appeared to assume a greater function among the later (Latin) writers. The earlier (Hellenic) authors were naturally talented ("plus ingenio quam arte valuerunt") and the later writers atoned for this deficiency by the polish of their verse. This statement of Quintilian, already found in Demetrius and repeated by other classic writers known to the sixteenth century,[27] is the lesson of the "Ode à Michel de l'Hospital."

Horace recognised that worthy critics of previous times, such as Democritus,[28] had admitted that nature was superior to art,[29] but held that art and nature were mutually dependent and necessary.[30] The idea of poetic fury he mocked even more extravagantly than had Plato.[31] Sikes, in his *Roman Poetry*, concludes that Horace "certainly seems to regard art as the predominant partner."[32] There are passages in the *Elegies* of Propertius where homage is paid to *ingenium* alone,[33] but even he grants that sometimes art may be as influential as genius.[34] Pliny recognises the common belief that the "archaic" poets wrote with more *ingenium* than *cura*, but adds that there was one exception to this rule in the person of Silius Italicus.[35]

One literary historian estimates the general attitude of the Romans as follows: "The premier place as a rule was assigned

[25] *De Finibus* iv, 10.

[26] Quintilian, *Inst. Orat.* xi, 3; ii, 19.

[27] Ovid, *Amores* i, 15, 14; *Tristia* ii, 424; Cicero, *De Oratore* i, 14.

[28] Also quoted by Cicero, *De Div.* i, 80.

[29] *Ad Pisones* 295–298.

[30] *Ibid.*, 408–411.

[31] *Ibid.*, 453 ff.

[32] E. E. Sikes, *Roman Poetry* (London, 1923), p. 62.

[33] Propertius, *Elegies* IV, i, 65–67; vi, 75–76.

[34] *Ibid.*, II, xxiv, 23–24.

[35] Pliny, *Epist.* iii, 7.

to Nature, but it was agreed that art should lend its aid and help to bring it to perfection."[36] In this rather obvious compromise, they remained more insistent upon the share of art than were the Greeks.

⚜ ⚜ ⚜

Into their new bottles the Renaissance writers poured this same old wine. As respectful spiritual offspring, they accepted the compromise slightly favoring nature which the classic authorities had handed down. In Italy, however, certain individuals familiar to the Pléiade openly took one stand or the other in the matter, and mention must be made of these.

Boccaccio, in his *Genealogia Deorum Gentilium*, bases his belief in natural genius as the foundation of poetry upon the testimony of his many predecessors. Let any fair-minded man read what Cicero says in his oration delivered in behalf of Archias. "The poets would declare with their own lips under whose help and guidance they compose their inventions, when for example, they raise flights of symbolic steps to heaven, or make thick-branching trees spring aloft to the very stars, or go winding about mountains to their summits."[37]

In his study of the Italian sources of the *Deffence*, Villey has stated that Du Bellay, Peletier, and Sébilet were probably influenced by such men as Bembo, Calcagnini, Giraldi, and Ricci, who gave all the advantage in this matter to the precepts of art. One might strike Sébilet from the list above, for he showed little inclination toward admitting the necessity of art. Villey shows that Du Bellay's advice about choosing an author to imitate who conformed to one's own natural powers has a possible source in the 1545 edition of Ricci.[38] We should be

[36] J. F. D'Alton, *Roman Literary Theory and Criticism* (London: Longmans, 1931), p. 472.

[37] Charles Osgood, *Boccaccio on Poetry* (Princeton, 1930), pp. 41–42.

[38] P. Villey, *Les sources italiennes de la Deffence* (Paris: Champion, 1908), p. 73.

more inclined to place the origin of this idea in the *Poetics* of Vida,[39] which served as a handbook for the Pléiade.[40]

Perhaps it was from Vida as well, rather than from earlier proponents of the idea, that the Pléiade got the notion that the "archaic" poets wrote spontaneously and naturally. Vida cites as proof of this contention the genius of Ennius, and later, Vergil.[41] But subsequent Latins dependent upon art or relying upon inadequate *ingenium* succeed only in defiling their language.[42] After filling three books with precepts and careful instruction in his *Poetics*, he concludes with the paradoxical remark that it is the gods, not rules, who guide the poet up Parnassus,[43] like a timid eighteenth-century rationalist who concludes his rationale with the qualifier that his rules are overshadowed by inexorable laws of Providence.

Scaliger's learned and technical discussion of poetry, with all its emphasis on rhetorical and stylistic devices, pays lip service to the doctrine of divine inspiration. For that generation of early poets whom the Muses favored more than any other J.-C. Scaliger borrows the significant name θεόπνευστοι; the temporal limits of this category Scaliger then extends down through Latinity, for he admits that Ennius and Horace must be accepted therein. But Scaliger was above all a rational critic. The remainder of the volume after the first few chapters is a monument to the conviction that only through a diligent study of *character*, *perspicuitas*, *proprietas*, *numerositas*, *sonus*, and a hundred other properties of poetry does one succeed in achieving them in his own work.[44]

All of these passages were more or less familiar to the Pléiade. They are reflected in the theoretical writings of the

[39] Vida, *Ars poetica* i, 39–50.

[40] Two tributes to Vida are found in Du Bellay's *Deffence*, Chamard edition, pp. 282–283, and poems, Chamard edition, VI, 130.

[41] Vida, *Ars poetica* i, 155; 170–171.

[42] *Ibid.* i, 180.

[43] *Ibid.* iii, 530 ff.

[44] J.-C. Scaliger, *Poetices libri septem* (Heidelberg: Commeliano, 1617), Bk. IV, chap. i.

Pléiade, which we shall consider after a momentary glance at the doctrine of nature in the Old French period.

Nature's predominant share in poetic composition was reiterated by the French as early as the *Prologue* of Guillaume de Machaut (1370) and the *Art de Dictier* (1392) of Eustache Deschamps. Machaut couched the idea in allegory, giving nature a personification. The specific natural talents with which she endowed him were Sense, Rhetoric, and Music.[45] Deschamps called poetry "natural music"; nature bestows it upon only a few, and for those naturally favored he was setting down "un petit de règle."[46] Even among the *rhétoriqueurs*, whose knowledge of the Greek and Roman treatises mentioned above was limited, the idea that poetry was a gift from God or nature was not uncommon. "Several of the Arts de Seconde Rhétorique intimate vaguely that poetry is a gift of Nature. It is not imparted; it is given, and to no great number."[47]

It might be added parenthetically that the device of presenting the doctrine of inspiration in allegorical form was not unknown to the Pléiade. Jodelle, in his "Hymenée du roy Charles IX," introduces Genius as an allegorical figure and has him explain his influence in figurative language.[48]

Before analysing the references to individual writers in the Pléiade's poetry, it will be necessary to examine the general position of the Pléiade on this issue, as revealed in their written theory. These theoretical works will be examined in chronological order.

First, however, we should like to quote momentarily from a neo-Latin contemporary of the Pléiade. Vulteius, who enjoyed a moderate popularity in the mid-century although not a member of the new school, was definitely interested in the

[45] Machaut, *Prologue*, in *Œuvres*, ed. by Hoepffner (Paris: Firmin-Didot, 1908), I, 1–2.

[46] Deschamps, *Œuvres complètes*, ed. by Raynaud (Paris: Firmin-Didot, 1891), VII, 270–272.

[47] W. F. Patterson, *French Poetic Theory* (Ann Arbor, 1935), I, 221, 228–229.

[48] Jodelle, M.-L., I, 299.

opposition of genius and technique. The "Ad Caussadum" of his *Epigrammatum libri* iiii (1537) is remarkable for its long list of the qualities which art contributes to poetry:

Natura an faceret bonos poetas,
Usu an assiduo suas Camoenas
Ornarent lepidi, & graves poetae,
Dicis Caussade saepe cogitasse.
Quis iam, quis rogo, nesciat poetas
Natura simul, et labori nasci?
Si natura nequit, iuvatur arte:
Ars tandem, improbus et labor parabunt,
Quod natura tibi negat Poetae.
Ars vincit Charites, nuvemq; Musas.
Plenum ars, dulce, sonans facit poema.
Ars dat lautitias, iocos, lepores,
Ars dat munditias, sonosq; dulces.
Ars dat divitias, opusq; complet.
Ars dat delicias, modosq; tornat.
Naturam labor improbus politq;
Quae iuncta efficiunt bonum poetam.[49]

This is an excellent sixteenth-century restatement of the Roman proverb "ars coronat opus," which the fourteenth line paraphrases. It is a further demonstration, by the way, that even the verses of a *latineur* may be extremely significant in an investigation of this sort.

Next in order of the works covering the theory of natural endowment is Sébilet's *Art poétique* of 1548. The third chapter of the initial book concerns invention, "the first part of poetry." Sébilet finds invention a gift of Minerva rather than an acquired art. Here he is following Horace.[50] He quotes the familiar proverb that poets are born, orators made. He interprets Horace's remarks upon art and nature as favoring neither of the two,[51] and admits both as "conjurateurs à la perfection

[49] Vulteius, *Epigrammatum libri* iiii (Lugduni, 1537), pp. 110–111. Later (p. 249), he writes to Macrin that art, nature, and labor combine to make a competent poet.

[50] *Ad Pisones* 385–386: "Tu nihil invita dices faciesve Minerva, *etc.*"

[51] Sébilet, *Art poétique*, ed. by Gaiffe, p. 25.

du poète." He finds in Horace's advice to assume only those poetic tasks which one's capacities permit a possible leaning toward nature as the first requirement.[52] He also quotes Quintilian, finding to his liking this rhetorician's contention that neither requisite can suffice without the other, and that the scales are slightly in favor of nature.

Mais qui pourroit raisonnablement affermer que la Poésie fust de nature et de première naissance, sans estude, doctrine, précepte, autrement que divinement donnée? Car ce qu'en Poésie est nommé art & que nos traitons comme art en cest opuscule, n'est rien que la nue escorce de Poésie, qui couvre artificièlement sa naturele sève et son ame naturèlement divine.[53]

In Sébilet, then, one finds the most consistent bias in favor of natural genius to be found in the mid-century.

On the other hand, as early as the *Deffence* (1549), Du Bellay takes the definite position that "le naturel n'est suffisant à celuy qui en poésie veult faire œuvre digne de l'immortalité." [54] As one who counselled tireless work and echoed the old Greek saying that there was no royal road to literary success, Du Bellay would certainly tend to deny the blunt simplification that "poets are born." Rather, the beginning of all good writing is acquired by knowledge, and Du Bellay mistranslates the *recte sapere* of Horace as *le sçavoir.* He points out on one occasion that it is common knowledge among scholars, "le naturel faire plus sans la doctrine que la doctrine sans le naturel," [55] but this chance statement cannot be taken as indicative of the tenor of his true feelings. Du Bellay is levelheaded, and realises that if this emphasis on nature is carried too far his entire campaign for stylistic and linguistic reform will be endangered. No, he objects, "Qu'on ne m'allègue point aussi que les poètes naissent, car cela s'entend de cette allégresse d'esprit qui naturellement excite les poètes et sans

[52] *Ad Pisones* 38–40: "Sumite materiam vestris, *etc.*"
[53] Sébilet, *op. cit.*, p. 10.
[54] *Deffence*, ed. by Chamard, p. 193.
[55] *Ibid.*, p. 193.

laquelle toute leur doctrine seroit manque et inutile." Granted this "allégresse d'esprit," or propensity, much more is required. Who would want literary fame if even the untutored, through a mere felicity of nature, could attain it as well? This use of "félicité" and the later statement that doctrine must be supplemented by a "félicité de nature"[56] indicate the extent to which Du Bellay will go in admitting natural endowment. It is a very significant word in his theory. Unwilling to grant that "poets are born," yet aware that some individuals make better poets than others independently of training, he will go so far as to say that they have a certain natural felicity. But in his theoretical writings he goes no further.

Jacques Peletier entitled the second chapter of his first book of the *Art poétique*, "De la Nature et de l'Exercise." This dates from 1555. Peletier shows how Democritus and Plato had apparently believed nature triumphant over art. He cites the familiar adage that poets are born, orators made, without attempting to find its provenance. He reminds us that by nature one may mean either the great external forces of the universe, which include even the supernatural and the contrary-to-nature; or nature may signify more particularly forces imposed within us, without our concern or intention. With this latter working definition, he concludes that art is more necessary than the ancients realised. But his conclusions are essentially a compromise. His decision is that nature demands the aid of an artisan hand, and that art can achieve nothing without the *naturel*.[57]

Published one year after Peletier's *Art poétique*, another theoretical work of the greater Pléiade group was Louis le Caron's *Dialogues philosophiques* (1556). The fourth dialogue is entitled "Ronsard, ou de la poésie." Here Le Caron takes up the problem of poetic inspiration, concludes that the poet cannot substitute art for nature in his effort to create memorable

[56] *Ibid.*, p. 198.

[57] Jacques Peletier, *Art poétique*, ed. by Boulanger (Paris, 1930), p. 74.

works. But if nature is essential to any literary enterprise, art is just as imperative a requirement. "La Nature et l'Art sont les dons communs de Dieu, sans lesquelz le poète ne doit espérer de rendre quelque œuvre louable et excellent." [58] That peripheral convert to the Pléiade movement, Jean de la Taille, ridicules the notion of natural genius more emphatically than any other, designating it "ceste sotte opinion de penser qu'on naisse et qu'on devienne naturellement excellent en cest art, avec une fureur divine, sans suer, sans feuilleter, sans choisir l'invention, sans limer les vers." [59]

And finally, Ronsard. In 1550 Ronsard subtly recognises but refuses to make any concession to the theory of the *doctus poeta*, with its emphasis on book learning and training. This is revealed by the presence of the adjective "indoctrinated" in his statement to Du Bellay that "le bon poète endoctriné par le seul naturel bien-né se haste de ravir le prix," whereas those scribblers who have learned with plodding, pains, and ruses, to their own shame create verses which run undisciplined outside the course of the Muses.[60] However, the famous ode to Michel de l'Hospital, composed two years later, is an unadulterated tribute to innate genius and divine inspiration. Often quoted is the celebrated quatrain,

> A fin (ô Destins) qu'il n'avienne
> Que le monde appris faussement,
> Pense que vostre mestier vienne
> D'art et non de ravissement.[61]

Ronsard's *Abbrégé de l'art poétique* (1565) repeats the idea contained in this ode and elsewhere in his works that for the earliest Helladic poets nature was all-sufficient, having to be replaced by art among the later Greeks and Romans. By 1565 the Christian inspiration had assumed a paramount rôle. Today,

[58] Quoted in Marcel Raymond, *L'Influence de Ronsard* (Paris: Champion, 1927), I, 316.

[59] La Taille, *Art de la Tragédie* (Manchester, 1939), p. 30.

[60] Ronsard, II, 150.

[61] *Ibid.*, II, 134.

Ronsard insists, to be a great poet one's inspiration must come from God. For the Muses, Apollo, Mercury, Pallas, Venus, and all those traditional deities are only manifestations of the forces of God, to whom the first men gave various names after the various effects of his incomprehensible majesty.[62]

By the term of his life, Ronsard had progressed to a belief in predestination (probably more Pythagorean than Calvinistic) and a denial of the will, which denial the Cartesians of the following century were to disparage. Poets are born, there is no doubt of it, but just as men are predestined to be poets, so are poets predestined to learn all of the art and wisdom of their profession. "Tout homme dès le naistre reçoit en l'âme je ne sçay quelles fatales impressions, qui le contraignent suivre plus tost son Destin que sa volonté."[63] The idea that poets, learning and all, were predestined — that although they were not learned at birth, their nature impelled them to study and attain greatness, this was the master stroke that cleft the problem, like Alexander's solution of the Gordian Knot. Had not Ronsard examined attentively those new theological tracts on predestination which he so scathingly condemned, he might not have happened upon this simple solution.

After this, the cautious compromises of Vauquelin, Pierre de Laudun, and Deimier have only a modicum of interest. We shall include them principally to round out our picture of the century. Vauquelin is sufficiently imbued with classicism to subscribe to *ingenium* and to reproduce the Platonic imagery of fury in his *Art poétique*. Although there are constant references to the parallel between nature and art, the following lines may be quoted as representative:

> C'est un point débatu par argumens divers,
> Si, de Nature ou d'Art, se compose un beau vers,
> Et laquelle des deux plus on estime et prise
> En vers, ou la Nature ou la Science aquise:

[62] *Ibid.*, VII, 46.
[63] *Ibid.*, VII, 77.

Quand à moy je ne voy que l'Art ou le Sçavoir
Sans veine naturelle, ait beaucoup de pouvoir:
Ni que sans la Science une veine abondante
Soit pour bien faire un vers assez forte et puissante:
Et tant bien l'un à l'autre aide sert et suvient,
Et d'amiable accord s'unit et s'entretient,
Que si Nature et l'Art ne sont tous deux ensemble,
Un vers ne se fait point bien parfait ce me semble.[64]

In his *Art poétique françoys* of 1598, Pierre de Laudun is illustrative of the *Zeitgeist* when considering art and nature. That is to say, he recognises that the poets of antiquity were natural artists. He suggests, however, that even modern poets have something divine about them. He cites the opinions of Aristotle, Plato, Democritus, and Horace, and concludes with the familiar legerdemain: Nature can get along without art, but art cannot dispense with Nature.[65] And Pierre Deimier held the completely categorical view that "poetry is a gift of Nature perfected by Art." [66]

Such were the opinions voiced by the mid-century and late-century theorists. Monotonous in their lack of imagination and analysis, occasionally inconsistent in their attempts at conciliation, they follow closely the patterns set down by the Greek and Roman rhetoricians. These Renaissance poets copied not only what the classic authors believed, as shown by the constant introduction of certain set ideas like the "poetae nascuntur, fiunt oratores," but copied from one another as well.

The idea of inspiration, however, was not always so stereotyped in their minds as the selections cited above would indicate. As the earlier chapters of this study have demonstrated, the Pléiade poets had a predilection for vivid imagery and varied in as many ways as possible the figures and conceits which they inherited, in essence, from the past. It is not until

[64] Vauquelin de la Fresnaye, *Art poétique*, ed. by Pellissier, p. 174.

[65] Pierre de Laudun, *Art poétique françoys*, ed. by Dedieu (Toulouse, 1909), pp. 77–78.

[66] Quoted in W. F. Patterson, *French Poetic Theory* (Ann Arbor, 1935), I, 789.

one studies the colorful vocabulary of the mechanism of inspiration in the Pléiade's poetry that one uncovers the real variety in their theory. A treatment of the Pléiade's various images of inspiration will be included later in this chapter. It is sufficient for the present to note that there is a sort of unanimity of opinion in their theory concerning the conflict between art and nature. It now remains to see whether their practice, their criticisms on individual writers, agreed with this theory.

⚜ ⚜ ⚜

Both for its importance and for the chronology of its subject matter, Ronsard's "Ode à Michel de l'Hospital" must be the first piece considered in this section. We have already discussed the main thesis of this important poem: that the ἀρχαῖοι composed with spontaneity and unmeditated artistry. These bards were Eumolpus, Musaeus, Orpheus, Hesiod, Linus, and Homer.

> Divins, d'autant que la nature
> Sans art librement exprimoyent:
> Sans art leur naïve escriture
> Par la fureur ils animoyent.[67]

But the second generation of Hellenic poets found that they had to labor over their verses:

> Par un art melancholique
> Trahirent avec grand soin
> Les vers, esloignez bien loin
> De la sainte ardeur antique.

This ode dates from 1552. Six years later Du Bellay took up the same theme in his *Divers jeux rustiques*. To Bertran Bergier he composed several stanzas on poetic inspiration, and more specifically on natural genius and studied art. He relates how Hesiod took one draught from the spring of Hippocrene and was changed from a herdsman into a perfect poet:

[67] Ronsard, II, 139.

Montrant que la seule nature
Sans art, sans travail & sans cure
Fait naistre le poète, avant
Qu'il ayt songé d'estre sçavant.

Les Bergiers, avec leurs musettes
Gardans leurs brebis camusettes
Premiers inventèrent les sons
De ces poétiques chansons.[68]

Whereupon he follows the ode to De l'Hospital with fidelity:

Aussi les vers du temps d'Orphée
D'Homère, Hésiode, & Musée,
Ne venoient d'art, mais seulement
D'un franc naturel mouvement.

Depuis geinant tel exercice
Soubs un misérable artifice,
Ce qu'avoient de bon les premiers
Fut corrompu par les derniers.[69]

Yet natural inspiration is not entirely obsolete; Du Bellay will good-humoredly concede that Bergier himself (as a *berger*) has been granted the direct gift of poetry. And in the *Deffence*, eight years before, he had shown that there was no reason why the great natural geniuses of Hellas might not have their modern counterparts, "for nature has hardly become so barren that she might not give birth to some Platos and Aristotles in our time." [70] Jacques Tahureau, it might be added parenthetically, voiced similar optimism.[71] As one might readily expect after examining his critical theory, however, these concessions do not always come willingly from Du Bellay. Generally, he holds that every poet since the first Helladic generation has been dependent upon training. If asked to explain the greatness of such Greek lyrists as Sappho and

[68] Du Bellay, V, 117; 119.
[69] *Ibid.*, V, 119–120.
[70] *Deffence, ed. cit.*, p. 133.
[71] Tahureau, Blanchemain edition (Paris, 1870), II, 193.

Corinna, the rival of Pindar, he insists that it was because they knew that they must work to develop their natural talents. For it is through art that one expresses the vital energy of nature.[72] Again the compromise.

The later Greeks could be held up as models of artifice (art). When Ronsard is trying to decide whether Garnier or Jodelle has inherited the primacy of Euripides, he sets up several criteria of comparison. These are the virtues and vices of Euripides's works, subject matter, sublimity of style, choice of words, but first and foremost he specifies the "vieil artifice des Grecs." [73]

In his congratulatory verses to Amadis Jamyn on his translation of Homer, Ronsard recalls the natural genius of this Hellenic author, as he had in the ode to Michel de l'Hospital. It is this innate artistry which made Homer inimitable.

> Mille Romains pour haut voler,
> Ont voulu ton vol égaler,
> Mais pournéant, car l'artifice
> Au prix de la nature est vice.[74]

But Du Bellay, in a poem addressed to Jeanne D'Albret, praises Homer for his excess of "artifice," noticeable especially in his inventions. Were he able to write the praises of the Queen, he would have no need of artifice, as had Homer.[75]

It is Pontus de Tyard who relates the matter of the natural versus the artificial to the problem of language. In his *Second Curieux* he is struck by the fact that Plutarch, Galen, and Ptolemy, who served the Roman emperors and whose acquaintances spoke Latin, composed faithfully in their native Greek. Tyard asks and answers the question why these writers should eschew the language of their benefactors in favor of Greek. His explanation is quite ingenious. "La response est facile: qu'ils tenoient pour résolution véritable, le naturel estre tous-

[72] *Deffence, ed. cit.*, pp. 155–156.
[73] Ronsard, VI, 435.
[74] *Ibid.*, VI, 436.
[75] Du Bellay, II, 224.

jours en l'homme, meilleur que l'artifice: et que chacun exprime en sa langue naturelle plus naïfvement les imaginations de son esprit."[76] This is indeed a strange choice of illustration designed to prove that one should avoid writing in antiquated tongues.

The Pléiade theorists were never quite consistent about the Roman poets. Though always agreed that the Hellenic masters composed as θεόπνευστοι, they will occasionally admit the Latins to this category, occasionally deny them admittance. In this vein Ronsard contrasts the "ingenious Greeks" with the "laborious Latins."[77] In the 1572 preface to the *Franciade* he makes a similar distinction, juxtaposing Homer and Vergil. Using the word "naïf," which had all the implications of *ingenium nativum*, he contrasts the spontaneity of the Greek with the labored care of the Roman. "J'ay patronné mon œuvre plustost sur la naïve facilité d'Homère que sur la curieuse diligence de Virgile."[78] It will be noted that "facilité" is used in the same sense as "félicité" in other passages of Du Bellay already encountered. But although Homer writes with native genius or felicity, his works may serve as well as those of Vergil to illustrate principles of studied composition. It is in fact the innate poets who first served as models for the artful poets.

> Homère de science et de nom illustré
> Et le Romain Virgile assez nous ont monstré
> Comment et par quel art, et par quelle pratique
> Il falloit composer un ouvrage Heroïque.[79]

In his "Poète courtisan," Du Bellay emphasises that art need not always be the same as artifice. That one must study and train himself for poetry is the underlying theme of the satire. But the studied artifice of the court poets repels him, and so tongue in cheek he commends this type of "art" to all would-be

[76] Pontus de Tyard, M.-L., p. 236.
[77] Ronsard, VI, 222.
[78] *Ibid.*, VII, 68.
[79] *Ibid.*, VI, 13.

court laureates. The passage where he ironically advises the court poet to forego studied training and rely upon his own talents merits inclusion at this point because of its mention of Pindar and Horace.

> Je veulx en premier lieu que sans suivre la trace
> (Comme font quelques uns) d'un Pindare et Horace,
> Et sans vouloir comme eux voler si haultement,
> Ton simple naturel tu suives seulement.
> Ce procès tant mené, et qui encore dure,
> Lequel des deux vault mieulx, ou l'art ou la Nature,
> En matière de vers, à la court est vuidé:
> Car il suffit icy que tu soyes guidé
> Par le seul naturel, sans art et sans doctrine.[80]

This ironical inclination toward nature over art is obviously a mere lampoon against the glib facility of the parasitic rhymers at court, and must not, of course, be regarded as inconsistent with Du Bellay's prose theory (*v. supra*).

One of Ronsard's most important critical passages was inspired by reflection upon the Greek and Roman writers. This text from the 1587 preface to the *Franciade* is interesting for the same reason as the preceding verses; it considers along with the follow-nature precept the idea (and here, distrust) of poetic "altitude" which one meets throughout the writings of the Pléiade. "Les autres plus rusez tiennent le milieu des deux, ny rampans trop bas, ny s'eslevant trop haut au travers des nues, mais qui d'artifice et d'un esprit naturel elabouré par longues estudes, et principalement par la lecture des bons vieux poètes Grecs et Latins, descrivent leurs conceptions . . . comme a faict Virgile."[81] For Ronsard, this is equivalent to saying that a good poet must supplement his natural gifts by a study of those who had greater natural gifts, certainly a modification or qualification of his stand in the ode to Michel de l'Hospital. This passage and the earlier couplet from the elegy to Christofle de Longueil, "Il faut garder le ton dont la grace despend,

[80] Du Bellay, VI, 132.

[81] Ronsard, VII, 82.

ny trop haut ny trop bas, suivant nostre nature," [82] seem to resume the classic golden mean so well to M. Laumonier that he concludes, "On croirait lire du Malherbe ou du Boileau." [83] Grévin, by the way, admits sweating over Plato and Aristotle, as does Ronsard.[84]

An interesting question that arose in connection with Roman literature was whether the Sibylline Books were written through divine inspiration or through studied art. It was not the Pléiade humanists, however, who first raised this vital issue. "Ciceron en parle au livre de *Divination*, voulant prouver par cete curieuse diligence que les vers des Sybilles étoint faictz par artifice, et non par inspiration divine." [85] One might add here that this puzzling question was also proposed in Vida's *Poetics*, which Du Bellay knew well, and that Vida drew the almost inevitable conclusion that the Sibyls had written naturally.[86]

The Pléiade's endeavors to reconcile contradictory concepts led to a familiar acknowledgment on the part of Du Bellay. This contends that art can replace nature by producing the effects of nature. In congratulating Des Masures for his translation of Vergil, Joachim passes beyond the Aristotelian dictum that art imitates nature in its creative processes and claims that art can replace nature if one judges by the results of these creative processes.

> Autant comme lon peult en un autre langage
> Une langue exprimer, autant que la nature
> Par l'art se peult monstrer, et que par la peinture
> On peult tirer au vif un naturel visage.[87]

Jacques Peletier uses somewhat similar language while paying tribute to this same Roman epicist. Both Renaissance poets

[82] *Ibid.*, V, 184.
[83] *Ibid.*, VIII, 136; also P. Laumonier, *Ronsard, poète lyrique* (Paris, 1909), pp. 283–284.
[84] Grévin, *Poésies choisies* (Paris: Garnier, 1922), p. 344.
[85] *Deffence, ed. cit.*, p. 280.
[86] Vida, *Ars poetica*, I, 539.
[87] Du Bellay, II, 171.

are interested in the idea of taking nature *au vif* which one meets so often in the mid-century discussions of mimesis. The conclusion which Peletier reaches, however, is a traditional one. His work is inferior to Vergil's in so far as art is inferior to nature.

> D'autant que l'art peut moins que la Nature
> Cest œuvre mien, qui sus le vif est pris,
> Est moins parfaict et moins digne de prix
> Que de Maron la divine facture.[88]

Just as Pontus de Tyard had discussed in his *Second Curieux* Greek writers who elected to compose in their native language, he also mentioned therein Cato, Varro, Cicero, Sallust, Caesar, Vergil, Horace, and Ovid as Romans who chose to write in Latin rather than in their fluent Greek. This analogy fits better than the other the case of the French Renaissance poets who had to choose between a native modern language and an imported dead language. "Mais qui est celuy d'entr' eux, qui n'aima mieux escrire en la sienne naturelle, qu'en celle qu'il avoit acquise par laborieux et artificiel estude?"[89] The implication seems to be that language is one of the natural gifts of the Muses, much like the skill of versifying itself. That is, one's own language is a natural gift whereas other languages than one's own must be acquired through learning. Although this distinction was a specious one, it afforded a good, practical argument against the neo-Latins of the period.

In Du Bellay's *Olive* we find the two creative forces of nature and art paralleled to the creative processes of invention and imitation. That invention depends upon *ingenium* and imitation upon learned procedures of composition is indicated by the adjectives Du Bellay affixes to each term in his second preface to the *Olive*. Those of his readers who are versed in the Latin poets will recognise this dependence; those who have read the works of Vergil, Ovid, Horace, Petrarch "trouverront

[88] J. Peletier, *Œuvres poëtiques*, ed. by Séché, p. 49.
[89] Pontus de Tyard, M.-L., p. 237.

qu'en mes escriptz y a beaucoup plus de naturelle invention que d'artificielle ou supersticieuse immitation."[90]

Statius, whom the Pléiade admired as an epicist, is cited as one of the early poets who composed under the influence of the divine fury, but who did not "enter into the temple of the Muses."

> Stace entre les Romains nous en monstra la voye:
> Combien qu'il fust sans art, de fureur transporté,
> Beaucoup plus ampoullé que plein de majesté.[91]

Such are the opinions and remarks of the Pléiade on the great names of Hellenic and Roman literature. Reflection upon the excellence of these ancients, those who were endowed with natural brilliance and those who had acquired masterful technique, elicited the cry from Ronsard, "A genous, Franciade, adore l'Aenéide, adore l'Iliade!" This humanistic appeal was first published in the year 1587.[92] Exactly one hundred years later, in 1687, Charles Perrault answered it in his *Siècle de Louis-le-Grand*, recalling the very wording of Ronsard! Of antiquity he testifies,

> . . . je ne crus jamais qu'elle fût adorable.
> Je vois les anciens sans plier les genoux.

⚜ ⚜ ⚜

In this chapter, as in others, the remarks of the Pléiade on early Renaissance authors are not numerous. Against the recent *rhétoriqueurs*, that generation of versifiers whose preoccupation with intricacies of rhyme was so distasteful to the Pléiade, Ronsard at least voices objections. Art, become effort in the unnatural ways of these rhymers, was the very reason for their mediocrity. It was against the *rhétoriqueurs*, according to M.

[90] Du Bellay, I, 20.
[91] Ronsard, VI, 16.
[92] *Ibid.*, VI, 13.

Laumonier, that Ronsard composed the lines of his ode to Joachim du Bellay which we reproduced above.[93]

Mention of the early-Renaissance Italians again raises the linguistic question. Ruminating upon those Latin works for which Petrarch and Boccaccio thought posterity would remember them, works, for example, like Petrarch's *De remediis utriusque fortunae* and Boccaccio's *De casibus virorum illustrium* or his bucolic eclogues, Du Bellay reaches conclusions similar to those of Tyard in the *Second Curieux*. One's own language is a gift of nature; one is attracted to it by an "inclination naturelle." Composition in a foreign or dead idiom is artificial and avails one nothing, as the experience of Petrarch and Boccaccio shows.[94] It is worth noting that Du Bellay, apologising in his *Regrets* for his Latin poemata, calls French not merely his native language, but his natural language.[95]

To a poet such as Vulteius, a neo-Latin himself, all of this reasoning was, so to speak, rubbish. A contemporary poet may compose in Latin and still remain naturally endowed, and this can be discerned in his verse. As proof he presents the neo-Latin Salmon Macrin:

> Res quae te faciunt bonum poetam,
> Sunt hae iudicio, Macrine, nostro,
> Ars, natura comes, labor gravisque.[96]

Leaving the linguistic issue to return to our chronology, we must again refer to Petrarch. Petrarchism illustrated so aptly the studied, artificial type of poetry that it was called an "art." Du Bellay twice inveighs against the "art de Pétrarquizer," [97] which same expression is used by Ronsard in his "Élégie à Cassandre." [98] One finds this interpretation of art as artificiality (even Boileau complained of the Petrarchists "qui s'affligent

[93] *Vide supra*, note 60.
[94] *Deffence, ed. cit.*, p. 148.
[95] Du Bellay, II, 60.
[96] Vulteius, *Epigrammatum libri* iiii (Lugduni, 1537), p. 249.
[97] Du Bellay, IV, 205, 211.
[98] Ronsard, I, 111.

par art")[99] in several of the discussions of art and nature. Such a meaning of *art* in this discussion may not be a perfectly legitimate one, but it is included as a reminder that in the Renaissance both *art* and *artifice* had favorable and pejorative values.

The Pléiade poets, as others before us have noted, were alternately kind and unkind toward Marot. In the matter of art and nature, he was weighed and found wanting. Ronsard admits that Marot had been a competent poet, but claims that he, Ronsard, was superior to him by the standards of both art and nature; in art, because he had studied more than Marot; in nature, because Ronsard was born to a better age and therefore enjoyed better natural endowments.[100] This idea that a "better" age may make a more natural poet, possibly based on a belief in inevitable human progress, seems contrary to the Pléiade's humanistic veneration of the past, and certainly a contradiction to their recurrent statement that the most natural and spontaneous artists were the earliest Helladic bards. It was advanced most seriously, of course, during the following century, when the proponents of modernism in the famous Quarrel of the Ancients and Moderns took hold of it. To avoid this apparent contradiction one may answer that Ronsard's conception of a better age had nothing to do with chronology, and that the goodness of an era is irrespective of time. In this way, the "best age" need not be the Age of Francis First, when this was written, but might be the Age of Augustus or the Golden Age of Hellas. One innovation remains, however, in this text of Ronsard. This is the idea that environment is part of nature's gift to the poet. This has already been indirectly hinted in the belief of Tyard that native language, one of the most important parts of environment, is a natural endowment.

Du Bellay was equally severe on Marot. Using artifice as a

[99] Boileau, *Art poétique*, II, 47.
[100] Ronsard, II, 103–104.

general term for art, as the Pléiade often did, Du Bellay complains that Marot and the Marotiques knew French well, possessed good native wit, "mais bien peu d'artifice."[101] This use of *artifice* in the favorable sense, by the way, should be contrasted with the many passages where it has a pejorative meaning. The reader should be constantly aware of one fundamental point: *art*, *artifice*, *ornement*, and *fantaisie* are all employed by the Pléiade in two ways, and in the pejorative acceptation have connotations of falsity.

We arrive finally at the Pléiade's opinions about their coevals. After perusing the discussions of art and nature in their theoretical treatises, we hardly expect to find the Pléiade considering many Renaissance poets as born artists. Yet such a possibility was occasionally entertained. One cannot forget the remark of Du Bellay that Mother Nature had not become so barren as to deny his century some Platos and Aristotles.[102] Or Jacques Tahureau's boast that France was full of an "infinity of Homers, Vergils, Euripideses, Senecas, Menanders, Terences, Anacreons, Tibulluses, Pindars, Horaces, Demostheneses, and Ciceros."[103] As one has seen throughout the previous chapters of this study, many of the remarks passed on the Pléiade's contemporaries were colored by prejudice and personal motives. Witness, for example, this passage from Du Bellay's *Vers lyriques*, addressed to Mellin de Saint-Gelays:

> Celuy qui n'a eu favorable
> La Muse lente à son secours,
> D'un artifice misérable
> Enfante les siens durs et lours.
> Pourquoy donques si longue nuit
> Veulx-tu sur tes labeurs estendre,
> Opprimant la voix de ton bruit,
> Qui malgré toy se fait entendre?[104]

[101] *Deffence*, p. 197. It is for this reason that M. Chamard concludes of Marot, "Ce poète naturel n'avait pas été véritablement un poète artiste," in *Joachim du Bellay* (Lille, 1900), p. 75.

[102] *Deffence*, p. 133.

[103] Tahureau, *Poésies*, ed. by Blanchemain (Paris, 1870), II, 195.

[104] Du Bellay, III, 96.

This advice to eschew labored study, contrary to the most fundamental beliefs of Du Bellay and evidently without irony, is the same counsel that he later gave to the "Poète courtisan" (1559). Here he advises the poet not to spend time in study, for there are other ways — social maneuvers — to achieve one's ends. The similarity of the phraseology in the two pieces (studying all night, *etc.*) lends support to the possibility that the "Poète courtisan" was after all directed at Mellin, and that in the year before his death Du Bellay was putting an ironic touch to the insincere advice and flattery he had penned earlier.

The reverse of this ironic advice of Du Bellay is Ronsard's elegy storming at the young courtier who mocked his works in public. Whereas Ronsard generally inclines toward nature and Du Bellay toward art, here it is Ronsard who demonstrates what a quantity of hard work and application the Pléiade thought necessary to the production of good poetry. This is what the Pléiade understood by *art*:

> Si tu sçavois ce qu'ils coustent à escrire,
> Si tu avois autant que moy sué
> Refueilleté Homère et remué
> Pour la science avec labeur apprendre,
> Tu n'oserois, petit sot, me reprendre.[105]

The same formula of work and more work is the theme of a poem by Jacques Grévin[106] and of an elegy of Ronsard composed to Grévin. The general burden of the latter is the unattainability of poetic perfection. But once again Ronsard's inclination toward nature over art reveals itself and he limits the benefits of study. A lawyer, physician, mathematician, or orator may become perfect in his vocation by dint of hard study. But the poet may not, for the Muse never gives herself completely to any individual or to any nation. The gift of poetry is like a fleeting will-o'-the-wisp that flashes over the meadows

[105] Ronsard, IV, 146.
[106] Grévin, *Poésies choisies* (Paris: Garnier, 1922), p. 344.

and streams, brightening now one country, now another, never favoring any particular one exclusively while favoring all.[107]

Olivier de Magny employs the word *félicité* with its special semantic value of natural endowment, a value which Du Bellay and Ronsard gave it in their discussions of art and nature. Magny is speaking of himself:

> La Nature m'a faict, & la Nature est belle
> Pour la diversité que nous voions en elle:
> Je suis donq' naturel, & ma félicité
> En matière d'amour c'est la diversité.[108]

Thumbing through the *canzoniere* of the Pléiade, one learns that latter-day congenital geniuses were not too uncommon in the Renaissance. In showering praises upon their friends, the Pléiade writers would occasionally overlook the convention of the *Grais ingenium*[109] and admit that their associates and coevals were born poets. Magny will admit that Ronsard is a product of nature.[110] Ronsard will admit that Des Autels is a product of nature.[111] In fact, Ronsard's celebrated poem to Christofle de Choiseul seems to set up natural inspiration as a rite of initiation into the confraternity of the Pléiade. Here, in one of the several poems where the personnel of the Pléiade is suggested, this εὐφυία seems to have destined Rémy Belleau for membership:

> Te concevant, Belleau, qui vins en la brigade
> Des bons, pour accomplir la septième Pléiade
> Qui as (comme bien-né) ton naturel suivi
> Et que les Muses ont naivement ravy.[112]

Successful translations, as contrasted with creative writing, depend upon art and learning rather than on nature. Thus, when one wished to congratulate a poet upon a translation, one might praise his "docte artifice," as Du Bellay praised that of

[107] Ronsard, VI, 404–405.
[108] Magny, *Odes*, Courbet edition, II, 134.
[109] *Ad Pisones*, 323–326.
[110] Magny, *Odes*, *ed. cit.*, I, 112.
[111] Ronsard, I, 117.
[112] *Ibid.*, V, 185.

Sébilet.[113] Yet the purpose of this art in translation is to catch the native spirit of the author translated. This was the aim of Peletier's vernacularization of the *Georgics* and Des Masures's version of the *Aeneid*, according to Du Bellay and to Peletier himself.[114] The same purpose may be ascribed to the imitation of genres as to the imitation of poets themselves. It is the true and natural style of the original pattern that one must copy. This was the great merit of Ronsard in recreating the Greek ode: ". . . et l'ode, quand à son vray et naturel stile, représentée en nostre langue par Pierre de Ronsard."[115]

⚜ ⚜ ⚜

Much of the Pléiade's speculation about inspiration is expressed not in the general and abstract terms with which we have been dealing, but rather in definite, concrete images and expressions which illustrate the great variety of ways by which nature may instill genius in the human soul. By their very essence, these images and conceits tend to view genius as the product of nature rather than art, of inspiration rather than perspiration, to use Thomas Edison's terms. This variety of poetic imagery describing the methods by which nature imparts the gift or grace of poetry reveals that the Pléiade borrowed from a wide number of sources. Many of the passages listed below will not contain specific judgments upon individual writers, but are included rather for their value in clarifying and amplifying the imagery of those passages which do, and to demonstrate again what a wealth of critical ideas lies scattered throughout the Pléiade's verse.

One of the most common forms in which the poet received the gift of inspiration was as nourishment. (It might be appropriate to note here that inspiration was not viewed as a breath,

[113] Du Bellay, IV, 181.
[114] *Vide supra*, notes 87 and 88.
[115] Du Bellay, I, 12.

an afflatus, by the Pléiade, despite the frequency of this image in classic times.) Poets were called "nourrissons des Muses." [116] This sustenance might be taken either in the form of food or, more commonly, of drink. Du Bellay indicates the basis for the former trope, writing in the second preface to the *Olive*: "J'ai tousjours estimé la poésie comme ung somptueux banquet," [117] and Ronsard extols the excellent Jean Dorat who was "nurtured by Apollo." [118] Such partaking might occur at the very table of the Muses. This is established in a passage of Ronsard embodying a possible reminiscence of Dante's *Paradiso XXIV* (1–9), where the Florentine, a new citizen of heaven, is to sup at the table of the fellowship of saints. The reminiscence we propose is strengthened by a mention of Dante in the preceding lines,

> Depuis que ton Pétrarque eut surmonté la Nuit
> De Dante, & Cavalcant, et de sa renommée,
> Claire comme un Soleil, eut la terre semée,
> Fait citoyen du Ciel: nul après luy n'a peu
> Grimper sur Hélicon, pour y estre repeu
> A la table des Sœurs de leur saincte Ambrosie,
> Qui seule donne l'ame à nostre poésie.[119]

The passage closes with the warning that the Muses do not give of their board to everyone.

Readers of Juvenal, the Pléiade knew that eating laurel leaves also inspired literary production.[120] More commonly, however, one drank in his inspiration. This drinking was done at one of the Boeotian springs of poetry, on either Mount Helicon, Pindus, Parnassus, or at Pimpla, and variously called Hippocrene, Aganippe, Castalia, Permessus, or less correctly, the Eurotas.[121] Lest they overwork the somewhat limited possibilities of this image, the Pléiade varied it, mostly by periphrasis, as much as possible. These springs or the waters that

[116] Ronsard, STFM, IX, 191.
[117] Du Bellay, I, 24.
[118] Ronsard, III, 241.
[119] *Ibid.*, VI, 27.
[120] Du Bellay, VI, 132.
[121] Ronsard, V, 37.

V. JOACHIM DU BELLAY

J'ay tousjours estimé la poésie comme ung somptueux banquet, où chacun est le bien venu, & n'y force lon personne de manger d'une viande ou boire d'un vin, s'il n'est à son goust.

(see page 218)

issued from them are called seriatim "the waters where the Ascrean drank," "the waters that flow on the mountain of the nine sisters," "the Chevaline spring," "the quick waters," and the like.[122] Adopting this nomenclature in his poem to Bertran Bergier and in the "Complainte du désespéré," Du Bellay makes the identification, common to his age, of Helicon with Parnassus, and places Hippocrene on the latter rather than the former mountain.[123] This addiction to mixing the elements of their tropes was not uncommon in the Pléiade, as we have noticed. Observe in the following lines by Ronsard the ideal of learning entering into an image of pure natural inspiration:

> A qui mieux d'un docte gosier
> A beu de l'onde Aganippide.[124]

The ways of obtaining this holy water were many and occasionally surprise one by their extravagance. One may drink the waters, as has been noted. Or one may "wash one's mouth in the waters of Permessus"; as unpoetic as this image seems, no less an authority than Ben Jonson called it the standard formula for describing inspiration.[125] Again, one might plunge into the flood or bathe himself nine times in the stream of Helicon.[126] Our favorite, however, remains that rite, described by Du Bellay, of leaping astride the steed of poetry, Pegasus, and diving nude into the stream.[127]

For a characteristic summary of the share which the sacred rivers have in the formation of a poet, one should consult the lengthy piece in *vers Baïfins* entitled "l'Hippocrène," in the second book of the *Poèmes*. It is a highly descriptive work,

[122] Ronsard, I, 81; I, 117; La Péruse, *ed. cit.*, p. 153; Du Bellay, IV, 105; V, 117; VI, 117; *etc.*

[123] Du Bellay, IV, 105.

[124] Ronsard, VI, 434.

[125] Ronsard, V, 364; see Ben Jonson, *Discoveries*, in R. P. Cowl, *Theory of Poetry in England* (London, 1914), p. 7: "and not think he can leap forth suddenly a poet by dreaming that he hath been in Parnassus, or having washed his lips, as they say, in Helicon."

[126] Ronsard, II, 379; V, 288.

[127] Du Bellay, II, 53.

replete with classic mythology, telling of the creation of the stream by Pegasus and explaining its magical powers.[128]

This thought of drinking in one's inspiration, by the way, was highly amusing to Rabelais, and he poked fun at it. In the prologue to the Third Book, he adopts the imagery, beseeching the reader, "Attendez un peu que je hume quelque traict de ceste bouteille: c'est mon vray et seul Hélicon, c'est ma fontaine Caballine: c'est mon unique Enthusiasme."

⚜ ⚜ ⚜

One of the most popular sciences of the middle sixteenth century was astrology. Although no reference to the idea that the stars influence the careers of individuals (found in Anaximander, Thales, Anaxagoras, and others) is found in ancient Greek writings of a purely literary character, it became common in the literature of the Romans. Brother Cornelia, in his excellent study of the classical sources of Ronsard's references to nature, shows that the idea was present in such writers as Horace and Vergil who were familiar to the Pléiade.[129] Although these Latins wrote that the conjunction of the stars influenced one's destiny, they did not speak of stars as making poets. This logical conclusion was reached by the Pléiade theorists themselves.

Before citing the texts which reveal this conclusion, one must examine some sample passages which indicate how everpresent

[128] Baïf, M.-L., II, 61.

[129] W. B. Cornelia, *The Classical Sources of the Nature References in Ronsard's Poetry* (New York: Columbia University, 1934), p. 187. *Cf.* on the subject of both astrology and demonology the excellent chapters in Lynn Thorndike, *History of Magic and Experimental Science*, vols. V and VI, "The Sixteenth Century" (New York, 1941). Thorndike recalls (V, 275) the following quatrain of Bonaventure des Périers:

> Pour ainsi donc, ô monde lunatique!
> Ayes pour tous cestuy seul prognostique
> C'est que, pour vray, tous les prognostiqueurs
> Sont et seront ou mocqués ou mocqueurs.

astrology was in their minds. Although the Pléiade, like Trissino, would probably conclude that Fortune was merely another name for Christian Providence, they half-believed in astrology, like men of today who scoff at superstition yet hesitate to light three cigarettes on one match. One or two of them were firm believers in the "science." Peletier, in his *De constitutione horoscopi* (1563) revealed himself an orthodox adherent with conventional ideas about division of the zodiac. Thorndike has pointed out that Latin verses of Dorat accompanied an astrological prognostication for the year 1570 by Jean Brochier. Credulous or not, they did not fail to perceive the poetic possibilities of astrology. In Petrarchist poetry it provided a splendid conceit, and one could coin such happy phrases as "l'Astre, guide à ma fatalité," [130] one could complain of his cruel star or rejoice in his benign star, as did Pontus de Tyard, Baïf, Ronsard, Du Bellay, and Magny.[131] It proved also a handy device to praise a celebrated or influential man, for one could explain how the stars had taken charge of his destiny. Magny discovered this while complimenting Charles Cardinal de Lorraine,[132] and Du Bellay while eulogising the Cardinal Du Bellay.[133]

It was inevitable that such a belief should enter the contemporary critical vocabulary. Whether one was to master the thorny art of poetry depended upon the astral conjunction at one's birth. One might say that the Pléiade paraphrased the Latin proverb into *ad aspera per astra*.

Pontus de Tyard remained unconvinced about astrological predestination. In the dialogue, "Mantice, ou Discours de la vérité de Divination par Astrologie," he seems to share the doubts of his collocutor Le Curieux.[134] It is our personal belief

[130] Pontus de Tyard, M.-L., p. 50.

[131] *Ibid.*, p. 50; Baïf, I, 161; Ronsard, I, 155; Du Bellay, I, 149; Magny, *Soupirs*, *ed. cit.*, p. 17; Jean de la Taille also accuses his star (*Œuvres*, III, p. 33).

[132] Magny, *Odes*, *ed. cit.*, I, 22.

[133] Du Bellay, III, 109.

[134] Pontus de Tyard, *Discours philosophiques* (Paris: L'Angelier, 1587), dialogue entitled *Mantice*.

that Mantice here is a portrait of Mellin de Saint-Gelays, whose *Advertissement sur les jugements d'astrologie*, published in 1546, held a brief for astrology and contained explanations similar to those found in the "Mantice" of Pontus.[135] Another Renaissance writer who voiced his scorn of astrology through a literary mouthpiece was François Rabelais. This he accomplished by that famous letter of Gargantua to his son Pantagruel, "Laisse moy l'astrologie divinatrice, et l'art de Lullius, comme abus et vanités." But on the whole, objections to the starmongers were rare.

Ronsard composed two major poems on stars, one the "Hymne des astres" and the other the "Hymne des Estoiles." [136] Probably the former hymn, appropriately dedicated to Mellin de Saint-Gelays, is his most important presentation of this intrusion of astrology into poetic theory.

> Cestuy là dès naissance est faict sacré Poète,
> Et jamais sous les doigts sa Lyre n'est muete,
> Qu'il ne chante tousjours d'un vers melodieux
> Les Hymnes excellens des hommes et des Dieux,
> Ainsy que toy, Mellin, orné de tant de graces.[137]

The piece begins with a general statement of the precepts of astrology, passing thence to their application to poetry. This is similar to the progression of the "Hymne des Estoiles"; Ronsard confides to the stars that he is following the destiny which they have allotted him personally.

> Tandis que tous les jours
> Vous devuidez vos cours
> D'une danse etherée:
> Endurant je vivray,
> Et la chance suivray
> Que vous m'avez livrée.[138]

[135] Mellin de Saint-Gelays, *Advertissement sur les jugements d'Astrologie*, in the "Trésor des pièces angoumoisines" (Angoulême: Société archéologique et historique de la Charente, 1866), Vol. II.

[136] Ronsard, VI, 276; IV, 255.

[137] *Ibid.*, VI, 281.

[138] *Ibid.*, IV, 259.

Tahureau twice links astrological influence with literary prowess. The first of these two poems, "A Messieurs les enfants de France," states merely that a child nourished on Parnassus has received the "benign favor of a good star at his birth." [139] In the second he shows how the influence of the stars may be malignant as well as benevolent for the poet:

> Car l'homme né durant un Astre
> Borgnoyant Phoebus de travers,
> Contreint, ne brouille que des vers
> Qui sentent l'air d'un Poestastre.[140]

That astral influence was for Tahureau merely a poetic motif, however, and not really a personal belief may be discerned in his prose *Dialogues*. Here he will not even go so far as to admit the dictum: "astra inclinant sed non necessitant." He calls almanacs and astral prognostications utter lies.[141]

Even if the stars do give the poet some natural talent, they may make him miserable nevertheless. Du Bellay, recalling the misfortunes of Euripides, Aeschylus, Plautus, and Ovid, curses the rigorous heaven that "assujetit ma naissance à l'indomtable puissance d'ung astre si malheureux." [142] But in another passage, from the exchange of sonnets with Jeanne d'Albret, Du Bellay states that he is no longer going to blame the stars for making poets out of mortals, for poetry is after all a noble profession.[143]

Sometimes the planets which exerted the influence were identified by name. In Du Bellay's "Les conditions du vray Poète," where he tells Bouju of the predestination that makes poets of men, it is apparently the planet Venus which makes amoristic poets of some: "Son estoile veut qu'il vive tousjours de l'amour amy." [144] The specific gifts of the four heavenly bodies, the

[139] Tahureau, *ed. cit.*, I, 31.

[140] *Ibid.*, I, 122.

[141] Tahureau, *Dialogues*, *ed. cit.*, p. 131.

[142] Du Bellay, IV, 106.

[143] *Ibid.*, II, 229.

[144] *Ibid.*, III, 121. Ronsard places the inspiration of Tyard's *Erreurs* with the "astre besson," more probably milady's eyes than the Gemini. (Ronsard, VI, 199.)

Sun, Mercury, Saturn, and Mars, are listed by Ronsard in his *Mascarades.* These natural endowments are power, prudent counsel, prosperity, and valor respectively.[145] Another mention of a specific star is found in Passerat:

> Ah l'on le disoit bien, que l'Estoille nouvelle
> A la sanglante queue, & aus cheveus ardents,
> Menaçoit les plus grands de tristes accidents:
> De meurtres, de mal-heurs, & de guerre cruelle! [146]

An interesting variation of this image of inspiration is encountered in the "Hymenée du roy Charles IX" of Etienne Jodelle. Genius, as an allegorical figure, speaks and tells how he collaborates with Mercury in endowing human beings at their birth. Mercury's gift is not prudent counsel, as in Ronsard, but the arts and particularly eloquence.[147] If the reader wishes to examine another contemporaneous piece which personifies the chief planets, let him read the "Chanson des astres," by the starstruck Saint-Gelays.[148]

In his *Odes*, Olivier de Magny rejoices that genethlialogy arranged the meeting of Ronsard and Paschal and the productive friendship which ensued from that meeting. When he sees the holy and fated bond which links these two together,

> Je beneiz l'estoile des cieux,
> Qui d'un accord si précieux
> Deux esprits si rares assemble.[149]

Another indirect benefit to poetry is ascribed to the planets by Du Bellay in the *Deffence*. The astral bodies conspire to enrich the French language. "Donques, s'il est ainsi que de nostre tens les astres, comme d'un accord, ont par une heureuse influence conspiré en l'honneur et accroissement de nostre langue." [150]

[145] Ronsard, III, 469–470.
[146] Passerat, *Poésies françaises* (Paris, 1880), II, 94.
[147] Jodelle, M.-L., I, 299.
[148] Mellin de Saint-Gelays, *Œuvres* (Paris, 1873), I, 121.
[149] Magny, *Odes, ed. cit.*, I, 44. [150] *Deffence, ed. cit.*, p. 319.

While treating of language, one might add that astrology and astromancy contributed two new words to the French vocabulary of the Renaissance. Although they did not remain in use, they provide us still another illustration that the Pléiade theorists practised what they preached regarding the enrichment of language. Both of these coinages appear as adjectival past participles. The first was invented by Jean-Antoine de Baïf:

> Mais, Tibaud, aussi tost qu'il naist
> Il faut que d'une douce œillade,
> Des Muses la chaste brigade
> L'enfant *bien-astré* favorise.[151]

The second was contained in "Les Parques" of Ronsard, where a child is characterised as "tout *en-astré* d'heur." [152]

In a characteristic sonnet already quoted, Du Bellay questions Ronsard on the source of his poetic inspiration. This sonnet abounds with the favorite tropes of the Pléiade. "De quel soleil, de quel divin flambeau vint ton ardeur?" [153] For purposes of completeness and to suggest what varied meanings the planets held for the Pléiade, one should mention parenthetically a neo-Platonist phase of the Pléiade's astrolatry. This is the belief, founded upon the *Timaeus*, that stars are the final resting places of human souls, and that the souls themselves become stars. Thus one finds the poets addressing their deceased friends as stars.[154]

The association of astrology with poetic or literary inspiration took hold, then, by the late sixteenth century, and one encounters it in subsequent treatises on poetic theory. Vauquelin de la Fresnaye is persuaded that it is astral influence which distinguishes the poets from the poetasters.[155] The insistence of the sixteenth century in proposing this belief gave it such

[151] Baïf, M.-L., II, 391–392.
[152] Ronsard, V, 135.
[153] Du Bellay, I, 124.
[154] See, for this doctrine, R. V. Merrill, *Platonism of Joachim du Bellay* (Chicago, 1925), pp. 31–35.
[155] Vauquelin, *Art poétique*, *ed. cit.*, p. 147.

an impetus that it reappeared in the following century in the very opening verses of Boileau's *Art poétique*:

> S'il ne sent point du ciel l'influence secrète,
> Si son astre en naissant ne l'a formé poète,
> Dans son génie étroit il est toujours captif.[156]

⚜ ⚜ ⚜

The idea of poetry being the product of a sacred, religious, or Corybantic exaltation is too well treated by other students of the Renaissance to invite full reproduction here.[157] Similarly, the Pléiade's judgments and opinions on other writers inspired with fury are too numerous and too uniformly routine; no attempt will be made to register more than a few here. One needs only to read the "Ode à Michel de l'Hospital" to perceive what an integral part of the doctrine of natural inspiration the Sacred Fury became. M. Franchet opines that this ode established the fame of both Ronsard and this doctrine.[158] For it is here that Jupiter defines poetry as a gift from himself, as a fury without which no writer becomes great. It is a colorful but dignified presentation of the old Platonic idea. Other passages treating of the *sacra pazzia* are more vivid and extravagant. For this reason we are tempted to regard fury as poetic imagery. More strictly speaking, it is an authentic philosophical doctrine, harking back to the *Phaedrus*. Equally important as the ode to De l'Hospital was the "Premier solitaire, ou Discours des Muses et de la fureur poétique," in which Pontus de Tyard expounds his Platonism. This prose work contains such inspired definitions of poetic fury as "l'unique escalier par lequel l'âme peut trouver le chemin qui la conduise à la source

[156] Boileau, *Art poétique*, I, vss. 3–5.

[157] On poetic fury in the Pléiade, see H. Franchet, *Le poète et son œuvre*, pp. 1–42; M. Raymond, *L'Influence de Ronsard*, I, 314–316; H. Chamard, *Histoire de la Pléiade*, I, 370–373; Patterson's index of *fureur poétique* in his *French Poetic Theory*, II, 482.

[158] Franchet, *op. cit.*, p. 17.

de son souverain bien & félicité dernière."[159] Well nigh unnoticed and unknown, this work is nevertheless the most complete contemporary analysis of enthusiasm and poetic frenzy.

Almost as significant is "La Lyre" of Ronsard (1569), in which the entire possession is described from the poet's viewpoint, from the initial seizure to the departure of the fury.[160] This exaltation is presented as the *sine qua non* of literary creation. The mooted question whether art or nature has the foremost share in making the competent poet suddenly seems faraway and futile. It is impossible for Ronsard to compose a line when he is not under this theoleptic influence, should the king himself ask him to rhyme. Perhaps he may wait a six-month or a twelvemonth before the fury descends upon him; then, after this long interval,

> Dedans mon cœur du Ciel elle devalle,
> Colère, ardant, furieux, agité,
> Je tremble tout, dessous la Déité. . . .

This emotional experience is further described until that moment when, the creation completed and "all passion spent," pen and paper drop weakly from his hands. Other passages of Ronsard[161] and his contemporaries[162] picture this excitation, but this is the most graphic attempt at introspective analysis.

The same physical exaltation is implicit in the word "enthusiasm" which the Pléiade frequently used. In fact, the Greek etymon implied violent ecstasy of creation or of possession. Typical Renaissance uses are Du Bellay's "ne sentant plus la première ardeur de cet Enthusiasme," Ronsard's reference to "l'Enthousiasme Limosin" and his tribute to Pontus de Tyard: "Il me faudroit non l'ardeur de ma ryme, mais

[159] Pontus de Tyard, *Discours philosophiques* (Paris: L'Angelier, 1587), fol. 8r.

[160] Ronsard, V, 44.

[161] See *Discours à De Troussily* (III, 312); the *Élégie au Roy* of 1584.

[162] For a comprehensive list, see Patterson, *op. cit.*, II, 482.

l'Enthousiasme aiguillon de Pontus." [163] To these examples might be added Magny's depiction of the "Enthusiasm which kindles my soul." [164] Among his incidental remarks in the 1574 edition of Saint-Gelays, Antoine de Harsy recalls that the literary giants of antiquity had held poetry to be divine, "disans la poésie n'estre autre chose qu'un enthousiasme ou celeste fureur." [165]

The conceit of fury was coupled with all the other conceits of poetic inspiration in an effort to achieve variety, an attempt which was not generally successful. Thus nature could impart this fury in many ways — by giving poets drink of the sacred streams of Boeotia,[166] by visiting them with demons,[167] by entrusting them to Apollo,[168] by giving them into the custody of the Muses,[169] and so on.

We have noted from our collection of references to inspirational fury that the mentions of individual writers included Renaissance writers as often as ancients. One cannot help feeling that this imagery was extremely inappropriate when applied to contemporary writers and that the Pléiade poet himself must have shared this feeling. How meaningless the image of fury could become is seen from Ronsard's compliment upon "la fureur de ton style," addressed to King Charles IX.[170] As was the case with the swan and bee imagery, the Pléiade's indiscriminate use of this image occasionally robbed it of its potential beauty and meaning.

Two distortions of the doctrine of poetic fury must be noted here. The first concerns the inventor of iambic verse, Archilochus of Paros, whose early satires were so sharp that he won eternal notoriety for his rage. It was probably Horace's statement that "Archilochum proprio rabies armavit iambo" which

[163] Quoted in Marty-Laveaux, "Pléiade françoyse" (Paris: Lemerre, 1896), *Appendice*, I, 78.

[164] Magny, *Dernières poésies*, *ed. cit.*, p. 4.

[165] Saint-Gelays, *Œuvres poétiques*, ed. by Blanchemain (Paris, 1873), I, 139.

[166] Ronsard, VI, 430.

[167] Du Bellay, V, 262.

[168] Ronsard, II, 134.

[169] Baïf, M.-L., II, 71.

[170] Ronsard, III, 180.

brought this poet and his rage to the attention of the Pléiade.[171] Whatever the source, this prodigy of wrath, this *fervens difficili bile jecur* caught the fancy of the Pléiade poets. Archilochus and his temper are mentioned with astonishing regularity in their verse. It was almost inevitable, considering their tendencies to dissociate elements of one metaphor or trope and apply them to another, that the Pléiade should associate the fury of Archilochus with the doctrine of theoleptic fury. Such a transfer is found in Du Bellay, Scève, Jodelle, and Ronsard.[172]

The second type of catachresis practised by the Pléiade concerned the fury of love. A parallel was established between the inspiration of love and the inspiration of verse, for to the amoristic poet both are the result of a heavenly fury. Thus, when Desportes exclaims, "O vers que j'ai chantez en l'ardeur qui m'enflame," he unconsciously reveals that the emotional experience one undergoes to produce amoristic poetry is the same as that inspiring other types of verse.[173] This identification of love's psychagogy and the Apollinic fury is a commonplace in the literature of the period and may be traced back through Ficino to the *Phaedrus* and the *Symposium.*

⚜ ⚜ ⚜

One aspect of the Pléiade's treatment of poetic fury deserves closer inspection than has yet been accorded it. This concerns demonology. The idea that poets are possessed by demons or a demon is best presented in the *Ion*, in the celebrated passage already quoted where Socrates explains how gods and demons incorporate themselves in the bards and inspire them. These demons were benevolent, not malevolent spirits like those of the New Testament. As such they became the masculine, or masculine and feminine, equivalent of the Muses.

[171] Horace, *Ad Pisones*, vs. 79.

[172] Du Bellay, IV, 94; Scève, *Poésies complètes*, ed. by Guégan (Paris, 1927), p. 240; Jodelle, M.-L., II, 140; for Ronsard it is a *despit furieux*, I, 90.

[173] Desportes, ed. by Michiels, p. 113.

Demons have resided in poets as far back in antiquity as hamadryads have inhabited oak trees. The notion of demoniac possession became a commonplace in the late classic period, as did the idea of Enthusiasm, a word meaning possession. Julian the Apostate spoke of Homer as θεόληπτος. Here again the spirit that bedevils the poet is an eudaemon, a favorable and not a malignant force.[174] But to later Christians of antiquity, the demon of poetry is charged with Satanism. Minucius Felix declared that the spirits which the poets praise as demons are unclean and steeped in vice. In their imparting of untruths to the poet they deceive and are deceived.[175] To Tatian, Apollo himself became a demon rather than a god and was to be condemned as vicious.[176] Theophilus also regretted the manner in which evil demons take hold of the poets; even Homer, Hesiod, and others were possessed by demons who abused them.[177] The view of Apollo as a malevolent demon is also found in Saint Augustine's *De Civitate Dei*, which the Pléiade knew.[178]

The intrusion of demonology into the literary theory of the Pléiade was abetted, as was the case with astrology, by the keen contemporary interest in the subject. The sixteenth century, like the seventh and sixth centuries before Christ, was definitely fascinated by this matter of spiritism. Books on the subject were plentiful.[179]

A general description of the state of these demons in the animal kingdom is furnished in "Les Daimons" of Ronsard, who records:

> Quand l'Eternel bastit le grand palais du Monde,
> Il peupla de poissons les abysmes de l'onde,

[174] See note 179.
[175] Minucius Felix, *Octavius* xxvii.
[176] Tatian, *Oratio ad Graecos* xxxviii.
[177] Theophilus, *Ad Autolycum* II, viii.
[178] Augustine, *De Civitate Dei* xix, 23.
[179] T. K. Oesterreich, *Possession, Demoniacal and Other* (New York, 1930), p. 156.

D'hommes la terre, et l'air de Daimons, et les cieux
D'Anges, a celle fin qu'il n'y eust point de lieux
Vuides en l'Univers. . . .[180]

And the basic function of the demons as they affect literature is posited by Du Bellay in his *Regrets*:

Tout œuvre qui doit vivre, il a dès sa naissance
Un Daemon qui le guide à l'immortalité:
Mais qui n'a rencontré telle nativité,
Comme un fruict abortif, n'a jamais accroissance. . . .

Virgile eut ce Daemon, et l'eut Horace encor,
Et tous ceulx qui du temps de ce bon siècle d'or
Estoient tenuz pour bons: les autres n'ont plus vie.[181]

These demons, he adds in an earlier work, purge and polish the poets with their divine flames.[182] This is the only mention of the flames of the demons which we have found in the Pléiade's writings.

Just as Ronsard had described the experience of Enthusiasm from the creative artist's viewpoint in "La Lyre," Jean Dorat relates how the demon of poetry comes to the writer and stirs him into action. In his "Epithalame au Duc de Joyeuse," Dorat recalls how "un esprit vint à moy" and caused him to compose a nuptial song of celebration.[183] To tell the truth, this demon acts more like the representation of a guilty conscience than like the demon of poetry.

Socrates honored the bard Homer by presenting him in the *Ion* as an illustration of spirit possession. In later years, penning his preface to the *Franciade* (1572), Ronsard remembered this. Altering the image somewhat to make those possessed by demons the sons of demons, he pictured the inspirational factor which led Homer to undertake his epic

[180] Ronsard, IV, 219.
[181] Du Bellay, II, 170. Ronsard mentions that these "guardian angels" look after the poets like faithful valets (II, 136).
[182] Du Bellay, II, 107.
[183] Dorat, M.-L., p. 22.

of the Trojan war: "cest Homère, lequel comme fils d'un Daemon, ayant l'esprit surnaturel, *etc.*" [184]

Sometimes this demon was called a "génie." The Latin *genius* became the equivalent of the Greek *δαίμων*. Jean Beaumont, in his *Treatise of Spirits, Apparitions, Witchcrafts, and other Magical Practices*, gave an etymological account of these two words, accepting them as suggesting the same idea.[185] An example of the substitution of "génie" for *δαίμων* is Ronsard's profession of belief:

> Toujours quelque Génie, ou l'influence dure
> D'un astre, nous invite a suyvre maugré tous
> Le destin qu'en naissant il versa de sur nous.[186]

At other times the demon is called a god, or a household tutelary, as in Du Bellay's "Aux dames angevines":

> Le docte Dieu, qui inspire en mon cœur
> Du sainct ruisseau la feconde liqueur,
> Mon sort fatal, & mon Dieu domestique
> Qui m'a voué au labeur poétique. . . .[187]

Or again, it might be called an angel; Baïf, in his *Passetems*, writes to M. de Marchaumont:

> Clausse, j'ay fait un bien gros livre:
> Son bon Ange sçait s'il doit vivre.[188]

Mention of the "docte Dieu" in the foregoing quatrain of Du Bellay brings into focus another complication of the idea of demonology. An interesting conflict arose which involved the old question of the respective functions of art and nature. As the Pléiade's theoretical treatises tended to show, the general consensus of this school was that a compromise must be effected between the two incompatible forces of natural genius

[184] Ronsard, VII, 68.
[185] Jean Beaumont, *Treatise of Spirits, Apparitions, Witchcrafts, and other Magical Practices* (London: Brown, 1705), pp. 2–3.
[186] Franchet, *op. cit.*, p. 22.
[187] Du Bellay, IV, 38.
[188] Baïf, M.-L., IV, 448.

and studied training. On the other hand, the extravagant imagery by which they dealt with the matter of inspiration tends to reveal a bias toward nature over art. Sometimes, however, even this imagery of inspiration is modified by considerations of training and technique. Even when speaking of seizure by the demon of poetry, they could not entirely forget the requisite of education. This impasse or contradiction might halt most theorists, but as we have seen, the Pléiade often resorted to the type of solution Alexander used on the knot of Gordius. As in the cases of sweetness and utility, sweetness and gravity, and other opposites, the Pléiade simply took the two irreconcilables and reconciled them. If the presence of a demon rendered education unnecessary for the poet, then it was because that demon was an educated one. This is similar to that logic employed by Ronsard in 1585 conciliating learning with predestination. The happy compromise is reached by both Du Bellay and Ronsard. It is found in the "Aux dames angevines," just quoted. And in his "Contre les envieux poètes" (1550), addressed to Ronsard, Du Bellay opines that his friend's demon is an educated one:

> Dont un Demon bien appris
> Les traitz, la douceur, la grace,
> Grava dedans tes espriz.[189]

In the same year, 1550, Ronsard published an ode to Du Bellay on the divine education of the learned poets, and refers again to supernatural pedagogy:

> Un Daemon les accompaigne
> Par sur tous le mieux instruit,
> Qui en songes toute nuit
> Sans nul travail les enseigne,
> Et demy-dieu ne desdeigne
> De les aller informant
> Afin que l'homme en dormant
> Toutes sciences appreigne.[190]

[189] Du Bellay, IV, 46.

[190] Ronsard, II, 170.

He proceeds to list the many arts which this "démon instruit" may impart to the poet by this novel indoctrination.

The close relationship between demonology and fury was noted in theoretical treatises as far back as the *Ion*, from which we have quoted above. The *Ars poetica* of Horace, of course, closes with the description of the *poeta vesanus*, or the lunacy-ridden poet. A most vivid picture of the possession of a poet by an Apollinic demon is found in Vida's manual of poetics.[191] This is an interesting coincidence, for these three works were the poetic treatises best known to the Pléiade. (Later on Vauquelin de la Fresnaye is to continue the tradition, describing just such a moonstruck poet as Horace's and concluding that his soul is seized by the "Demon tormenteux.")[192] Demons and fury are often coupled in Pléiade poems. Sometimes this fury was tempered by sweetness or softness. Thus, when Du Bellay asks De Mesmes

> Quel Démon a ceste fois
> De sa fureur la plus doulce
> Jusqu'aux estoilles te pousse
> Sur les aelles de ta voix? [193]

the fury may be interpreted as a mild experience or else as an intensely sweet, hedonistic thrill.

The transfer of the powers of the demon to the poet made the poet a sort of demon himself, just as his affiliation with the gods gave him a sort of divinity. Jodelle was one of the first to note this, as the following two passages attest. In one of these, a vision of the renowned authors of antiquity, including the eight masters of lyric poetry — and these visions were common to the Renaissance writers after Dante and Petrarch — he hears the songs of "ces grands Démons humains, ces Chantres et Poètes." [194] But the bards of antiquity were not the only demons; Jodelle declares that he and his friends be-

[191] Vida, *Ars poetica* II, 429 ff.
[192] Vauquelin, *Art poétique*, *ed. cit.*, p. 181.
[193] Du Bellay, V, 262–263.
[194] Jodelle, M.-L., II, 123.

come such spirits, that he enjoys thus greater powers of communication with others of his profession:

> Ma Muse ou ce Démon qui me fait tant de dons,
> Que l'on me met moymesme au rang des hauts Démons,
> Se masquant lors de toy se présente a ma veue.
> Par luy donc je te voy, en luy je t'entretien,
> Et des vers du Démon, qui est et tien & mien,
> Présent, absent, je pais l'âme à toy toute deue.[195]

Almost a response to this was a sonnet from the *Regrets* of Du Bellay, where Joachim grants that Jodelle is a demon. Then he echoes the Platonic image of the *Ion* in its completest form. Socrates had said that the gods entered the souls of the great creative artists like Homer, and that the spirit of the Homers in turn took possession of the minds of the lesser poets and rhapsodists. These latter poets and rhapsodists he then condemned as interpreters of interpreters. This primary and secondary inspiration is implicit in Du Bellay's tribute describing in detail the Corybantic possession by which Jodelle holds him:

> Mais je ne sçay comment ce Daemon de Jodelle
> (Daemon est-il vrayement, car d'une voix mortelle
> Ne sortent point ses vers) tout soudain que je l'oy
> M'aiguillonne, m'espoingt, m'espouvante, m'affolle,
> Et comme Apollon fait de sa prestresse folle,
> A moymesme m'ostant me ravit tout a soy.[196]

There are further references to the demon of poetry by Jodelle,[197] Du Bellay,[198] Vulteius,[199] and others, but the essential character and functions of the demon are summed up by the preceding passages. Only one observation remains to be set down.

The same catachresis which the Pléiade devised to identify poetic and amoristic fury may be recognised in the Pléiade's

[195] *Ibid.*, II, 174.
[196] Du Bellay, II, 177.
[197] Jodelle, M.-L., II, 220.
[198] Du Bellay, I, 10.
[199] Vulteius, *Epigrammatum libri* iiii (Lugduni, 1537), p. 173.

identification of the poetic demon with the demon who instigates the fury of love. Once again the parallel types of inspiration, that of love and that of the arts, are assimilated. Thus Ronsard could write in the first book of the *Amours* about

> Quelque Démon par le congé des Cieux
> Qui présidoit à mon ardeur première.[200]

The foregoing paragraphs show how the details and vocabulary of one of the popular contemporary sciences, demonology, were incorporated into the literary credo of the Pléiade. This volume has more than once shown that the Pléiade borrowed terms from sixteenth-century sciences (alchemy, astrology, *etc.*) and embodied them in their critical vocabulary. It is irrefutable that their first interest in poetic demons came from Plato, but no small impetus was given this interest by the contemporary preoccupation with the subject. If one would know to what a great extent demons, witches, and black magic were a part of the daily life of the sixteenth century, let him read the contemporary history and bibliography contained in the *Compendium Maleficarum* of Fra Francesco Maria Guazzo.[201]

⚜ ⚜ ⚜

The function of the Muse or the Muses was often the same as that of the poetic demons. The belief that the Muse enters the poet's spirit and creates through him is at least as ancient as Homer himself: Μῆνιν ἄειδε, θεά —Ἄνδρα μοι ἔννεπε, μοῦσα. It probably dates from the Helladic or Aegean culture, being tied up with the beliefs in oracles and divination. Imagery involving the Muses became a stereotyped stylistic device throughout classical literature, but once the Pléiade had adopted them

[200] Ronsard, I, 92.

[201] A modern edition of this work first published at Milan, "apud Haeredes Augustini Tradati," in 1608, has been edited by the Rev. Montague Summers (London, John Rodker, 1929).

into their poetic vocabularies, the office of these ladies varied radically from mere spirit-possession.

With the Pléiade the sisters' personalities became as diverse as their duties, and none sums the matter up better than Pontus de Tyard:

elles ont prins surnom, comme Siciliennes, de Sicile: Hilissiennes d'un fleuve Attique: Thespiennes de Thespie, ville de Boeotie; Libethriennes, d'une fontaine en Magnésie; Pimpléades, Castalides, Aonides, ou Aoniennes, Coriciennes, Olympiennes, Pieriennes, Aganippides, Pegasiennes, Citheriennes, Meoniennes, & en plusieurs semblables sortes. En outre, elles ont esté accompagnées d'epithètes tirez d'autre part, comme doctes, éternelles, delicates, plaisantes, plaintives, songneuses, saintes, musiciennes, babillardes, laborieuses, douces, sacrées, & autrement, *etc.*[202]

Tributes to the Muses are most common in the Pléiade, as are poems describing their agenda. Baïf composed two pieces entitled "Les Muses." One of them is a long relation of classic mythology apparently intended to rival Ronsard's ode to Michel de l'Hospital, in which the Muses are likewise the center of interest.[203] The other is a dizain in the *Passetems*, where the functions of the goddesses are recorded in almost as many lines as there were sisters:

Calliope inventa l'Héroique chanson,
Et Clion de la lyre enseigna le doux son:
La voix tragique fut par Euterpe elevée,
Melpomène premier l'épinette a trouvée,
Des flutes les tuyaux Terpsichore entonna,
Eraton des grans Dieux les louanges sonna,
La docte Polymnie acorda la cadence,
Polymnie à tous chans ajousta l'acordance,
Uranie chanta le bal que font les cieux,
Thalie du Comic les jeux facecieux.[204]

To demonstrate further the variety of the Muses' activities,

[202] Pontus de Tyard, *Discours philosophiques* (Paris: L'Angelier, 1587), fol. 33r.
[203] Baïf, M.-L., II, 71.
[204] *Ibid.*, IV, 395.

we shall list several representative functions as set down by several representative poets. Recalling the fourth book of Ovid's *Tristia*, Du Bellay says that the Muse comforts him in adversity, dries his tears, gives him repose, life, humility, sense of values, and the sacred presents of the gods.[205] She succors the poet so that he will not compose with "miserable artifice." [206] Both Belleau and Ronsard note that the Muses store their gifts to poets in a sacred treasure chest (*sacré cabinet*, *cabinet saint*).[207] Baïf and Ronsard describe the dance which the Muses execute around Apollo.[208] They are loved by Phoebus Apollo.[209] As Hesiod had written, they send sweet songs into the air with their bows; [210] they put these bows into the poets' grasp; [211] they put the arrows into the poets' hands, and apparently these sagittal symbols denote the songs themselves.[212] They govern a man's fame and make his name fly from mouth to mouth.[213] They pronounce who are the worthy poets.[214] They safeguard the sweetness of song.[215] As Horace had written,[216] they furnish the very subject matter of verse to their favorites.[217] Whence Ronsard's complaint to Des Masures that the Muses gave all the arguments of poetry to the ancients, so that few if any were left.

Not always were the references to the Muses complimentary. Instead of being regarded as kindly sources of inspiration, they were censured by Belleau for beguiling men with their songs and their *piperie*,[218] by Tahureau for their *chant jazard*,[219] and by Du Bellay for their *bavardage*.[220] Passerat chides the

[205] Du Bellay, II, 47.
[206] *Ibid.*, III, 96.
[207] Belleau, M.-L., II, 155; Ronsard, II, 342. Also Marot (Garnier edition), I, 203.
[208] Baïf, M.-L., I, 90; Ronsard, III, 194.
[209] Du Bellay, IV, 187.
[210] *Ibid.*, III, 61.
[211] *Ibid.*, II, 157.
[212] *Ibid.*, I, 78.
[213] *Ibid.*, III, 83.
[214] *Ibid.*, II, 184.
[215] Magny, *Odes*, *ed. cit.*, I, 29.
[216] Horace, *Ad Pisones*, vss. 83–85.
[217] Ronsard, IV, 364.
[218] Belleau, M.-L., I, 206.
[219] Tahureau, *Poésies* (Paris: Librairie des Bibliophiles, 1870), II, 35.
[220] Du Bellay, VI, 116.

jazardes Muses, and Ronsard the *Muse babillarde*.[221] Du Bellay even complains in his "Lyre chrestienne":

> Quand j'oy les Muses cacqueter
> Enflant leurs motz d'ung vain langage,
> Il me semble ouyr cracqueter
> Ung perroquet dedans sa cage:
> Mais ces folz qui leur font hommage,
> Amorcez de vaines doulceurs,
> Ne peuvent sentir le dommage
> Que traynent ces mignardes Sœurs.[222]

This censure is interesting, for it reveals how the Pléiade humanised the Muses, made flesh and blood women of them. This tendency has been noted in Ronsard by Franchet, who writes, "Where Ronsard separates himself completely here from neo-Platonism is in his conception of the Muses. They live, they breathe, the Muses of Ronsard, those 'brunettes aux beaux yeux' whom he really loved." [223] This statement might be qualified with a reminder that this love and this humanisation were not at all restricted to the verse of Ronsard. Most of the Pléiade indulged in it. Tahureau called the Muses "mes folastres Déesses, mes petites maistresses";[224] he claimed that Paschal "returned the thousand caresses of the sisters." [225] Passerat speaks of the poet's "paying court to the nine sisters," [226] whom he pictures in one poem as "aus yeux bruns" [227] (although to Ronsard they were "aus yeux noirs") [228] and in another as "aus cheveus blonds." [229] Ronsard relates to Pierre Lescot that his father had accused him of loving the Muses too well. This is perhaps too faithful a memory of the first book of Vida's poetics to be taken seriously. Vida had described the physical passion which youth feels for the Muses, comparable to animal spirits, and shows the futility of parental objections

[221] Passerat, *Poésies françaises* (Paris, 1880), I, 87; Ronsard, II, 151.
[222] Du Bellay, IV, 142.
[223] H. Franchet, *Le poète et son œuvre*, p. 19.
[224] Tahureau, *Poésies*, *ed. cit.*, I, 171.
[225] *Ibid.*, I, 91.
[226] Passerat, *ed. cit.*, I, 177.
[227] *Ibid.*, I, 78.
[228] Ronsard, VI, 95.
[229] Passerat, *ed. cit.*, II, 161.

once the boy's passion has been aroused.[230] A second Latin treatise which the Pléiade knew and which made frail humans of the Muses was the *De Consolatione Philosophiae* of Boethius; when Philosophy comes to Boethius in his prison, she inquires who has allowed those strumpets of the theater to draw near the sick man.[231]

Granted then that the poets "pay court to the daughters of Memory," as Du Bellay and Ronsard both wrote,[232] another variation on this metaphor becomes possible. The daughters may favor the Swans with their attentions and gifts, but what will be the relations between the Muses and the Crows — the poetasters? These latter versifiers may dishonor the Muses, may abuse them. This dishonoring of the humanised sisters was *allzumenschlich* itself, and it aroused chivalrous indignation among the competent poets. Du Bartas, in his "Uranie," makes the Muse Urania appeal for protection against those poets who are making bawds of her sisters: "Je ne puis d'un œil sec voir mes sœurs macquerelles des amoureus François." [233] And in a prefatory piece to the works of Desportes, Nicolas Vauquelin depicts in detail the manner in which the poor poets of the period lay their evil hands upon these virgins:

> Les Muses ont perdu toute leur chasteté,
> Et comme on voit en tout nostre siècle effronté
> A ceste heure chacun met la main sous leur robe,
> Entre dedans leur temple et leurs secrets desrobe . . .
> Ces pudiques beautez, à la fin trop faschées
> De voir de gens de peu leurs faveurs recherchées,
> Leurs saints ruisseaux troublez, et par impunité
> Tout le monde attenter à leur virginité,
> Laissent le temple ouvert, et toutes en colère,
> En retournant s'asseoir aux costez de leur père,
> Abandonnent leur art sans honneur et sans pris,
> Profané par la voix de tant de bas espris.[234]

[230] Vida, *Ars poetica*, I, 286 ff.
[231] Boethius, *De Cons. Phil.* I, 1.
[232] Du Bellay, II, 116; Ronsard, II, 146.
[233] Du Bartas, *Œuvres* (Chapel Hill, 1938), II, 172.
[234] Desportes, *Œuvres* (Paris: Delahays, 1858), pp. 5, 6–7.

Sometimes the three Parcae were credited with the function of predestination and presumably, by extension, of inspiration. Ronsard complains that at the hour of his birth one of these sisters blackened his thread of life.[235] Du Bellay considered that Robert de la Haye had been favored by the Parcae.[236] But the spinning sisters were not humanised so attractively as the Muses. They were pictured as aged and ugly.[237] Clotho, Lachesis, and Atropos remained inviolate from the versifiers.

We have consistently found that at one time or another the Pléiade modified these classical images of inspiration and genius by considerations of the complementary factor of art and training. This present image is no exception. Just as the Pléiade struck a compromise with the expression "démon instruit," the identical concession to art is implicit in the expression "muses apprises" coined by Ronsard.[238] Despite their enthusiasm for the doctrine of natural inspiration, they were never able to forget completely the contributory functions of training and education.

⚜ ⚜ ⚜

Before leaving the question of art and nature, we shall consider briefly the two incidental matters of *naïveté* and of direct emotional or sensory inspiration.

One of the most frequent synonyms of "le naturel" in the sixteenth century was "le naïf." The Latin meaning of *nativus* was still the principal meaning of this word before 1600.[239] Like the ἁπλοικός of Demetrius, "naïf" assumed the two meanings of ingenuous and inborn, but in the Pléiade's critical vocabulary it had only the latter value. The natural genius

[235] Ronsard, I, 28.

[236] Du Bellay, V, 271.

[237] Ronsard, II, 141.

[238] Ronsard, STFM, II, 121.

[239] On *nativus* in this sense, see Cicero *Part. Or.* 5, 16; Quintilian, viii, 3, 36. References from Harper's *Latin Dictionary* (New York, 1907), p. 1188.

of a literature or language, its ethos, is sometimes called its "naïveté" by the Pléiade. Rémy Belleau, for example, remarks that in his translation of Anacreon he has attempted to capture the naïveté of the Greeks.[240] And Du Bellay in the *Deffence* avers that even if Homer and Vergil were alive again, they would be unable to capture the naïveté of the Tuscan vernacular of Petrarch.[241] Pontus de Tyard holds that only in one's own language can one write "naïvement." [242]

The term "naïf" may serve to describe the ethos of the individual poet as well. Ronsard pays tribute to the innate sweetness ("naïve douceur") of Horace.[243] If he is unwilling to admit that any writers since the bards of Hellas have possessed an entirely natural genius, he will concede that some components of one's style may be native. Others than Ronsard made this compromise. Charles Fontaine granted that a poet may have a native gayety.[244] Ronsard wrote that he patterned his work after the "naïve facilité" of Homer.[245] The tribute to Horace was rephrased and paid by Du Bellay to Baïf, "Nul mieux de toy, gentillime Poëte, façonne un vers doulcimement naïf." [246] A similar expression is used to describe the results of a warm poetic inspiration, an ardor that makes itself felt in verse:

> Autant que me semble doulx
> Le traict de ma flamme vive,
> Autant mes vers, soyez-vous
> Rempliz de doulceur naïve.[247]

If this ardor is intense enough to be considered a fury, then it creates a natural style that is anything but mild. Those whose compositions are the exclusive product of their nature were

[240] Belleau, M.-L., I, 4.
[241] *Deffence*, p. 89.
[242] Pontus de Tyard, M.-L., p. 236.
[243] Ronsard, VII, 4.
[244] Charles Fontaine, preface to the *Fontaine d'amour* (Paris, 1545), quoted in M. Raymond, *Influence de Ronsard* (Paris: Champion, 1927), I, 57.
[245] Ronsard, VII, 68.
[246] Du Bellay, II, 286.
[247] *Ibid.*, IV, 39.

said to have been "naïvement ravy" by the Muses.[248] Or, as in the case of the early Greeks, they had a "naïve escriture." [249]

The Pléiade toyed further with this notion. Thus Pontus de Tyard explains to the lady of his *Erreurs* that there are degrees of spontaneity to a style, and that she must help him to write more natural verses:

> Melline, estrainte en l'amoureux lien,
> Rend plus mielleux l'esprit Catulien
> Au vers mignard de son heureux Baïf.
> Donq adouci la rigueur qui me touche:
> Car si je voy ta beauté moins farouche,
> Je te peindray d'un pinceau plus naïf.[250]

This brief mention of love as an inspiration enabling one to compose natively or naturally raises the question of direct emotive inspiration in general. Any emotion, and this we noted in Demetrius and Longinus, could serve as a direct stimulus to spontaneous composition, independent of learned technique or training. Du Bellay, for example, wrote to his uncle, the cardinal, that hot anger inspired some of the sonnets in his *Regrets*. However, the one affection by which the Pléiade generally illustrated the theory was love.

In a passage reminiscent of Dante's definition of the direct poetic impulsion of love, the definition addressed to Bonagiunta in *Purgatorio XXIV*, Baïf describes love's spontaneous dictation of the sonnets in his *Amours de Francine*: "Hélas, je n'écri rien, rien hélas je ne chante, que ce qu'il veut ditter." [251] This was the familiar contention of Dante and Guido Cavalcanti. Desportes makes two admissions that love directs his pen:

> Amour guide ma plume et me donne l'adresse, *etc.*[252]
> Escrivant de l'amour, Amour guide ma plume.[253]

[248] Ronsard, V, 185.
[249] *Ibid.*, II, 139.
[250] Pontus de Tyard, M.-L., p. 105.
[251] Baïf, M.-L., I, 221.
[252] Desportes, *Poésies*, ed. by Michiels, p. 413.
[253] *Ibid.*, p. 50.

He cautions Belleau that Belleau must not think himself the author of the *Bergerie*, for it is obvious that the real author is love.[254] Jacques Tahureau writes that it is not Phoebus, Calliope, or the Parnassian troupe, but rather love which inspires him. "C'est l'œil vainqueur qui tient le mien surpris, le seul outil qui polist mes ecriz." [255] And finally two passages from Du Bellay:

> Je me contenteray de simplement escrire
> Ce que la passion seulement me fait dire.[256]
>
> Ce que je puis de mon amour escrire
> Naïvement, sans art et fiction,
> Comme sans art est mon affection.[257]

The theory of sensory or emotive inspiration, then, could be summed up adequately and economically in a single line which one finds in the third book of the hendecasyllables of Vulteius, a line in the dedication of Brixius to Vulteius: "Id quod sentio, sum tibi locutus." [258]

Emotions had a way of stifling as well as inspiring literary productions. Jean Passerat relates how the spectacle of civil strife in France takes out of him any enthusiasm for creative activity. In perhaps the only contemporary verse passage where a direct relationship between the civil wars and literary production is established, Passerat decries the passing of his inspiration before the attrition of war:

> On a joué deux fois la mesme tragédie,
> A la tierce on verra secher les lauriers verds
> Du roc Parnassien: tout s'en va de travers,
> L'on n'imite l'accord des peuples de Candie.[259]

[254] *Ibid.*, p. 434.
[255] Tahureau, Blanchemain edition, II, 145.
[256] Du Bellay, II, 55.
[257] *Ibid.*, V, 134. The religious poet and psalmist employs this same image, but it is God who "guides one's pen"; Du Bartas, ed. by U. T. Holmes, I, 224.
[258] Vulteius, *Hendecasyllables*, Book III, dedication.
[259] Passerat, *op. cit.*, I, 186.

It might interest the reader to recall that quite the contrary opinion was maintained by Diderot. Discoursing on dramatic poetry, Diderot saw in civil war a splendid stimulus to verse. He, too, adopts the image of the laurel. "C'est lorsque la fureur de la guerre civile arme les hommes de poignards, et que le sang coule a grands flots sur la terre, que le laurier d'Apollon s'agite et verdit." [260]

One final theory of intuitive genius must be recorded. This is the theory of the *intelletto* which Michelangelo propounded so skillfully: Art is something which exists whether artists exist or not. Like the troubadour who finds harmonies, the artist merely discovers the harmony and art which have existed before him and will survive him. God places these harmonies in the materials themselves,

> Si come per levar, Donna, si pone
> In pietra alpestra e dura
> Una viva figura
> Che la più cresce, u' più la pietra scema;

and it is logical that no artist will be able to find what is not there, that is, conceive works greater than or different from the predestined art. Once again taking an illustration from sculpture, Michelangelo gives us the famous quatrain with the most significant last line, the line copied by Desportes:

> Non ha l'ottimo artista alcun concetto
> C'un marmo solo in sè non circoscriva
> Col suo soverchio; e solo a quello arriva
> La mano che ubbidisce all'intelletto.

This is merely a variation upon the theme of natural genius which we have encountered in so many forms in the foregoing pages, related to the system of *trobar clus*. A special intellect is given to the elect who are favored at birth, a *trovatore* spirit. To illustrate his theory of *ingenium* Michelangelo applies it to writing as well as sculpture. "Just as in pen and ink lie high

[260] Diderot, *De la poésie dramatique*, XVIII.

and low and mediocre styles, and in marbles rich and vile images, in so far as our power is able to draw them out," begins the artist in a letter to Cavalieri.[261] Indeed, this idea derived from antiquity found no more earnest apostle in the Renaissance than Michelangelo Buonarroti. Although the *Rime* of Michelangelo were not translated into French until 1860, they were published during his lifetime and accessible to the *italianisants* of the era of the Pléiade. That his theory of the *intelletto* was familiar to at least some of the French poets is attested by Desportes's free translation of the quatrain quoted just above:

> Le sculpteur excellent desseignant pour ouvrage
> Une plante, un lion, un homme, un élément
> Si la main obeyt et suit l'entendement,
> Trouve en un marbre seul toute sorte d'image.[262]

One cannot tell how many besides Desportes knew the *Rime*. Had the Pléiade known them well, they would probably have reproduced some of their picturesque imagery in their own works. The constantly recurring theory of the *eletto* in Michelangelo resembled very closely the predestination and grace of the Protestants. But although the Pléiade sometimes called the gift of poetry a *grâce*,[263] they made a conscious effort to avoid the term "elect" and any other imagery of inspiration which had connotations of Protestantism.[264]

⚜ ⚜ ⚜

In chapter XLVII of the Fifth Book of Rabelais, "Comment

[261] *Lettere di Michelangelo Buonarroti*, ed. by Papini (Lanciano, 1913), letter lxv.

[262] Desportes, *ed. cit.*, p. 186.

[263] For poetry as a gift, as grace, see the following uses of *grâce* in connection with inspiration. In the "Ode à Michel de l'Hospital" (Ronsard, II, 136), where Jupiter states, "Those whom I choose to make poets by the *grace* of my bounty, *etc.*"; "Les Muses," of Baïf (M.-L., II, 90); also, the poem to Christofle de Choiseul (Ronsard, V, 185).

[264] Wishing to show the supremacy of the Christian God over the pagan Fates, Ronsard lapses into the term "les esleus de Dieu" at least once (Ronsard, VI, 204).

Panurge et les autres rithment par fureur poétique," Friar John looks at Panurge, who is about to declaim some doggerel and cries in wonderment:

> Es-tu fol devenu ou enchanté? Voyez comme il escume: entendez comme il rithmaille. Que tous les diables a il mangé? Il tourne les yeux en la teste comme une chèvre qui se meurt: se retirera il à l'escart? fiantera il plus loin? mangera il de l'herbe aux chiens pour descharger son thomas? ou à l'usage monachal mettra il dedans la gorge le poing jusqu'au coude afin de se curer les hypochondres?

Pantagruel allays his friend's apprehensions, stating, "Croyez que c'est la fureur poétique." The objection of Rabelais to the doctrine of divine fury has a rational basis. Anyone will grant that a writer may become subject to a certain enthusiasm while composing, but this hardly constitutes an actual possession. The excessive physical disturbances which Ronsard pictures in his poem on the lyre no poet of his time actually experienced — not even the most exalted or ecstatic poet of the mid-century, Marguerite d'Angoulême. As long as they realised this as practitioners, why did the Pléiade poets propound the idea of fury so insistently as theorists? Such was the poser of Rabelais.

The two most inconsistent features of these passages about native genius and hard work, however, remain their attempt to apportion inspiration and technique in absolute quantities and their inability to understand the qualifier of the personal equation. Not everyone can become a Dante or a Goethe, of course. The importance of the personal equation no one will deny. But the admission of personal differences in theories about artistic aptitudes is quite a different matter from believing in the divinity of the artist and predestination.

The fact that the Pléiade found the imagery of this divinity and predestination — Muses, demons, Corybantic fury, astromancy — in the classic writers with whom they were familiar inclined them somewhat toward a belief in nature over art. All these images were more than meaningless conceits; they possessed a definite literary and critical meaning and indicated an emphatic personal persuasion. The Pléiade's own contributions to this imagery, like their variations upon the tropes based on sweetness, were considerable and in some cases most original.

In trying to determine whether the Pléiade school was more inclined toward nature or art, one is confronted with three categories of information, different and dissident. We shall classify them as follows:

PRO NATURA: the varied imagery of inspiration describing how poets are given the bounty of genius by divine or mechanical intervention, imagery found in various poems and in tributes to writers of genius.

PRO ARTE: the counsel regarding composition and style found in the Pléiade's few texts of instruction and personal epistles.

AUREA MEDIOCRITAS: the prose treatises which attempt a compromise between the two extreme viewpoints.

Worthy of note are the insistent attempts at compromise which the Pléiade made, weighing art against nature. Troubled by the suspicion that art and nature must coöperate and yet fond of their demons and Muses, the Pléiade found a way out by making these demons and Muses educated creatures. One silenced all partisans of *la doctrine* by referring to one's learned Muse or demon. Faced with the alternatives of predestination and the disciplines of learning, the Pléiade poet concludes that one may be foredestined, of course, but that such determinism presupposes the idea of working hard anyway. Another form of compromise is the decision that some parts of one style may be native, although one's total gifts are not. We have seen how the poets pay tribute to the natural mildness, sweetness, gayety, or fluency of an author. Such compromises show that the Pléiade theorists were not so dogmatic and intransigent as certain historians have made them out to be.

This chapter reveals another sidelight on Pléiade theory concerning the possible acceptance of one's native language as a gift of nature. As one did not learn it through the same diligent study by which one learned a foreign language, it was accepted as innate; the foreign idiom, on the other hand, could be considered art and effort, for it demanded long hours of concentration and training. The Pléiade theorist does not say that one is born speaking his native language, but rather with an innate propensity (what the Greeks called λόγοι σπερματικοὶ) for expressing himself in that language alone. Speroni had called this the "inclinatione del nascimento" which makes one eschew foreign languages (*cf.* Du Bellay's "inclination naturelle")[265] and inferred clearly that one is born to one particular language.[266] If one attempts to compose in a tongue other than his own, that is, through artifice, one's work will lose its natural force and beauty, as experience invariably shows. One's own language affords a native grace and facility that neither a foreign tongue nor an ancient one could offer. Thus, an excellent argument was born to support the linguistic reforms of the Pléiade.

In this chapter on art and nature as in the chapter on sweetness, we have found the daily life of the Renaissance providing the Pléiade with imagery to adapt to their critical theory. The alchemists and brewers had supplied new tropes based on distillation, for example. Here, in their discussions of inspiration, the current interest in astrology enabled them to particularise genethlialogy to their own ends. Again, the contemporary vogue of demonology made the Pléiade much more conscious of the poetic demons, and the theological disputations over free will induced them to adopt the idea of poetry as a grace. If one is to enrich his language by borrowing from everyday arts and sciences, as they preached, one might as well enrich the figures of that speech from them as well.

The distinction between a poet and a versifier, by the way, was readily apparent if one accepted innate genius as the touchstone. A versifier was one who made an end rather than a

[265] The text is reproduced in P. Villey's *Les sources italiennes de la Deffence* (Paris: Champion, 1908), 121. [266] *Ibid.*, p. 130.

means of verse. He was also a writer so poor in sentiment and subject that all his poetry possessed was rhyme. In either case, his preoccupation with rhyme was particularly distasteful to the Pléiade. Ronsard is never more vehement than when he is condemning rhyme and the excessive importance attached to it. One of the principal aims of art is to teach the rules of versifying and rhetoric. Versifiers may be said to have mastered some of the principal teachings of art; they might conceivably master every precept of art. All that cannot be learned comes from nature. Art can make versifiers; art cannot make natural poets. A versifier may be defined then as an exclusive product of art; a poet must be defined as an exclusive or at least a partial product of nature. It is all as clear as a syllogism. Accordingly, one will not find the Pléiade praising an author as the exclusive product of art or training, whereas they frequently compliment authors on being the exclusive product of nature. This fact reveals once again a bias toward nature over art, never formally articulated.

Not everyone in the sixteenth century, of course, favored nature over art. Cotgrave's dictionary cites a contemporary proverb, "Nourriture passe nature." [267] But the partisans of art were in the minority. Even Montaigne admits in the *Essays*, "Ce n'est pas raison que l'art gaigne le poinct d'honneur sur nostre grande et puissante mère nature." [268] The epigram quoted by both Pliny and Quintilian that nature cares so little for man as to deserve the name of step-mother rather than mother (reproduced quite frequently in the works of the Pléiade) should not be accepted as a reaction against nature in favor of art.[269] The nature which is so selfish toward man is here external nature, the physical forces of the earth. It is the cruel parent which Leopardi pictured so aptly in the *Ginestra*, where he himself uses the phrase of Pliny. None of the

[267] Edition of 1632.

[268] Montaigne, *Essais* (Paris: Chronique des lettres françaises, 1928), II, 41.

[269] Quintilian, *Inst. Orat.* xii; Pliny, *Hist. Nat.* VII, i, 1; see also, Chamard edition of the *Deffence*, pp. 45–50.

Pléiade, to our knowledge, had the gift of creative talent in mind while echoing the phrase.[270]

Despite the obvious contradictions and compromises which might be taxed against the partisans of nature, their position was the one which remained most popular. It was to remain the predominant viewpoint until the eighteenth century was to redefine the issue as a choice between enthusiasm and verve, on the one hand, and reason and taste, on the other, with the latter elements overbalancing the former. René Bray, in his competent study of seventeenth-century classicism, states that "even when it could not define this mysterious genius, the seventeenth century denied neither its existence nor its necessity." [271] He shows that the superiority of nature was acknowledged by Mairet, Corneille, even Chapelain and Boileau. Bray concludes, "Contentons-nous de ces images: la conclusion de notre enquête, c'est que tout le XVIIe siècle a consideré le génie comme la première qualité du poète."

In Spain the controversy continued. In 1614 Cervantes published his allegorical *Viaje al Parnaso* and records that in the symbolic Garden of Genius:

> Naturaleza y arte allí parece
> Andar en competencia, y está en duda
> Qual vence de las dos, qual más merece.

But William Shakespeare, writing a year or two earlier than Cervantes, corroborates the conclusion of Bray and adopts a type of reasoning which we noted in the manual of Jacques Peletier.

> . . . Nature is made better by no mean
> But nature makes that mean: so, over that art
> Which you say adds to nature, is an art
> That nature makes.

[270] Ronsard, VI, 340; Du Bellay, *Deffence*, ed. by Chamard, p. 46; Du Bellay, I, 115; II, 86; *etc.*

[271] R. Bray, *La formation de la doctrine classique en France* (Lausanne, 1931), p. 87.

Bray's conclusion about the seventeenth century is a more positive one than we should be justified in making for the sixteenth century. There were a great many reserves and compromises occasioned by the knowledge of the Pléiade that poetry was hard work, that poetry was a profession, that poetry demanded both a humanistic and a prosodic education. However, their Hellenism, their imagination, and their egotism inclined them to set genius over art. And their remarks and criticisms on other writers reveal that this inclination was even more pronounced than their theoretical treatises indicated.[272]

[272] Franchet concludes his chapter on poetic fury by showing how the problem maintained its interest down into the nineteenth century, citing such notable examples as the *Moïse* of Vigny and the *Mazeppa* of Hugo: "Combien Ronsard eût aimé ces poèmes qui font resplendir d'un éclat nouveau l'éternelle vérité de sa doctrine," *Le poète et son œuvre d'après Ronsard* (Paris: Champion, 1923), p. 42.

VI

CONCLUDING REMARKS

> Die Literaturgeschichte ist die große Morgue wo jeder seine Todten aufsucht, die er liebt oder womit er verwandt ist.
>
> — HEINRICH HEINE, *Die Romantische Schule*

THE following paragraphs are a by-product. They represent a few critical reactions which still lingered after the individual conclusions to each chapter had been recorded. They are of a most general character. They are incidental thoughts which suggested themselves during the composition of the preceding chapters, but were set aside and temporarily forgotten, only to reappear now at what should be a more propitious moment. They are like the words of the Arismapians and Nephelibates in Rabelais, thoughts which accumulate frozen in the air but suddenly thaw out and make themselves heard long after they are articulated. For the specific results of the five investigations undertaken in this volume, the reader must turn to the summarising pages of the individual chapters.

He who creates literary criticism is more fortunate than he who records it. The critic may set up an outline which, if followed, will build for him an organic monument of unity, a finite and orderly world of ideas. Centrifugal ideas which try to elude his regulated world, driving out toward the chaotic megacosm of his imagination, he governs and fits into his finite system. In no way limited or directed by the nature or amount of his materials, he may order or dispose of them with free will. By synthesising, he knows that he will shape these materials into an integral organism, like the Logos which makes order out of darkness and chaos.

The literary historian is not so fortunate. The unity of his work is established for him by his materials themselves. These may have a will of their own, may be "d'une forme au travail rebelle," to quote Gautier. Sometimes they resist him, fighting his attempts to reduce them to unity. The literary historian who would record the story of the nineteenth-century French drama, for example, finds himself hard put to find the unifying elements or community of purpose in the theater of Pixerécourt, Dumas père, Hugo, Augier, Scribe, Rostand, and Curel. Where will the literary historian find the elements unifying the Flaubert of *Salammbô* with that of *Bovary* or with that of the *Tentation de saint Antoine*? Often the literary chronicler can find no unity, and his work's only unity (as Croce wrote of the *Orlando Furioso*) is the intention of the author himself.

In this volume, our function has been solely that of literary historian. Consequently his problem has been ours. The unity of this study was not determined by us, but rather by the Pléiade poets themselves. Whatever organic quality the investigation assumed was due to the materials themselves. In this they favored us. Although this study was originally designed to supplement the Pléiade's partially organised critical system, that is, form part of a greater unity, it turned out to have a certain unity and completeness of its own. This unity, brought out by the comments of the Pléiade on other writers, lies in the basic character of the criteria established. For in selecting what have been the most frequent criteria of judgment in the Pléiade's prose and poetry, one discovers that they concern, after all, the most basic problems of literary theory. These might be restated in order as the ethical and moral character of literature, the expression and communication of ideas, the rewards and social nature of art, the purpose and function of literature, and the inspiration and technique of poetry. All other criteria which we have uncovered are subordinately related in one way or another to these rudimentary matters. Such issues as stylistic altitude or sublimity, linguistic media, and the like, which exist as less frequent criteria of judgment, may be considered as merely contingent facets of these five major issues.

As only one of these five major criteria, the last one, was treated at any considerable length in the poetical documents of the period, two of them merely mentioned, and two utterly non-existent in the theoretical vade mecums, they have remained relatively unnoticed in discussions on Pléiade theory of recent date. The conflict between art and nature, recognised as a live issue by the Renaissance critical treatises, has been dealt with as such by modern scholars. The latter have also touched upon certain minor facets of the four other issues discussed in the first four chapters. Thus, they have noted the Pléiade's fetish of poetic glory, without recording the subtle but universal reaction against poetic glory. Certain lacunae still remained in the reconstructions of a Pléiade poetics undertaken in this and the past century. For this reason it was stated at the outset that the purpose of this study was to fill in some of the intervals in the critical system which the Pléiade itself did not take time to formulate. As these lacunae and contradictions concerned basic matters, the method adopted here proved to be a relatively productive one. By classifying the many unexploited judgments of the Pléiade on classic, mediaeval, and Renaissance writers and delving into poems which have sometimes been considered of secondary importance, one brings into relief several sides of the Pléiade's aesthetics which might otherwise escape notice. This method also brings to light the vast accumulation of criticism to be found cloaked in the verse of this school of poets — in many schools of poets — in their offhand and most spontaneous observations. It is in these impromptu passages that they are often the most unconsciously and therefore the most honestly critical. Some of the truest literary criticism, then, is couched in practice rather than formal theory.

⚜ ⚜ ⚜

One conviction has strengthened itself during the course of our study. This persuasion concerns the word "Pléiade" which we have used in our title and throughout the volume. It seems to us a most specious bit of reasoning to associate this term with the number seven. We have found MM. Laumonier and Chamard both conceding that there were more than seven poets in the mind of Ronsard himself, even though a recent letter from M. Laumonier to this writer shows him still inclined toward the limitation of seven.[1] In his notes to the Lemerre edition of Ronsard (VII, 496), Professor Laumonier states that the term may be considered to include nine poets, listed in the "Isles fortunées" (1553), the epistle to Jean de la Péruse (1553), and the hymn to Henry II (1555). However, one should consider the views of the other participants in this movement. Others as well as Ronsard drew up registers which have significance. Du Bellay admitted that the Muses had not restricted to a small elect "tout ce qui se peut dire de bonne grâce en nostre poésie."[2] If one is to make up the membership list of the Pléiade from the Pléiade's actual poems, the method suggested by M. Laumonier, then one should consult and consider poems by others than Ronsard, such as those of Du Bellay, Baïf, Dorat, and Tyard, which we enumerated in our introductory chapter. In these works also, the outstanding poets representing the mid-century humanism and literary reforms are catalogued, and if one accepts these additions, the number of candidates eligible for the constellation of the Pléiade swells considerably.

In 1563 Ronsard declared that he had appropriated the term "Pléiade" from the "sept estoilles de la Pléiade, comme autrefois on avoit fait des sept excellens poètes Grecs qui florissoient presque d'un mesme temps." However, the cluster of stars in Taurus which the astronomers call the Pleiades contains

[1] In a letter dated February 8, 1939, M. Laumonier wrote the author, "Si d'autre part vous étendez votre sujet sur quatorze ou quinze poètes, il ne s'agit plus de la Pléiade qui ne comprenait que sept poètes."

[2] Du Bellay, I, 21.

not seven but hundreds of stars. And the venerable company of the Pleiad, the Alexandrian Pleiad of the third century B.C., consisted of more than seven members if one is willing to accept different authorities. Moreover, the minimum number which we may allow if we accept Ronsard himself as the arbiter (taking the sum of names from the "Élégie à Jean de la Péruse," the "Hymne de Henry II," and Binet's *Vie de Ronsard*) is ten members: Ronsard, Dorat, Du Bellay, Baïf, La Péruse, Belleau, Jodelle, Des Autels, Peletier, Tyard. How can one construct a historical picture of the Pléiade's works and reforms by eliminating three of these names, by restricting the movement to seven participants? And if the number seven must be discarded, why ought one settle on any definite number?

To indulge in lengthy pettifoggery debating whether the Pléiade included seven, eight, nine, or ten members would certainly seem a mark of pedantry rather than scholarship. There are after all valid criteria to determine who belongs to a consistent literary movement and who does not. Is it not a community of sources, education, prejudices, enthusiasms, reforms, language, and imagery which makes a poetic or literary school? Between 1545 and 1575 all the humanistic poets of France were absorbing the same classical texts, were adopting the same poetic vocabulary, were attempting the same reforms of prosody. The more one reads of the major and minor writers of these decades, the more one is struck by their common "tone." In presenting an inventory of certain poetic images, we have occasionally been obliged to cite other poets than the original group for which we were to hold ourself responsible. Sometimes Tahureau or Magny illustrated a Pléiade tenet better than any of those whom Ronsard would admit in his narrow definition of the Pléiade. Or again, it might be a poet recognised by Ronsard as belonging to the Pléiade who offends against Pléiade doctrine more flagrantly than another whom Ronsard would not recognise. An example? Compare Jacques

Tahureau's condemnation of obscurity in the "Avis au lecteur" of his *Admirée*[3] with the justification of obscurity in Tyard's *Premier Solitaire*.[4] There is no question which poet conforms more closely to the written precepts of the nucleus of the Pléiade.

Other recent scholars have noticed this problem and have circumvented the limitations of seven. M. Marcel Raymond, in his excellent study on the contemporary influence of Ronsard,[5] separates the poets of the mid-century into "major" and "minor" members of the Pléiade. In her study on the influence of Ariosto on the Pléiade, Miss Cameron simply adopts the nomenclature, "Ronsard's group." Neither of these expedients seems completely satisfactory. The first, because no two scholars would inevitably agree on a rigid classification between "major" and "minor" as regards the Pléiade poets. The second, because it emphasises Ronsard's rôle too exclusively. M. Chamard, in his recent study on the Pléiade, writes that while wishing to respect the conventional limitation of seven, he must add as an eighth member Jacques Peletier, "qui a donné de la doctrine la formule la plus complète, la plus intelligente et la plus modérée." It is true that the term Brigade exists as a sort of compromise, even less clearly defined than the word Pléiade. Some scholars have resorted to the term Brigade, but it is beyond doubt a word with no tradition or historical importance behind it. Instead of falling back on these or other alternatives, it seems best that one should continue to use the appellation "Pléiade." But the word should be understood to include any number of coeval poets from seven upwards, provided that these contemporaries offered evidence of the humanistic interests, the prosodic revisions, the linguistic reforms, the critical prejudices, and the creative enthusiasms of Pierre de Ronsard and Joachim du Bellay.

⚜ ⚜ ⚜

[3] Tahureau, *Sonnets, odes, et mignardises à l'Admirée*, 1554 edition. This "Avis" is not reproduced in the 1870 edition undertaken by Blanchemain.

[4] *Vide supra*, chap. III, note 31.

[5] See tome I, chap. ix.

The foregoing pages reaffirm once again the wide humanistic and classic culture of the Pléiade school. In studying the Pléiade's thoughts on five fundamental problems of critical theory, we have been obliged to preface each of our chapters with a recapitulation of Hellenic and Roman theories which left an indelible imprint on the thinking of the Pléiade. The Pléiade's cult of Greek and Latin letters is of course familiar to any student of the Renaissance. Every manual or history of this movement quotes such passages as the exhortation in the *Deffence*, "Ly donques et rely premièrement (ô poète futur), fueillete de main nocturne et journelle les exemplaires grecs et latins," a phrase reproduced almost verbatim in the "Poète courtisan." Or the tribute by Ronsard in his panegyric to Greece, "mère des Arts, des Philosophes mère." One has only to look into the curricula of the contemporary colleges, inspect a bibliography of the translations from the classics coming off the busy presses of Paris and Lyons, or tabulate the nationalities of the authors whom the Pléiade poets were reading to appreciate how completely classical was their culture. Let us take, for example, the writers mentioned by Ronsard, collected and classified in our card file:

French	98	German	1
Classic Greek	38	Polish	1
Latin and neo-Latin	24	Flemish	1
Italian	12	Spanish	1
Swiss	2		

Of Spanish literature they knew only the *Amadis*, and this in translation. Although Ronsard predicted that many Swans would come to settle upon the banks of the Thames, unknowingly forecasting the literature of the Elizabethan Age, the Pléiade knew only More in England. More was mentioned once by Scève and twice by Faciot and qualified as Morus, a neo-Latin. The only German writer they knew was Luther, whom they classed among the *pseudoprophetae*. Buchanan, the

"Scotch humanist" of Bordeaux, composed only in French and the classic languages.

Adding the thirty-eight Greek to the twenty-four Latin authors, we note that a total of sixty-two classic authors and critics are mentioned by Ronsard, as a representative member of the Pléiade. Of some hundred and seventy-eight writers mentioned by Ronsard, sixty-two, or over a third, are classics.

It is not surprising, then, having established the five most frequent criteria upon which the Pléiade based their remarks on literature, to discover that these were part of the active critical theory of the classic grammarians and poets. The Pléiade knew Greek and Roman literature so well that they borrowed not only along general lines, but lifted the most minute bits of imagery as well. Vida had advised them to steal even the smallest details from the classics, and Du Bellay pointed out in the second preface to the *Olive* that there is no law against borrowing figures and mannerisms from the ancients.[6] Thus, when we have found Vergil, Martial, and Propertius all calling mediocre poets geese and then meet Ronsard using this same image, we have very probably uncovered the source of his inspiration. Although the definitive editions of several of the Pléiade poets give evidence that the editors have ferreted out borrowings from the classics with perseverance and ingenuity, this type of research is one that is never finished.

Ronsard's mentions of these hundred and seventy-eight writers occupy over a thousand references in his works. The presence of these many references in the pages of Ronsard and his associates attest the Pléiade's passion for shop talk. They never forgot for a moment that they were more than poets, that they were literary arbiters. The fact that they did not compose a greater number of prose works did not prevent them from setting down innumerable remarks about the great and near great of literature. Not only did they digress about other

[6] Du Bellay, I, 20.

writers, but filled long stanzas with divagations about the trade of letters and about themselves as poets. Thus, poetry retained its classic function as a medium of expression for every sort of exposition, a function which was later usurped by prose. With the Pléiade, poetic works were called upon to express ideas on aesthetics, philosophy, morals, religion, and politics. Poems treating of these subjects did not assume special verse forms, were even cast in lyric forms, alien though they were to lyricism. Of the five topics just suggested, politics was the least frequently discussed in these poems. Whether or not we consent to accept this as a fault or lack of social consciousness, it merely corroborates what we have already pointed out, that to the Pléiade literature was not supposed to have a political or social utility.

The question might well be raised whether all these mentions of writers, however useful they are to a literary historian, really belonged in the poems of the Pléiade, consisting to a great extent of love sonnets, heroic odes, eclogues, and the like. In a hundred and fifty-four sonnets, Shakespeare never once refers to another writer; in the sequence of the *Passionate Pilgrim* he mentions only Dowland and Spenser by name. A rule of thumb in art is that one should not write plays about playwrights, novels about novelists, or poems about poets, especially poems judging poets. The Pléiade overstepped this restriction constantly. At least, they mentioned poets in poems of every sort. But the results were not always successful. In many cases the digressions contributed nothing to the poem; in some cases they seemed as inappropriate as ostentatious.

⚜ ⚜ ⚜

In their sustained campaign for the enrichment of the vernacular language, the leaders of the Pléiade felt the values of translations so keenly that they held them to be of equal value with the creative literature. As a matter of fact, they often spoke of translators in the same terms and judged their works by the same criteria which they employed for the creative writers themselves. This betrays how fine a line of distinction was drawn between the translation and the original work. Among the poetic genres which Sébilet treats in his *Art poétique françoys* (II, xiv) is the *version*, which he characterises as "aujourd'huy le poème plus fréquent et mieus receu des estimés Poètes et des doctes lecteurs." Considering how common the practice of *innutrition* was, there might be actually little difference between a creative work and an imitation. Du Bellay's "D'un vanneur de blé," from the Latin of Naugerius, illustrates how the translator and the creative artist may coincide. While the poems presented as original works had a large element of translation in them, these pieces presented as translations had often a large share of free creation in them. An interesting study of the Renaissance poet's efforts to copy from others and yet remain original is found in Gmelin's "Das Prinzip der Imitatio in den romanischen Literaturen der Renaissance." [7] Sometimes the distinction became so fine that the Pléiade poet must have been uncertain whether to call the work a translation or not. Some of the mid-century translations from Petrarch could be considered either original or plagiarised works, as you wish.

To prove our point, let us take a contemporary sonnet which might be called an independent work or a literary steal, depending upon the indulgence of the reader. It was composed by Desportes, and to our knowledge no scholar at this date has yet noticed that it was an *innutrition* of Petrarch:

> Vante-toy maintenant, outrageuse déesse,
> D'avoir fait tout l'effort de ta plus grand' rigueur,
> Privant Amour de traits, d'allegresse mon cœur,
> La terre d'ornement, de gloire et de richesse.
> On ne sçait plus que c'est de vertu ny d'adresse,
> L'honneur triste languit sans force et sans vigueur;

[7] R. Gmelin, "Das Prinzip der Imitatio," *Romanische Forschungen*, XLVI (1932), 85–359.

Bref, de cent deïtez ton bras s'est fait vainqueur,
Morte gist la beauté, la grâce et la jeunesse.
  L'air, la terre et les eaux cet outrage ont pleuré,
Le monde, en la perdant, sans lustre est demeuré,
Comme un pré sans couleurs, un bois sans robe verte,
  Tandis qu'il en jouit, il ne la connut pas;
Moy seul je la connus, qui la pleure icy-bas,
Cependant que le ciel s'enrichit de ma perte.[8]

  Lasciato hai, Morte, senza sole il mondo
Oscuro e freddo, Amor cieco ed inerme,
Leggiadria ignuda, le bellezze inferme,
Me sconsolato ed a me grave pondo;
  Cortesia in bando ed onestate in fondo:
Dogliom' io sol, nè sol ho da dolerme:
Che svelt' hai di virtute il chiaro germe.
Spento il primo valor, qual fia il secondo?
  Pianger l'aer e la terra e 'l mar devrebbe
L'uman legnaggio, che senz' ella è quasi
Senza fior prato, o senza gemma anello.
  Non la conobbe il mondo mentre l'ebbe:
Conobbil' io, ch' a pianger qui rimasi,
E 'l Ciel, che del mio pianto or si fa bello.

This type of composition the theoretical treatises condoned, even encouraged. Jacques Peletier stated in his *Art poétique* that translation is the truest kind of imitation.[9] Imitation in the Aristotelian acceptation was not understood in France until late in the century. The Pléiade's conception of imitation was merely the plagiaristic type which had been identified with Dionysius of Halicarnassus and perpetuated by Quintilian,[10] but which the Pléiade knew best from Vida. The earliest Renaissance reference to Aristotelian mimesis was in the first book of Trissino's poetics in 1529.[11] Professor Bullock has

[8] Desportes, ed. by Michiels, p. 486.

[9] Peletier, *Art poétique*, ed. by Boulanger (Paris, 1930), p. 105.

[10] R. McKeon, "The Concept of Imitation," *Modern Philology*, XXXIV (1936), 1–37.

[11] W. L. Bullock, "The Precept of Plagiarism in the Cinquecento," *Modern Philology*, XXV (1928), 293–312.

shown that the best poets practiced plagiarism unabashed well after the year 1550 and that the Aristotelian acceptation was not generally understood until after 1550, even in Italy. We would amplify this statement and say that it was misunderstood by the French poets until after the late sixties at least, even though the *Poetics* of Aristotle had been mentioned by Du Bellay as early as 1549.[12] Our cards show many references to Aristotle by the Pléiade, for every sort of connection other than his theory of art imitating nature. It was a sheer coincidence, then, that the Pléiade, not understanding the implications of the Aristotelian definition, viewed *imitatio* as a type of creation just as Aristotle had considered mimesis to be creative. And their own definition was even more important for their purposes, since it excused their plagiaristic methods of enriching their language and introducing new poetic forms into the fallow and weed-choked garden that was French poetry of the early 1500's.

The acceptance of imitation as a form of creation invites a closer examination of the meaning of the term. Several kinds of imitation are listed in the *Deffence* and other prose writings of Du Bellay:

> Traducteurs: Translate verbatim (*transcrire*).
> Translateurs: Reproduce ideas closely (*tourner*).
> Paraphrastes: Reproduce ideas freely (*rapporter*).
> Imitateurs: Practise innutrition (*enter*).

One would normally be tempted to conclude from this that only the *paraphrastes* and *imitateurs* could be classed as creators by the Pléiade, and the *traducteurs* and *translateurs* as mere copyists. This did not always prove to be the case, however. Jamyn, Lavardin, Salel, Belleau (as translator of Anacreon), who did no more than translate, were praised for the natural qualities (naïveté), originality, sweetness, utility of

[12] Du Bellay, *Deffence*, ed. by Chamard, pp. 282–283. In his *Joachim du Bellay* (Lille, 1900), p. 54, M. Chamard rightly cautions that one cannot conclude from this that Du Bellay knew the *Poetics* well.

their writings, just as though they were creating new works out of their own imagination, and were judged as independent artists.

This manner of thinking may seem to indicate a lack of critical acumen and discrimination to us nowadays, even though so late a critic as Voltaire declared a good imitation to be the most perfect originality. We are likely to concur with Tolstoy that all this is nothing more than fraud. But one must judge this "imitatio" pragmatically, by the standards of the sixteenth century itself, with the contemporary needs and aims. Just as we found their apparent distinction between native language as nature and foreign tongues as art utterly incompatible with the linguistic ideas of the present day, but an admirable distinction to justify their own language campaign, so must we regard their conception of imitation from the viewpoint of 1550, not of today. Yet, even while endeavoring to understand the Pléiade's attitude, we cannot help but wish that the newly discovered classic literatures had served less as models to copy and more as examples of literary independence and originality to rival.

⚜ ⚜ ⚜

By seeking out the criticisms contained in the Pléiade's poetry, one is occasionally enabled to clarify and amplify materials presented by their theoretical treatises. Perhaps the greatest amount of clarification has concerned their critical imagery. One of the chief talents of the Pléiade was their versatility in varying and reshuffling the fund of poetic imagery which they inherited from the classics. (They evinced greater originality at this than in adopting the limited imagery of Petrarchism, with its "sweet enemies" and "sweet lights.") Given the fact that poets are to be likened to bees or swans, for example, they sought and found ingenious new ways to illustrate this comparison. On a few occasions the results were confusing. At one moment, for instance, one could not be sure whether it was the Muse who shot the song from her bow or whether it was the poet to whom she gave the bow who did the shooting. At another, it might be Pegasus who drinks at the Parnassian spring rather than the poet. At still another moment, one is at a loss to explain whether the sweetness a Pléiade writer is discussing belongs to the *utile dulci* type, the *dolce stil* type, or both. However, in the majority of cases the results of the reshuffling are clever and successful.

Some of the most inventive fruits of this toying with classical imagery are the tropes describing imitative processes. In several instances the use of these figures reveals how omnipresent the doctrine of imitation was. Told by the ancients that the poet is a honeybee, they set up a figure of imitation from the bee's culling the honey from flowers. Told by the ancients that the poet was a swan, they imagine an imitative process from the quills of the swan. Given the process of distillation to work on, they proceed to make a mimetic figure of it.

There is another specific way in which the Pléiade manipulated poetic imagery. The Pléiade poets were amoristic writers, even in their old age. (Old age arrived early for the sonnet writers of the Renaissance, if one is to believe their verse; Ronsard deplores his old age at thirty-five [13] and Michelangelo complains of senility in sonnets composed over forty years before his death.) As amorists, they associated as much of their critical imagery as possible with the imagery of love. One finds them identifying the fury of poetic creation with the ardor of physical passion. They identify their Muses with their mistresses or their mistresses with their Muses, and the inspiration of poetry becomes the same as the inspiration of love. They are told that the swans are poets and they promptly confirm this by recalling that the swan is a bird sacred to Venus. One of the reasons why they will agree that the bee is like a poet is that he is continually amorous of all sweet plants. They will accept the belief in predestination of poets by astral

[13] Ronsard, STFM edition, X, 296.

conjunction and will proceed to claim that the star under which they were born was Venus. We have noted just above that they sometimes identified the Horatian concept of sweetness with the sweetness of love. These will serve as sufficient examples to illustrate one aspect of the Pléiade's versatility in varying their imagery and creating a new figurative language out of the old.

Granting all this versatility at their command, it can scarcely permit us to overlook a basic weakness of the Pléiade. This was the fact that they relied too constantly upon a certain general set of formulae and images to achieve their poetic effects. When the same product is cultivated in a field again and again, no matter how rich the loam in the beginning, the field becomes sterile and the product inferior. Even Maurice Scève, who passed for an ingenious inventor, has a monotony of effects with his stags, basilisks, archers, Hecates, and the rest. No matter what one calls the river of Helicon, whether one rinses his mouth in its waters or merely drinks them, the image grows tedious after endless repetition. When we read about heroes or poets deserving or winning a laurel, an olive branch, the sweet live plant of Apollo, an Olympian palm, the leaf of victory, the branch of victory, and the like, the inevitable consequence of this repetition is to weary the critical reader.

Certain aphorisms and beliefs are advanced *ad absurdum.* Throughout the entire poetry of the period, cropping out in various phrasings and in various genres, we find them reiterated with regrettable frequency. Typical examples are:

> Sleep is the brother of death.
> A lover's battlefield is the bed.
> Homer advises us to drink wine.
> Liars always succeed at court.
> Nature is the step-mother of man.

One explanation for the abuse of certain imagery, of course, was simply that it was part of the standard baggage of the classic poets and that the Pléiade was too imbued with the cult of the classics to be eclectic, to realise that Hellenism was a tonic to be taken in moderation. Another reason was that much of the production of the Pléiade was poetry of circumstance, put together on the spur of the moment and addressed to individuals who possessed no critical acumen whatsoever. Tolstoy, by the way, complained that this was a characteristic of most of the literary works of the Renaissance. Unfortunately, these works appear with a magnified importance in the modern editions of these poets, occupying equal space with works of merit. The fact that so much of their poetry was in sonnet form, a fixed medium offering a minimum of opportunity for novelty, might be proposed as another explanation. The basic reason, however, and this was one of the fundamental weaknesses of the entire movement, remained the Pléiade's somewhat limited discrimination, originality, and vision. For if they were adept at creating new variations upon minor and stereotyped conceits, they could nevertheless have become more original poets. They could have enlarged to a somewhat greater extent the scope of poetry and the creative initiative of the poet.

Other shortcomings they had, of course — and here we are speaking of them as practitioners rather than theorists. One peccadillo was their artistic self-consciousness, and this we have deplored before. We have demonstrated that they would talk about poetry, their Muse, or their own rôle as poets at every turn, in epithalamiums, epinician odes, elegies, or *gayetez*. Another *hamartia* which emerges from the foregoing pages is their lack of self-discipline about their inspirations, and particularly their basing poems upon puns on personal names. This was a bad habit they may have picked up from Petrarch. Typical are poems referring to:

Honey (Mellin de Saint-Gelays)
Shepherds (Bertran Bergier)
Flowers (Simon Bouquet)

Gold (Dorat)
Joy (Anne de Joyeuse)
Heroic verse (Héroët)
Altars (Des Autels)
The constellation Ara (Des Autels)

Lanson pointed out one error of the Pléiade which arraigns them as practitioners of poetry, but which is really a consequence of their theory. This was the Pléiade's preference for verisimilitude over verity, that is, the generally true or the classically true over the realistically true. Put in other words, this means that the Pléiade was never to achieve the humble and intimate sincerity which one feels in the pages of a Montaigne or a Villon or even a Marot. It also means that the Pléiade could not paint word pictures or portraits with vivid naturalism — or, as they themselves phrased it, "au vif." We shall grant that this was a failing of Ronsard, Dorat, Tyard, and to a somewhat lesser degree, of the rest of the Pléiade. Du Bellay in his *Regrets*, Tahureau in his *Dialogues* occasionally attain a "sincere" style. But as a whole, the criticism of Lanson is just. Perhaps one must expect this shortcoming in a group of poets intent upon creating a more exalted style. It is also an inevitable result of the Pléiade's disdain for the common reader, which we recognised in Chapter II as a short-sighted imperfection of the new school.

We must not forget that if the fundamental literary tenets of the Pléiade prevented them from composing more candid ("Romantic") or more graphic ("Realistic") verses, such composition was not after all characteristic of or consonant with classic aesthetics. The Pléiade poets were classicists. Neglecting those values which we have come to associate with romanticism and realism, they made amends by striving to attain in their creations Form, Beauty, and Truth, the three desiderata of classic aesthetics.

The positive merits of the Pléiade easily counterbalance and offset the few shortcomings we have enumerated. These poets justified their birthright of living in the period of the Renaissance by their many reforms and contributions and their untiring effort to create "quelque plus haut et meilleur style." When we contemplate the static condition of French letters under Lemaire and Marot, under the Puy de Rouen, we realise that some of these contributions were remarkable, especially those dealing with prosody. Outside of Italy, none among the Western European nations of the middle Cinquecento could boast of a group of such purposeful literati developing a new literature and literary language out of the gothic heritage of the second rhetoric, creating by both precept and example. Their benefactions to the development of a new prosody and literary idiom are generally regarded as their chief title to fame. This one cannot deny. But their opinions on the fundamental problems of literature, inadequately formulated and consequently less appreciated by the seventeenth and succeeding centuries, remain no less a notable contribution. For although some of the most basic of them never found articulate expression in the Pléiade's few formal treatises and prefaces, as this volume has attempted to show, these ideas were constantly in their thoughts, "nihil magis ad manum."

BIBLIOGRAPHY

BIBLIOGRAPHY

Editions of the Sixteenth-Century Poets Included in this Study

Baïf, Jean-Antoine de. *Œuvres en rime.* Edited by Ch. Marty-Laveaux. 5 vols. Paris: Lemerre, 1881–1890.

Belleau, Rémy. *Œuvres poétiques.* Edited by Ch. Marty-Laveaux. 2 vols. Paris: Lemerre, 1878.

Desportes, Philippe. *Œuvres.* Edited by A. Michiels. Paris: Delahays, 1858.

Desportes, Philippe. *Amours de Diane.* Lyon: Vaganay, 1928.

Dorat, Jean. *Œuvres poétiques.* Edited by Ch. Marty-Laveaux. Paris: Lemerre, 1875.

Du Bellay, Joachim. *Œuvres poétiques françaises.* Edited by H. Chamard. 6 vols. Paris: Société des textes français modernes, 1908–1919.

Du Bellay, Joachim. *Poésies françaises et latines.* 2 vols. Paris: Garnier, 1918. Includes the Latin *Poemata.*

Du Bellay, Joachim. *Lettres.* Edited by P. de Nolhac. Paris: Charavay, 1883.

Grévin, Jacques. *Théâtre complet et poésies choisies.* Edited by L. Pinvert. Paris: Garnier, 1922.

Héroët, Antoine. *Œuvres poétiques.* Edited by F. Gohin. Paris: Société des textes français modernes, 1909.

Jodelle, Etienne. *Œuvres poétiques.* Edited by Ch. Marty-Laveaux. 2 vols. Paris: Lemerre, 1868.

Jodelle, Etienne. *Amours et autres poésies.* Edited by Van Bever. Paris: Sansot, 1907.

Magny, Olivier de. *Œuvres complètes.* Edited by E. Courbet. 6 vols. Paris: Lemerre, 1871–1880.

Peletier, Jacques. *Œuvres poétiques.* Edited by L. Séché. Paris: Revue de la Renaissance, 1904.

Péruse, Jean de la. *Poésies.* Vol. II, "Le Trésor des Pièces Angoumoisines inédites ou rares"; Angoulême: Société historique et archéologique de la Charente, 1866.

Ronsard, Pierre de. *Œuvres complètes.* Edited by P. Laumonier. 8 vols. Paris: Lemerre, 1914–1919.

Ronsard, Pierre de. *Œuvres complètes.* Edited by P. Laumonier. Vols. I–XI. Paris: Société des textes français modernes, 1914–1942. Edition incomplete at present date.

Scève, Maurice. *Délie, object de plus haulte vertu.* Edited by E. Parturier. Paris: Société des textes français modernes, 1916.

Scève, Maurice. *Poésies complètes.* Edited by Guégan. Paris: Garnier, 1927.

Tahureau, Jacques. *Œuvres.* Edited by P. Blanchemain. 2 vols. Paris: Librairie des Bibliophiles, 1870.

Tyard, Pontus de. *Œuvres poétiques.* Edited by Ch. Marty-Laveaux. Paris: Lemerre, 1875. In same volume with poetry of Jean Dorat.

Theoretical Treatises (French) of the Century Consulted

Aneau, Barthélemy. *Le Quintil Horatian*, contained in the E. Person edition of the *Deffence* of Du Bellay. Paris, 1892.

Autelz, Guillaume des. *Réplique aux furieuses défenses de Louis Meigret.* Lyon: Jean de Tournes, 1551.

Deimier, Pierre. *L'Académie de l'art poétique*, reproduced in large part in the *French Poetic Theory* of Patterson (Ann Arbor, 1935).

De Laudun, Pierre. *L'Art poétique françois.* Edited by J. Dedieu. Toulouse: au Siège des facultés libres, 1909.

Du Bellay, Joachim. *Deffence et illustration de la langue françaíse.* Edited by H. Chamard. Paris: Fontemoing, 1904.

Du Bellay, Joachim. *Défense et illustration de la langue française.* Paris: Garnier, 1918. Includes the research of Villey on Italian sources omitted in the Chamard edition.

Du Bellay, Joachim. First and second "Préface à l'*Olive*," included in the edition of the poetry by Chamard, Vol. I. Paris: Société des textes français modernes, 1908–1919.

Fabri, Pierre. *Le Grand et vray art de pleine rhétorique.* 3 vols. Rouen: Société des bibliophiles normands, 1889–1890.

Foclin, Antoine. *Rhétorique françoise*, quotations from the Chamard edition of Du Bellay's *Deffence.*

Fontaine, Charles. Preface to *La Fontaine d'amour.* Paris, 1546.

Jodelle, Estienne. Prologue to *Eugène*, in *Œuvres poétiques*, Vol. I. Paris: Lemerre, 1868.

Le Blanc, Richard. Preface to the translation of the dialogue of *Ion*, quoted in Patterson, *French Poetic Theory.*

Le Caron, Louis. Dialogue IV of the *Dialogues philosophiques*, quoted in Raymond's *Influence de Ronsard.*

Malherbe, François de. *Commentaire sur Desportes* of 1606, in *Œuvres complètes de Malherbe.* 5 vols. Paris: Hachette, 1862–1869.

Montaigne, Michel de. Any edition, the chapters: "Des livres" (II, x), "De l'art de conférer" (III, x), "Deffense de Sénèque et de Plutarque" (II, xxxii).

Pasquier, Etienne. *Recherches*, Book VII, chap. vii. Paris: Menard, 1643.

Peletier, Jacques. *Art poétique.* Edited by A. Boulanger. Paris: Les Belles lettres, 1930.

Ronsard, Pierre de. Preface to the *Odes*; *Préface sur la musique au Roy François II*; *Abbrégé de l'Art poétique*; first preface to the *Franciade* (1572); third preface to the *Franciade* (1587); all included in the Laumonier-Lemerre edition of Ronsard.

Scaliger, J.-C. *Poetices libri septem.* Heidelberg: Bibliopolio Commeliano, 1617.

Sébilet, Thomas. *Art poétique françois.* Edited by Félix Gaiffe. Paris, 1910.

Tahureau, Jacques. *Les Dialogues.* Edited by F. Conscience. Paris: Lemerre, 1870.

Tahureau, Jacques. *Oraison au Roy,* in *Œuvres.* Edited by Blanchemain. Paris: Librairie des Bibliophiles, 1870.

Taille, Jean de la. *L'Art de la tragédie.* Manchester: Éditions de l'Université, 1939.

Tory, Geoffrey. *Champfleury.* Edited by G. Cohen. Paris, 1932.

Tyard, Pontus de. *Discours philosophiques.* Paris: L'Angelier, 1587.

Studies on the Individual Poets of the Middle Sixteenth Century

Baïf, Jean-Antoine de:

Augé-Chiquet, Mathieu. *La Vie, les idées et l'œuvre de Jean-Antoine de Baïf.* Paris: Hachette, 1909.

Ingraham, Edgar S. *The Sources of the "Amours" of Jean-Antoine de Baïf.* Columbus, Ohio: J. F. Hoor, 1905.

Nagel, Heinrich. *Die Metrischen Verse Jean-Antoine de Baïf's.* Leipzig, 1878.

Wiley, W. L. "Antoine de Baïf and the Ovidian Love-Tale," *Studies in Philology*, XXXIII (1936), 45-54.

Belleau, Rémy:

Eckhart, Alexandre. *Rémy Belleau, sa vie, sa Bergerie.* Budapest, 1917.

Van Bever, Adolphe. *Amours, échanges de pierres précieuses de Rémy Belleau.* Paris, 1909.

Wagner, Franz A. *Rémy Belleau und seine Werke.* Leipzig, 1890.

Desportes, Philippe:

Lavaud, Jacques. *Un poète de cour — Philippe Desportes.* Paris: Droz, 1936.

Vaganay, Hugues. "Du nouveau sur Desportes: Desportes et Malherbe," *Bulletin du bibliophile*, 1928, pp. 502–506.

Dorat, Jean:

Marty-Laveaux, Ch. "Notice sur Dorat" in *Œuvres poétiques*. Paris: Lemerre, 1875.

Du Bellay, Joachim:

Bordeaux, M. *La Jeunesse de Joachim du Bellay*. Angers, 1912.

Chamard, Henri. *Joachim du Bellay*. Lille: Bigot, 1900.

Kerr, W. A. R. "The Pléiade and Platonism," *Modern Philology*, V (1907–1908), 407–421.

Le Bourgo, L. *De J. Bellaii latinis poematibus*. Cognac, 1903.

Merrill, Robert V. "Considerations on *Les Amours de I. Du Bellay*," *Modern Philology*, XXXIII (1935–1936), 129–138.

Merrill, Robert V. "Lucian and Du Bellay's *Poète Courtisan*," *Modern Philology*, XXIX (1931–1932), 11–20.

Merrill, Robert V. *The Platonism of Joachim du Bellay*. Chicago: University of Chicago Press, 1925.

Plötz, Gustave. *Étude sur Joachim du Bellay et son rôle dans la réforme poétique de Ronsard*. Berlin, 1874.

Villey, Pierre. *Les Sources italiennes de la Deffence et illustration*. Paris, 1908.

Grévin, Jacques:

Maloigne, M. *Jacques Grévin, sa vie, son œuvre*. Laval, 1926.

Pinvert, Lucien. *Jacques Grévin*. Paris: Fontemoing, 1898.

Héroët, Antoine:

Arnoux, Jules. *Un précurseur de Ronsard: Antoine Héroët*. Digne, 1912.

Kerr, William A. R. "Antoine Héroët's *Parfaite Amye*," *Publications of the Modern Language Association*, XX (1905), 567–583.

Jodelle, Estienne:

Colletet. "La Vie de Jodelle," in Van Bever edition of *Amours et autres poésies*. Paris: Sansot, 1907.

Kahnt, Paul. *Gedankenkreis der Sentenzen in Jodelle's und Garnier's Tragödien*. Marburg, 1887.

Magny, Olivier de:

Cambon, Paul. *Olivier de Magny, poète de Cahors*. Cahors, 1925.

Favre, Jules. *Olivier de Magny*. Paris, 1885.

Peletier, Jacques:

Chamard, Henri. *De Jacobi Peletarii Cenomanensis Arte Poetica*. Lille, 1900.

Jugé, Clément. *Jacques Peletier du Mans; essai sur sa vie, son œuvre, son influence*. Paris, 1907.

Péruse, Jean de la:

Banachévitch, Nicolas. *Jean Bastier de la Péruse.* Paris: Presses universitaires de la France, 1923.

Ronsard, Pierre de:

Bishop, Morris. *Ronsard, Prince of Poets.* New York: Oxford, 1940.

Champion, Pierre. *Ronsard et son temps.* Paris, 1925.

Cohen, Gustave. *Ronsard, sa vie et son œuvre.* Paris, 1924.

Franchet, H. *Le poète et son œuvre d'après Ronsard.* Paris: Champion, 1922.

Laumonier, Paul. *La "Vie de Ronsard" de Claude Binet.* Paris, 1910.

Laumonier, Paul. *Ronsard poète lyrique.* Paris, 1909 and 1933.

Longnon, Henri. *Pierre de Ronsard.* Paris, 1912.

Nolhac, Pierre de. *Ronsard et l'humanisme.* Paris: Champion, 1921.

Raymond, Marcel. *Bibliographie critique de Ronsard en France.* Paris, 1927.

Raymond, Marcel. *Influence de Ronsard sur la poésie française.* 2 vols. Paris: Champion, 1927.

Silver, Isidore. *The Pindaric Odes of Ronsard.* Paris, 1937.

Scève, Maurice:

Baur, Albert. *Maurice Scève et la Renaissance lyonnaise.* Paris, 1916.

Brunetière, Ferdinand. "Un Précurseur de la Pléiade: Maurice Scève," in his *Études critiques*, Vol. VI. Paris, 1899.

Also see the *Notices* in the Parturier and Guégan editions.

Tahureau, Jacques:

Chardon, H. *La Vie de Tahureau, documents inédits.* Paris, 1885.

Tyard, Pontus de:

Flamini, Francesco. "Du rôle de Pontus de Tyard dans le Pétrarquisme français," *Revue de la Renaissance*, I (1901), 43–55.

Jeandet, J. P. Abel. *Étude sur le seizième siècle, France et Bourgogne, Pontus de Tyard.* Paris: Aubry, 1860.

Jeandet, J. P. Abel. *Études bibliographiques sur Pontus de Tyard.* Mâcon, 1894.

General Poetic Histories, Literary Movements, Zeitgeist: 1500–1600

Allais, G. *Malherbe et la poésie française à la fin du XVIe siècle.* Paris: Thorin, 1891.

Atkinson, G. *Les Nouveaux horizons de la Renaissance française.* Paris: Droz, 1935.

Baldwin, Charles S. *Renaissance Literary Theory and Practice, 1400–1600.* New York, 1939.

Banville, Théodore de. *Petit traité de poésie.* Paris: Charpentier, 1881.

Bédier et Hazard. *Histoire de la littérature française illustrée.* 2 vols. Paris: Larousse, 1923–1924.

Blanchemain, Prosper. *Poètes et amoureuses, portraits du XVIe siècle.* Paris: Willem, 1877.

Bourciez, E. *Les Mœurs polies et la littérature de cour sous Henri II.* Paris: Hachette, 1886.

Bray, R. *La Formation de la doctrine classique en France.* Lausanne: Payot, 1931.

Brunetière, F. *Manuel de l'histoire de la littérature française.* Paris: Delagrave, 1898.

Brunot, F. *La Doctrine de Malherbe d'après son Commentaire sur Desportes.* Paris: Masson, 1891.

Bullock, W. L. "The Precept of Plagiarism in the Cinquecento," *Modern Philology*, XXV (1928), 293.

Burckhardt, J. *Die Kultur der Renaissance.* 2 vols. Leipzig: Seeman, 1877–1878; 1885.

Busson, Henri. *Les Sources et le développement du rationalisme dans la littérature française de la Renaissance.* Paris: Letouzey et Ané, 1922.

Cary, Henry Francis. *The Early French Poets.* New York: Albert & Charles Boni, 1925.

Chamard, Henri. *La Doctrine et l'œuvre poétique de la Pléiade.* Paris: Guillon, 1931.

Chamard, Henri. *Histoire de la Pléiade.* Paris: Didier, 1939–.

Chamard, Henri. "L'Invention de l'ode et le différend de Ronsard et Du Bellay," *Revue de l'histoire de la littérature française*, VI (1899), 21–54.

Chamard, Henri. *Les Origines de la poésie française de la Renaissance.* Paris: Boccard, 1920.

Charbonnel, R. *La Pensée italienne au XVIe siècle et le courant libertin.* Paris: Champion, 1919.

Chasles, Ph. *Études sur le XVIe siècle en France.* Paris: Charpentier, 1876.

Clark, D. L. *Rhetoric and Poetry in the Renaissance.* New York: Columbia University, 1922.

Coindreau, M. E. "Actualité du seizième siècle," *Mélanges Laumonier* (Paris: Droz, 1934), 611–621.

Cons, Louis. *Anthologie littéraire de la Renaissance française* (introductory chapter). New York, 1931.

Cornelia, W. B. *The Classical Sources of the Nature References in Ronsard's Poetry.* New York: Columbia University, 1934.

Crépet, E. *Poètes français depuis les origines à nos jours.* Paris: Gide, 1861–1863.

Darmesteter et Hatzfeld. *Le XVIe siècle en France.* Paris: Delagrave, 1919.

Dejob, Charles. *L'Influence du Concile de Trente sur la littérature.* Paris: Thorin, 1884.

Deschamps, G. "Poésie française au XVIe siècle," *Revue Encyclopédique*, 1902.

Dulon, *Histoire littéraire de Lyon pendant la première moitié du XVIe siècle.* Lyon, 1866.

Egger, Émile. *L'Hellénisme en France.* 2 vols. Paris: Didier, 1869.

Faguet, É. "L'Humanisme français au XVIe siècle," *Revue Bleue*, 1891.

Faguet, É. *Le Seizième siècle.* Paris: Boivin, several editions.

Faguet, É. *Histoire de la poésie française de la Renaissance au Romantisme.* Paris: Boivin, 1923.

Feugère, L. *Les femmes poètes au XVIe siècle.* Paris: Didier, 1860.

Fouquières, Becq de. *Traité général de versification française.* Paris: Charpentier, 1879.

Françon, Marcel. "La Tradition littéraire au Moyen Age," *Harvard Studies and Notes in Philology and Literature*, XVI–XVII (1935), 47–53.

Gmelin, H. "Das Prinzip der Imitatio," *Romanische Forschungen*, XLVI (1932), 85–359.

Gosse, E. *Malherbe and the Classical Reaction.* Oxford: Clarendon, 1921.

Gramont, F. *Les vers français et leur prosodie.* Paris: Hetzel, 1876.

Guy, Henry. *Histoire de la poésie française au XVIe siècle.* 2 vols. Paris: Champion, 1910; 1926.

Hauser, H. *Études sur la Réforme française.* Paris: Picard, 1909.

Hawkins, Richmond L. *Maistre Charles Fontaine, Parisien.* Harvard University Press, 1916.

Hecq, G., et Paris, L. *Poétique française au moyen âge et à la Renaissance.* Paris: Bouillon, 1896.

Julleville, Petit de. *Histoire de la langue et de la littérature française.* 8 vols. Paris: Colin, 1896–1899.

Kastner, L. E. *History of French Versification.* Oxford: Clarendon, 1903.

Kaulen, F. *Geschichte der Fr. Poesie im XVI. Jahrh.* Hannover, 1882.

Keating, L. Clark. *Studies on the Literary Salon in France, 1550–1615.* Cambridge, 1941.

Lachèvre, F. *Bibliographie des recueils collectifs de poésie du XVIe siècle.* Paris: Champion, 1922.

Lanson, G. *Histoire de la littérature française.* Paris: Hachette, many editions.

Lanson, G. "Comment Ronsard invente," *Revue universitaire*, 1906.

Lecky, W. E. H. *Rise and Influence of Rationalism in Europe.* New York: Appleton, 1871.

Lefranc, Abel. *Grands écrivains français de la Renaissance.* Paris: Champion, 1914.

Lefranc, Abel. *La Vie Quotidienne au temps de la Renaissance.* Paris: Hachette, 1938.

Macintire, E. J. "French Influences on the Beginnings of English Classicism," *Publications of the Modern Language Association*, XXVI (1911), 496–527.

McKeon, R. "Concept of Imitation," *Modern Philology*, XXXIV (1936), 1–37.

Morf, H. *Geschichte*, Vol. I, "Das Zeitalter der Renaissance" (Sixteenth century bibliography). Strassburg: Trübner, 1914.

Nitze and Dargan. "The Renaissance," Part II, *History of French Literature.* 3d ed. New York: Holt, 1938.

Nolhac, P. de. *Pétrarque et l'humanisme.* Paris: Bouillon, 1892.

Oliver, Revilo P. "Recent Interpretations of the Renaissance," *Italica*, XII (1935), 130–135.

Owen, J. *Skeptics of the French Renaissance.* New York: Macmillan, 1893.

Patterson, W. F. *Three Centuries of French Poetic Theory.* 2 vols. Ann Arbor: University of Michigan, 1935.

Peyre, Henri. *Qu'est-ce que le classicisme? Essai de mise au point.* Paris: Droz, 1933.

Picot, E. *Français italianisants au XVIe siècle.* 2 vols. Paris: Champion, 1906–1907.

Piéri, Marius. *Pétrarque et Ronsard.* Marseille: Laffitte, 1896.

Plattard, J. *L'Œuvre de Rabelais.* Paris: Champion, 1910.

Plattard, J. *Vie de Rabelais.* Paris and Bruxelles: van Oest, 1928.

Poole, H. B. "The Idea of Poetic Justice in the Criticism of the Sixteenth Century in France," *University of Colorado Studies*, XV (1925–1927), 133–145.

Raymond, Marcel. *L'Influence de Ronsard sur la poésie française.* 2 vols. Paris: Champion, 1927.

Renaudet, A. *Préréforme et humanisme.* Paris: Champion, 1916.

Rosenbauer, A. *Die Poetischen Theorien der Pléiade nach Ronsard und Du Bellay.* Leipzig: Deichert, 1895.

Sainéan, L. *Problèmes littéraires du XVIe siècle.* Paris: Boccard, 1927.

Sainte-Beuve, C.-A. *Tableau historique de la poésie française au XVIe siècle.* Paris: Charpentier, 1843.

Saintsbury, George. *Classical Criticism*, Vol. I, and *Renaissance Criticism*, Vol. II of *A History of Criticism and Literary Taste in Europe*. Edinburgh and London; Blackwood, 1922–1929.

Shorey, Paul. "*Le Double Mont* in French Renaissance Poetry," *Modern Philology*, XIX (1921–1922), 221–222.

Smith, Preserved. *Age of the Reformation*. New York: Holt, 1920.

Spingarn, J. E. *Literary Criticism in the Renaissance*. New York: Columbia University, 1908.

Symonds, J. A. *The Renaissance in Italy*. 7 vols. New York: Holt, 1887–1888.

Taylor, H. *Thought and Expression in the Sixteenth Century*. 2 vols. New York: Macmillan, 1920.

Texte, Joseph. "Influence italienne dans la Renaissance française," in his *Études de littérature européenne*. Paris: Colin, 1898.

Tilley, A. *The Dawn of the French Renaissance*. Cambridge, England: University Press, 1918.

Tilley, A. *Literature of the French Renaissance*. Cambridge, England: University Press, 1904.

Toffanin, G. *Storia dell'Umanesimo*. Naples: Perrella, 1933.

Toffanin, G. *La fine dell'Umanesimo*. Turin: Bocca, 1920.

Vianey, J. *Le Pétrarquisme en France au XVIe siècle*. Montpellier: Coulet, 1909.

Villey, P. *Les sources et l'évolution des Essais de Montaigne*. 2 vols. Paris: Hachette, 1908.

Vossler, K. *Poetische Theorien in der Italienischen Frührenaissance*. Berlin: Felber, 1900.

Weidinger, A. *Die Schäferlyrik der franz. Vorrenaissance*. Munich: Wolf, 1893.

Will, Samuel F. *A Bibliography of American Studies on the French Renaissance*. Urbana: University of Illinois Press, 1940.

Wright, C. H. C. *French Classicism*. Cambridge: Harvard University Press, 1920.

SELECTIVE INDEX

SELECTIVE INDEX